DATE DUE

DE 18'98			
JУ 12'00			
DE 6 '01			

DEMCO 38-296

THE ORDEAL OF INTEGRATION

ALSO BY ORLANDO PATTERSON

NONFICTION

The Sociology of Slavery: Jamaica, 1655–1838

Ethnic Chauvinism: The Reactionary Impulse

Slavery and Social Death: A Comparative Study

Freedom in the Making of Western Culture

Rituals of Blood (forthcoming)

Ecumenical America (forthcoming)

FICTION

The Children of Sisyphus

An Absence of Ruins

Die the Long Day

ORLANDO PATTERSON

THE ORDEAL OF

INTEGRATION

Progress and Resentment in America's "Racial" Crisis

CIVITAS

COUNTERPOINT

Washington, D.C.

LIBRARY OF CONGRESS CATALOGING-IN-PUBLICATION DATA
Patterson, Orlando, 1940–
The ordeal of integration: progress and resentment in
America's "racial" crisis / Orlando Patterson.
Includes bibliographical references and index.
1. United States—Race relations   2. United States—Ethnic relations   I. Title
E185.615.P35   1997
305.8' 00973—dc21   97-29254
ISBN 1-887178-61-9 (hardcover: alk. paper)

Printed in the United States of America on acid-free paper that meets the American National Standards Institute Z39-48 Standard

Composition, book and jacket design by Caesar Jackson

CIVITAS/COUNTERPOINT
P.O. Box 65793
Washington, D.C. 20035-5793

3 5 7 9 10 8 6 4 2

For Anita
"One Love"

CONTENTS

In the attempt to understand and come to terms with the problems of Afro-Americans and of their interethnic relations, the country has been ill served by its intellectuals, policy advocates, and leaders in recent years. At present, dogmatic ethnic advocates and extremists appear to dominate discourse on the subject, drowning out both moderate and other dissenting voices.

A strange convergence has emerged between these extremists. On the left, the nation is misled by an endless stream of tracts and studies that deny any meaningful change in America's "Two Nations," decry "The Myth of Black Progress," mourn "The Dream Deferred," dismiss Afro-American middle-class status as "Volunteer Slavery," pronounce Afro-American men an "Endangered Species," and apocalyptically announce "The Coming Race War." On the right is complete agreement with this dismal portrait in which we are fast "Losing Ground," except that the road to "racial" hell, according to conservatives, has been paved by the very policies intended to help solve the problem, abetted by "The Dream and the Nightmare" of cultural changes in the sixties and by the over-breeding and educational integration of inferior Afro-Americans and lower-class Euro-Americans genetically situated on the wrong tail of the IQ "Bell Curve."

If it is true that a "racial crisis" persists in America, this crisis is as much one of perception and interpretation as of actual socioeconomic and interethnic realities. By any measure, the record of the past half century has been one of great achievement, thanks in good part to the success of the government policies now being maligned by the left for not having gone far enough and by the right for having both failed and gone too far. At the same time, there is still no room for complacency: because our starting point half a century ago was so deplorably backward, we still have some way to go before approaching anything like a resolution.

This work is the first of a trilogy on the sociology, history, and culture of what is erroneously called "race" in America. The present volume explores, through closely linked essays, the current economic sociology of this problem, the ways we have tried to interpret it, and how we might begin to solve it. The second volume, *Rituals of Blood,* shifts the focus from socioeconomic issues and interethnic relations to the cultural aspects of the Afro-American experience, intraethnic dilemmas, and the historical sources of these problems. The third volume, *Ecumenical America,* will explore the rise of an overarching national culture in America, its diffusion as the first genuinely global culture, and the extraordinary role of Afro-Americans in both its development and diffusion.

All of the essays are either new or completely rewritten and expanded versions of previously published works. While there have been important continuities in my ideas over the years, change and evolution have been more characteristic of my thought. A short preliminary version of the first essay, "The Paradoxes of Integration," appeared in the *New Republic* on November 6, 1995. The ideas developed in the second essay were first explored in my article "The Moral Crisis of the Black American," which appeared some twenty-five years ago in the *Public Interest.* I have significantly altered or developed most of my views on this subject since that time, and the present essay not only reflects my present thinking, but takes account of changes in the subject itself and of relevant works by others. An earlier version of the fourth essay appeared in *The Bell Curve Wars,* edited by Steve Fraser (1995). The present version shifts the focus from Richard Herrnstein and Charles Murray's book, *The Bell Curve,* to the broader question of the genetic interpretation of inequality and the cultural meanings and contradictions of this approach to our "racial" crisis.

◧

For reasons explored in several of the essays, I find present nomenclature on Afro-Americans and their ethnic relations unsatisfactory. Indeed, I think the terms we use contribute to the problem. The term *race* itself is one that I attempt to avoid; when its use is necessary, it will be placed in quotation marks. Afro-Americans are not a "race" in any meaningful sense, but an aggregate of 33 million people that is better described as an ethnic group if one must speak of the entire collectivity. I therefore use the term *ethnic* instead of *racial* and refer to an *ethnic group* instead of a *race.*

I think the time has come to abandon the terms *black* and *white* in reference to Americans. They are linguistically loaded terms and emphasize the physical, which is precisely what we want to get away from in inter-ethnic relations. The term *Afro-American* will be used to refer to persons of African ancestry who identify themselves with this ethnic group. Although I have no special objection to *African American,* I think this term is inadequate for reasons mentioned recently by Charles C. Moskos and John Sibley Butler in the preface to their excellent book, *All That We Can Be: Black Leadership and Racial Integration the Army Way* (1996). Afro-Americans are not Africans; they are among the most American of Americans, and the emphasis on their Africanness is both physically inappropriate and culturally misleading. Furthermore, in light of increasing immigration of Africans from Africa into the United States, it is best to reserve the term *African American* to describe this group. I will therefore use the term *Afro-American* throughout this and other works. If we abandon the term *black,* however—whether in favor of *African American* or *Afro-American*—it makes no sense to continue to use the term *white.* I therefore use the term *Euro-Americans* to describe the people elsewhere known as *whites.*

◧

I would like to thank Christopher Jencks for his comments on the draft of the essay "For Whom the Bell Curves" that appeared in *The Bell Curve Wars* and for our many conversations on American ethnic inequality while we taught a graduate seminar together at the Harris School of the University of Chicago. I would also like to thank Ms. Sarah Flynn for her excellent advice and editorial work on these essays. Finally, I wish to thank my wife, Anita Patterson, for her love and support and for her many insights on American culture, especially its mainstream intellectual and literary traditions and the unexpected ways in which they have influenced Afro-American life and thought.

THE ORDEAL OF INTEGRATION

INTRODUCTION

Nearly half a century ago, America began seriously to confront the enormity of its "racial" problem. Overcoming the accumulated injustices of centuries has been an ordeal that has tested the mettle of the nation, especially its constitutional commitment to the ideals of equality and freedom. The objective economic, sociological, and political record clearly demonstrates that this painful period of transition has not been in vain. In almost all areas of life, progress—sometimes quite dramatic—has been made in surmounting the ingrained and institutional evils of racism and oppression. Only a fool or a bigot would deny that a great deal remains to be done, that indeed, in some areas, we have seen intolerable stagnation and even regression. But there is no gainsaying the clear trend lines of progress in changing ethnic attitudes and in the improved condition of the vast majority of Afro-Americans.

One cannot help wondering, then, why President Clinton has chosen this moment to call for a national debate on "race." The answer perhaps is that something has gone terribly wrong with the way we view and talk about "race" in America. If what the President proposes is yet another inquiry into America's "racial" dilemma, his well-meaning initiative is likely to do more harm than good; but if what he has in mind is a debate about how we talk about and evaluate "race," it might do some good.

For the truth is that we no longer make sense on the subject of "race." We have talked ourselves into a hole full of rhetorical quicksand. Our attempts to clarify merely confound, and language itself has become a trap. For Euro-Americans and Afro-Americans alike, saying what one means or meaning what one says about "race" is naive, at best. At worst, one risks lifelong verbal abuse. As Paul Sniderman and Thomas Piazza bluntly put it, "Anger and resentment have become the common currency, as much among racial liberals as among racial conservatives."[1] This quagmire may explain why President Clinton has called for a great debate on "race" at a time when relations between ordinary Afro-Americans and Euro-Americans are, in fact, the best they have ever been, although still far from ideal.

How we interpret and talk about "race," and how professional leaders from both ethnic groups verbally interact, especially in competitive situations, often bears little relation to the progress achieved by ordinary people in their cross-ethnic relations. Attempting to understand the realities of American "race relations" based on the talk and behavior of professional "race leaders" is the sociological equivalent of an economist attempting to understand the American economy based on the talk and behavior of professional stockbrokers.

Any reference to Afro-Americans by Euro-Americans that does not acknowledge the totality of racism or flatter all things Afro-American risks sneers of contempt or the charge of racism. Any but the most professionally qualified expression of sympathy is likely to be dismissed as liberal patronage. Any suggestion that an Afro-American person might be responsible, even in some minor way, for his or her condition invites the knee-jerk response that one is blaming the victim. The result is that no Euro-American person, except one insensitive to the charge of racism, dares say what he or she really means.

For Afro-Americans who talk about "race," especially professional "race" advocates, it is difficult to know what people mean, since so much "race" speech has become ritualized and rhetorical. Racism, an undeniable fact of life for most Afro-Americans, has become for too many the explanation for every problem, the excuse for every failing, the moral whip with which to lash out at anyone who dares to criticize.

The overwrought nature of ethno-"racial" talk results in curious forms of self-censorship and privileged speech among ethnic groups in their interactions with each other. For example, a Euro-American person is privileged to say, "I like brown skin," and risk the horrors of skin cancer if he wishes to turn his skin brown by exposing himself to the sun's rays. An

Afro-American person dares not say, "I prefer straighter hair," even though Afro-Americans spend an inordinate proportion of their disposable income actualizing just such a preference. On the other hand, an Afro-American person is privileged to say, "I love my blackness," or "I take pride in the great cultural achievements of my race," or any such chauvinistic claptrap. No Euro-American person dares say the very same thing, not if she cares about her reputation, even though it is true that nearly all Euro-Americans cherish their appearance and cultural heritage.

But informal communication is the least of this communicative quagmire. The problem also besets and distorts academic and policy analyses and statements about the Afro-American condition, which leads to badly flawed public policy and unworkable programs if not crippling inaction. The norm of subjectivity dominates even academic discourse and scholarship. Every Afro-American is presumed to be an expert on all aspects of the subject of "race." The most misinformed statement about the "black condition" by an ignorant resident of the ghetto is accepted as the truth about the plight of the poor. And nothing is more lamentable than to behold an Afro-American college freshman with an upper-middle-class suburban background "telling it like it is" about racism to a senior Euro-American scholar with a lifetime of accumulated knowledge on the subject.

As I point out in the first of the six essays that make up this volume, the view that being a member of a minority group endows one with special insights into its problems has had devastating consequences for the academic study of Afro-American life and intergroup relations. To take the most egregious example, serious scholarship on the urban ghetto by Euro-Americans was effectively censored for a decade and a half from the early seventies by hostile Afro-American scholars who declared "the death of white sociology" and insisted that only Afro-Americans were qualified to study and discuss their condition.

The return of Euro-Americans to the field in recent years has, if anything, exacerbated another problem in the study and discussion of Afro-Americans: the tendency to racialize all issues relating to them. We insist on calling Afro-Americans a "race," even though we claim that there is no scientific basis for such a designation. We then racialize areas of Afro-American life having nothing to do with Afro-Americans' ethnic background. Most of what the typical Afro-American does in daily life has little or nothing to do with being Afro-American. There is no specifically Afro-American way of being healthy, sick, or dying; of falling in and out of love; of doing a good job or making a mess of it; of being happy or being depressed; of being victimized or being a victimizer; of being nice or being just another mean son of a bitch. But one would never think so reading or listening to Afro-American writers and spokespersons. According to the Afro-American press, every conceivable thought or act of the Afro-American is somehow "black," an expression of a black soul that is different in every way. But this is not confined to Afro-American journalists.

When they are not proving that "race" as a concept has no scientific meaning, most social scientists and even medical researchers are busily controlling away all other variables in a relentless effort to prove that one, and only one, variable explains the condition of Afro-Americans: "race." Having abolished the ontological basis of "race" in biology, American social scientists vie with each other to reestablish its ontological essence as social fact. And this, in turn, has led to the idea of "race" creeping back into natural science. The consequences are not just flawed science and policy, but sometimes literally life-threatening situations. A recent study in the *Annals of Internal Medicine* cites several cases where misdiagnoses due to the racialization of medical classification resulted in the deterioration or death of the patient.[2]

The overracialization of Afro-American life is related to another problem in current talk and scholarship about Afro-Americans: the tendency to homogenize them as a single group beset by crises and intractable dilemmas. The traditional racist assumption that all Afro-Americans are an inferior caste of loafers finds its direct counterpart in the liberal racist assumption that all Afro-Americans are helpless victims of institutional and individual "racial" forces over which they have absolutely no control. For the television news producers the only news, other than sports and entertainment, worth reporting on Afro-Americans is bad news: "blacks" as underclass criminals and "blacks" as victims. In the ideal newscast, all are merged, which explains the media obsession with "gangsta" rappers, ghetto violence, the criminal behavior of athletes, and that apotheosis of modern television broadcasting, O. J. Simpson: super-ghetto child, super-athlete adult, super-entertainer, super-stud, super-killer.

Social scientists, while less sensationalist, are no less homogenizing and deterministic in their accounts of Afro-Americans. American social science is either uninterested in, or befuddled by, the fact that the vast majority of Afro-Americans, including the majority of those born and brought up poor, overcome their circumstances and lead healthy, happy, productive lives. For the same reason that they exhibit little interest in the growing number of poor Euro-Americans, who now greatly outnumber their Afro-

American counterparts and are as crime committing, violent, wife batter-
ing, child abusive, and drug addicted—alcohol and amphetamines being
their drugs of choice—with economic and health consequences for the
nation that are absolutely and proportionately greater than those caused
by any other group. It is, however, consistent with the obsessive overracialization of social problems and their confinement to a homogenized
population of 33 million Afro-Americans that the rapid development of
this other underclass remains one of the best-kept secrets among American
journalists and social scientists. No wonder, then, that Jacqueline Jones's
excellent study, *The White Underclass,* documenting these developments,
fell like a lead balloon upon the nation's scholars and journalists.

◻∎

In this book I explore the present state of Afro-Americans, the progress
they have made toward full equality, the nature of their relations with
Euro-Americans, and our perceptions as well as our mode of talking about
and evaluating these issues.

Chapter 1 begins by demonstrating the remarkable facts of Afro-
American progress, while fully acknowledging the very serious persisting
problems of the lower classes among them. Yet the overwhelming popular
and academic view is that Afro-Americans are now in the depths of some
intractable crisis and that relations with Euro-Americans have never been
worse. This pessimism is so deep-seated and pervasive that it is becoming self-fulfilling, which, in turn, plays right into the hands of the racist
extremists among both groups. "Racial" separatism and the pernicious
old Southern dogma of separate-but-equal "races" is alive and well once
again. The second objective of chapter 1, then, is to explain this pessimism
and the reasons that progress seems to breed resentment and anger among
members of both groups.

Having set the stage with this overview of where we are, and how we
misrepresent what has been achieved, the following three chapters examine
the three main forms of "racial" discourse in America—the liberal, conservative, and hereditarian or genetic—and their implications for public policy.

At its best, liberalism can take credit for much of the progress made
by Afro-Americans over the past half century. Modern American liberals
share with classical liberals a strong commitment to individualism and
self-determination but differ from them in two important respects: they
have far more faith in the role of government than their classical coun-

terparts do, and they rely heavily, and indiscriminately, on social determinism in explaining the condition of the poor, and especially the Afro-
American poor. This is the source of major contradictions, especially among
liberal Afro-American leaders and intellectuals. Determinist arguments are
used to explain the absence of self-determination and, to compound the
absurdity, determinist policies are advocated as the best means toward
the abolition of dependency.

Chapter 2 examines these contradictions and their implications, most
notably the bizarre cult of the victim that has become the hallmark of late
twentieth-century liberal doctrine. Other than being born rich and privileged, or owning a government subsidized corporation, being a victim has
become the main path to entitlement or any kind of social support in
America today. America seems mesmerized by the image and status of the
victim. On talk shows, in the news media, and in popular books, the victim as hero reigns supreme. The best-seller lists of the nation are dominated by tales of incest, rape, wife battery, child abuse, compulsive ill-
nesses, and every other imaginable kind of torture. Implicit in all this, I
argue, is an oversocialized view of human beings as wholly determined
products of their environment and a neglect or downright denial of all
agency in accounting for, or remedying, one's condition. It is very likely
that the liberal "racial" discourse has been the model and inspiration for
this extraordinary development. The same week that the *New York Times*
reported on its front page that the nation's publishers were "preparing to
release a torrent of confessionals that offer competing visions" of victimization and "true torment," the eldest son of the Reverend Martin
Luther King Jr. met with his father's convicted killer live on CNN and told
him, "In a strange sort of way, we're both victims."

While I am extremely critical of these developments, I remain firmly
committed to the view that not less but more government action is needed on behalf of the nation's poor. Contrary to what conservative critics
imagine, autonomy and self-determination, far from being incompatible
with an activist government, often require it. Chapter 3 defends this view
with a theory of representational agency that is presented as part of a
broader critique of conservative "racial" discourse. There I argue that,
contrary to the conservative view, which holds to an undersocialized conception of human nature that is as flawed as the oversocialized conception
of the liberals, the surrender to market forces and advocacy of government inaction in the face of nightmarish ghettos, growing impoverishment
in the midst of affluence, spreading homelessness, inadequate health insur-

ance for millions of working people, and multigenerational rural poverty are themselves dehumanized forms of determinism. There is no logical or moral difference between dependence on the tyranny of the marketplace and dependence on government. Only a hopelessly limited view of the relationship between the individual and society deludes one into thinking so.

The conservative outlook is in no way necessarily racist, despite the fact that many racists are conservative. Conservatism is consistent with a principled antiracist position, one that was already fully developed in Alexander Hamilton's writings and goes further back to the conservative Quaker fathers of the abolitionist movement.

Conversely, American radicalism has had a long, vicious streak of racism. Andrew Jackson and his era, the crucible of radical democracy in America, were rabidly racist. Southern populism went hand in hand with militant Negro-phobia; George Fitzhugh, one of nineteenth-century America's most brilliant critics of capitalism, was vehemently racist; the progressive movement did nothing to alleviate the racist horrors of the early twentieth century; and it is to the eternal shame of the American labor movement that, up until the civil rights era, it always favored Euro-American racist solidarity over worker solidarity. Indeed, so-called American exceptionalism, namely, its failure to develop a strong tradition of social democracy with a universal welfare state, in sharp contrast to the rest of the industrial world, can be largely attributed to the chronic racism of America's labor leadership and its members.

Though not racist, the conservative view of the poor in general, and the Afro-American poor in particular, is hopelessly self-contradictory—in the conflict between its self-serving economic rationalism and its traditionalism, between its individualism and its nationalism, and between its antideterminism and propensity toward determinist cultural explanations. In recent years these contradictions have become so glaring that they have begun to disturb numerous thoughtful conservatives. After lecturing the working classes and advocates of the poor for the past century and a half about the sovereignty of the market and the need to adapt to its "discipline" and "rationality," many conservatives, including some of the nation's leading capitalists, have lately begun to sing a different tune as they stand by helplessly and, with the conditioned incapacity of a third-generation welfare mother, watch the so-called global economy and international market forces erode their most cherished traditions and undermine the sovereignty of the states they have long ruled. The chickens of economic rationality, with its self-serving and cockeyed view of human nature and society, are finally coming home to roost.

The hereditarian approach to "race" is, of course, based on the genetic explanation of human differences. Class, gender, and ethnic differences are to be largely accounted for by genetic inheritance. Beginning with the misappropriation and distortion of Darwinian biology by Herbert Spencer and the social Darwinists of the late nineteenth century, genetic explanations of observed group differences have been advocated by a vocal minority of racialists throughout the twentieth century. This hard core of racialists has had periodic success in appealing to a broader audience. Late nineteenth-century social Darwinism rationalized the devastating assault on all laws aimed at alleviating the conditions of the poor, including child labor. In its wake followed the eugenics wave during the teens and early 1920s, which had a major impact on the nation's immigration policy and created a climate hostile to the interests of Afro-Americans and other ethnic groups, such as Italians and Jews, not then considered equal to Americans of Anglo-Saxon ancestry.

Another, smaller resurgence of biological determinism occurred during the late thirties and early forties, partly a reflection of the early successes of the Nazi and Fascist movements in Europe. The Nazi Holocaust seemed to have delivered a deathblow to biological theories of "race," and between the mid-forties and late sixties there was a strong antihereditarian ethos accompanying the civil rights movement. However, conservative Euro-American reaction against the Great Society programs aimed at ameliorating the Afro-American condition and reducing racism provided the opening for the revival of hereditarian advocacy during the early seventies. The controversy died down by the mid-seventies, only to reappear in the "Bell Curve" wars of the mid-nineties like an intellectual comet of ice and dust with a twenty-year cycle.

Genetic hereditarians are necessarily racists, but not all racists are hereditarian, and many conservatives are openly hostile to this most extreme form of determinism. The problem for the hereditarians is that a consistent pursuit of their position leads them into headlong conflict with both traditional conservatives and many lower-class Euro-Americans, for reasons discussed in chapter 4. Charles Murray's most egregiously hereditarian remarks in the recent controversy were directed against what he called "white trash." White "trash" who read—an increasing proportion —have long learned to be wary of eugenics and other "scientific" defenses of their anti–Afro-American views. It is now common knowledge among even the "trash" that within-group genetic differences are greater than

8

between-group ones. Sauce for the genetic goose of anti–Afro-American discrimination and exclusion is too obviously sauce for the gander of anti–white "trash" discrimination. A minority of Euro-Americans no doubt continue to find biological explanations of inequality, especially ethnic inequalities, appealing, but here again the trend in American attitudes is unambiguously progressive. The most recent poll on the subject shows that less than 20 percent of Americans believe in biological determinism, and 40 percent take the extremely liberal position that genetic factors play no role whatsoever in accounting for human differences.[3]

In chapter 5, I turn to an examination of affirmative action, which, for all its faults and declining political support, remains the most successful policy initiative in the fight against racism and ethnic discrimination against working- and middle-class Afro-Americans. The volume of elite opposition to this policy is truly extraordinary, and shows no sign of letting up. The most unusual aspects of this debate, as I show, are that only a minuscule number of Euro-Americans even claim to have been adversely affected by it, and the majority of Euro-American workers actually express support for it when it is explained in unbiased terms. The problem, then, is to explain where the opposition is coming from, and why. The answers reflect badly on those who dominate the media and public discourse in America, including quite a few public figures who continue to imagine themselves in favor of Afro-American progress and improvement in intergroup relations.

Afro-Americans, women generally, and other disadvantaged groups have long been told by the more candid among the fortunate that life is unfair. Nothing is more hypocritical than people who have acquired their status largely by virtue of their ancestry and good fortune, or whose parents benefited from the massive postwar "affirmative action" program in suburban housing subsidies that explicitly excluded Afro-Americans, or who now earn incomes and exercise power out of all proportion to their modest talents, moralizing about fairness and merit. With the exceptions of academia, the professions, certain areas of commercial science and high technology, and those cutting-edge areas of business demanding original entrepreneurial talent, America is not, has never been, and will never be a meritocracy.

As long as people are able to pass on to their children, however average their native intelligence, most of their tangible wealth and power as well as their intangible assets—their *social* capital, or network of contacts, and their *cultural* capital, by which I mean those learned patterns of mutual trust, insider knowledge about how things really work, encounter rituals and social sensibilities that constitute the language of power and success—America will remain what it has been since the turn of the last century. This country is a very successful plutocratic democracy with a highly engaged elite public, a vigilant press, and a largely demobilized mass electorate whose rights and freedoms are constitutionally protected.

I share the current liberal concern over the mass apathy of the electorate—although I see it more as deliberate demobilization—and the sorry state of campaign financing, but I consider these the correctable excesses of any vigorous plutocratic democracy. No one with a knowledge of the real history of American democracy, or of democracies in general, including Plato's Athens, is likely to be complacent about current trends, but neither will he be unduly alarmed, especially where the system operates under the rule of law. What is unjust, however, and what should excite far greater outrage, is the systematic exclusion of certain groups from the social and cultural capital essential for success in this society. Democracy is, quintessentially, about inclusion. Its inherent flaw, which emerged with the original version invented by the Greeks, is a tendency to forge this inclusion by means of the exclusion of certain groups, most notably women and the descendants of slaves. America followed Greece to the letter in the historic construction of its democracy. It is time to put an end to this shameful flaw in what is, otherwise, the best system of governance and society. Afro-Americans and women are unique among all other disadvantaged groups, precisely in that their socially imposed differences were historically used as the contradistinctive mortar for the construction of the inclusively exclusive male, Euro-American citizenry that was the foundation of this great capitalist democracy. After centuries of such exclusion, it becomes impossible for such groups to penetrate the elite or even the upper reaches of the middle classes even if the preliminary task of removing overt political obstacles to inclusion has been achieved.

Affirmative action, I argue, seeks to perform this historic correction of democracy. It is a form of state-sponsored mobility that permits the entry of a critical mass of members of the formerly excluded groups into the elite spaces where real democracy works. Once this has been achieved —once the language and culture of power and elite status have been learned and the social capital acquired by a generation of these formerly excluded groups—we can expect them to pass on these intangible assets to their descendants, at which point affirmative action should be phased out.

There is evidence that this elite is rapidly emerging among Afro-Americans and that the intergenerational transfer of social and cultural capital has begun. I expect affirmative action to be gradually phased out over the course of the next fifteen years and make several proposals about the best way to achieve this. It would be a tragedy to abort it just when it is in its last phase before coming to term.

The volume concludes with a brief summary of what is required to restore sanity to intergroup relations, and a few general pointers toward the kind of policies that might promote self-determination among the bottom quarter of the Afro-American population.

Clearly, this work is not another compendium and analysis of statistical data on "race" in America. There is currently a vast outpouring of such works, in academic journals and texts, governmental research, think-tank reports, and popular books. "Race" is currently the happy hunting ground of the nation's army of policy wonks. I have drawn on the better of their works in addition to doing my own culling of the available data, especially in the first chapter. However, what we badly need now are more works attempting to understand not only the deeper underlying factors at play in this area of social relations, but the ways we go about the task of making sense of them, and it is in this vein that this work is presented. My emphasis is on the assumptions, intellectual frameworks, and ideological orientations that frame, filter, sometimes enlighten, and often distort analysis, discourse, and action in relation to Afro-Americans and their interethnic relations.

■

My own biases and intellectual orientations should be obvious to the careful reader of what follows. Alas, only a few seem to read carefully these days, especially on this subject. What tends to pass for reading and criticism is the search for cues on the basis of which snap judgments are made in classifying the author as "liberal," "conservative," "racist," "Tom," "feminist," "sexist," or whatnot. We have extended the way we view television to the way we read.

I have given up trying to explain to semiliterate American magazine editors and sound-bitten television producers why it is laughable to categorize me as a conservative, for the same reason that I long ago gave up attempting to explain to angry bourgeois Jamaicans that I have never been a pro-Castro communist. In both cases I have been condemned by association and by my tendency not to care where my ideas originated— as long as they strike me as sound—or where the chips fall as a result of what I write and say.

My intellectual development originated in the anti-imperialist tradition of West Indian scholarship and activism. I graduated from the University of the West Indies in 1962, the same year Jamaica graduated from three centuries of colonialism. My most formative years, however, were those spent in Britain during the sixties, as a graduate student at the London School of Economics, then as a member of its faculty, and a member of the editorial board of *New Left Review,* a budding novelist, and a founding member of the Caribbean Artist Movement. What emerged from my London years, combined with my pre- and post-colonial West Indian heritage, was a strong commitment to academic irreverence and public intellectual involvement; an agonistic engagement with European culture that is the hallmark of West Indian intellectualism, including the admittedly quixotic belief that the Caribbean version of the appropriated game of cricket is the ultimate model of civilized conduct; and a deeply rooted exilic impulse that led me, inevitably, to America, along with more than a third of my fellow nationals.

My intellectual baggage upon leaving Britain also included a dogmatic commitment to democratic socialism as the only solution to the problems of the poor and "non-white" everywhere, including America. It is not often that one has the opportunity to see the theories one fervently shares with others put into practice, but we were so unfortunate. For most of the seventies I was Special Advisor to the late Jamaican prime minister Michael Manley, whose regime attempted to restructure the Jamaican economy along democratic socialist lines. The ensuing disaster, unnecessarily aided and abetted by the American CIA, disabused me of all totalizing ideologies and policies that attempt in any way to micro-manage an economy. At the same time, the ensuing obscenities of inequality in Jamaica following the return to free market forces in the eighties, along with parallel developments in Latin America and post-Soviet Eastern Europe, have reinforced my conviction that the free market is a clumsy and pernicious tool for distribution and social justice.

As I argue in chapter 3, there are no logical reasons for believing, and abundant empirical grounds for discarding, the conservative capitalist dogma that the terms and modes of exchange between individuals optimal for economic production are the same as those ensuring even a minimally fair distribution of income. What the philosopher Karl Popper aptly termed "piecemeal social engineering" is essential for both the productive and distributive ends of any fair society, especially one committed to self-determination. In my younger years in Britain, I used to mock this piece of wisdom from the old philosopher, along with my fellow New Left gadflies. I now treat it as gospel.

What has most fashioned my thinking throughout the years, however, has been my academic work as a historical sociologist. I abandoned economics for sociology when it became clear to me that the social and cultural aggregates that constitute societies can never be reduced to the sum of the choices made by individuals. Understanding how these structures came into being and how they are rationalized, sustained, and reproduced over time is my abiding intellectual preoccupation. I have focused on the structures and culture of domination in human life, particularly on the structure of human slavery and its dialectical relation to the processes of liberation and the resulting construction of the idea of freedom in the West.

This dialectic informs everything I write, including the essays in this volume. Relations between Afro- and Euro-Americans are very much the product of the Manichaean dialectics of legal slavery and the institutional neoslavery of the post-reconstruction South. The second volume in this trilogy of essays will directly address this history. The present volume examines its consequences for the present. We are most certainly the product of the past, but we are in no way determined by it. That is because, as moral agents, our ancestors were all party to the construction of the past as it unfolded, including the slave in his or her relation with the slaveholder and the wider hostile world of Euro-American freemen. As one of my intellectual heroes, the great ex-slave philosopher Epictetus, pointed out some two millennia ago, the slave and former slave could always choose, however cruel and constraining the fetters of domination. In Epictetus's time, the best proof of this was the extraordinary way in which slaves and former slaves came to dominate and reconstruct the culture, language, and economy of ancient Rome. As the greatest of Latin poets, Horace, himself the son of a former slave, put it: "Captive Greece held her captor captive."

In our own time, and our own far greater "Rome," America, the best proof of Epictetus's audacious view is the extraordinary harvest of Afro-American culture and its powerful impact on the American cultural mainstream, an influence dating from the earliest colonial times. Culture is the distillation of our ancestors' choices—both those they made together and those they made alone. The vitality of Afro-American culture, as well as its past and continuing impact on the mainstream culture of America, is the most powerful argument against the surrender to determinist and victimist dogma. The essays that follow are mere footnotes to this living proof.

1 THE PARADOXES OF
INTEGRATION

After two and a half centuries of slavery, followed by a century of rural semiserfdom and violently imposed segregation, wanton economic discrimination, and outright exclusion of Afro-Americans from the middle and upper echelons of the nation's economy, it was inevitable that when the nation finally committed itself to the goal of ethnic justice and integration the transition would be painful, if not traumatic. The prejudices of centuries die hard, and even when they wane, the institutional frameworks that sustained them are bound to linger.

What is more, Afro-Americans, like once-oppressed peoples and classes everywhere, were bound to develop strategies of survival and patterns of adaptation to their centuries of discrimination and exclusion that were to become dysfunctional under newer, less constrained circumstances. Only supermen remain unimpaired by sustained systemic and personal assault. Centuries of public dishonor and ritualized humiliation by Euro-Americans were also certain to engender deep distrust, not only of those who actively humiliated and exploited them, but of all those who passively benefited from their oppression, which is to say, all persons of European ancestry.

In light of all this, the achievements of the American people over the past half century in reducing racial prejudice and discrimination and in improving the socioeconomic and political condition of Afro-Americans are nothing short of astonishing. Viewed from the perspective of compar-

15

ative history and sociology, it can be said, unconditionally, that the changes that have taken place in the United States over the past fifty years are unparalleled in the history of minority-majority relations. With the possible exception of the Netherlands—which is really too small to be meaningfully compared to America—there does not exist a single case in modern or earlier history that comes anywhere near the record of America in changing majority attitudes, in guaranteeing legal and political rights, and in expanding socioeconomic opportunities for its disadvantaged minorities.

Throughout Latin America, for example, the ideology of "Third World" solidarity and "racial democracy" merely adds insult to the dismal injuries of persisting racist attitudes and outright racial discrimination against minorities of African and Indian ancestry (in fact, Indians receive murderous treatment verging on genocide in parts of Central America and the Amazon). In the Islamic world, religious and ethnic minorities, especially those of African ancestry, continue to suffer discrimination that is so taken for granted it is not even permitted on the agenda of public issues. In extreme cases such as Mauritania, the Sudan, and some of the oil emirates, the enslavement of sub-Saharan Africans thrives. And in only a few states of sub-Saharan Africa are the rights and freedoms or economic security of the mass of the African populations respected by the dictatorial and kleptocratic elites that despoil the lands they make a mockery of ruling.

And yet, in spite of this comparative and historical record, we find America now mired in "racial" disharmony. What is going on? Is the "racial crisis" we read and hear about every day real? Or is it largely a crisis of perception, which, I hasten to add, can become real if people genuinely believe what they falsely perceive? Nations have been known to talk themselves into war through misperceptions and miscommunications about genuine but objectively tractable problems. Are we facing such a crisis?

In what follows I attempt to make sense of the sociological knot of "race" in America, fraught with paradox at almost every turn. I argue that the present condition of Afro-Americans is itself paradoxical, and the perceptions of this condition and the attempts to understand it are further riddled with paradoxes and contradictions. Observing this is like watching the foreplay of two octopuses through the distorting window of a glass-bottom boat. They appear to be consuming each other when, in fact, they are really trying to connect.

Let us begin by looking directly at the paradoxical knot that is the present Afro-American condition.

THE PARADOX OF PROGRESS:
THE BEST AND WORST OF TIMES

The paradox is this: for the great majority of Afro-Americans, these are genuinely the best of times, but for a minority they would seem to be, relatively, among the worst, at least since the ending of formal Jim Crow laws.[1]

THE BEST OF TIMES

On the one hand, there is no denying the fact that, in absolute terms, Afro-Americans, on average, are better off now than at any other time in their history. The civil rights movement effectively abolished the culture of postjuridical slavery, which, reinforced by racism and legalized segregation, had denied Afro-American people the basic rights of citizenship in the land of their birth.

Afro-Americans are now very much a part of the nation's political life, occupying positions in numbers and importance that go well beyond mere ethnic representation or tokenism. Quite apart from the thousands of local and appointed officials around the country—several having served as mayors of the nation's largest cities—Afro-Americans have held positions of major national importance in what is now the dominant power in the world. They have served as governors, senators, and powerful congressmembers chairing major House committees, and as appointed officials filling some of the most important offices in the nation, including that of the head of the most powerful military machine on earth.[2] In 1995 the Colin Powell phenomenon bedazzled the nation, and with his high-profile appointment as chairman of the national campaign to encourage volunteers to help children there is renewed speculation about his candidacy in 2000. For the first time in American political history, an Afro-American is seriously under consideration for the nation's highest office, with his strongest support coming from quarters often considered conservative on ethnicity.

It would be ridiculous to dismiss these developments as aberrations. What they demonstrate, beyond a doubt, is that being Afro-American is no longer a significant obstacle to participation in the public life of the nation.

What is more, Afro-Americans have also become full members of what may be called the nation's moral community and cultural life. They are no longer in the basement of moral discourse in American life, as was the case up to about forty years ago. Until then Afro-Americans were socially "invisible men" in the nation's consciousness, a truly debased ex-slave people. America was assumed to be a Euro-American country. The mainstream media, the literary and artistic communities, the great national debates about major issues, even those concerning poverty, simply excluded Afro-Americans from consideration in spite of the contributions they had made to the nation's cultural life.

No longer. The enormity of the achievement of the last forty years in American ethnic relations cannot be overstated. For better or worse, the Afro-American presence in American life and thought is today pervasive. A mere 13 percent of the population,[3] Afro-Americans dominate the nation's popular culture: its music, its dance, its talk, its sports, its youth fashion; and they are a powerful force in its popular and elite literatures.[4] "American culture," as Albert Murray insisted a quarter of a century ago, "even in its most rigidly segregated precincts, is patently and irrevocably composite...incontestably mulatto."[5] An Afro-American music, jazz, is the nation's classical voice, defining, audibly, its entire civilizational style. So powerful and unavoidable is the Afro-American popular influence that it is now common to find people who, while remaining racists in personal relations and attitudes, nonetheless have surrendered their tastes, and much of their viewing and listening time, to Afro-American entertainers, talk-show hosts, and sitcom stars. The typical Oprah Winfrey viewer is a conservative Euro-American, lower-middle-class housewife, and 66 percent of all Americans are of the belief that she is either "somewhat likely" or "very likely" to go to heaven, a state of cherishment exceeded only by Mother Teresa in the hearts of her fellow Americans.[6] Among the young, the typical rap fan is an upper-middle-class, Euro-American suburban youth[7] and Michael Jordan the ultimate hero.

This is a truly amazing situation, which finds no parallel in any other society or culture in the world today, and it is confirmed by a 1991 poll that compared the attitudes of the majority populations of several nations toward their main domestic minorities. The United States came out far ahead of all other nations in its level of ethnic tolerance. Thus, 42 percent of French people expressed dislike for their North African minority; 21 percent of the English openly detested the Irish among them; 45 percent of West Germans held unfavorable views of the Turkish minority; and 49 percent of Czechoslovakians expressed dislike for the Hungarians among them. In comparison, only 13 percent of Americans responded that they disliked the Afro-American minority.[8] The skeptical response to this survey is, of course, that Americans have simply become more adept at hiding their true feelings about race. It is hard to see why Americans should be any more hypocritical than other nations on this score. Indeed, one would think that the French and British, who pride themselves on their traditions of tolerance—who indeed even claim to have invented these traditions—would have more reasons to be hypocritical.

Closely related to the achievement of full political and cultural citizenship has been another great success of the postwar years: the desegregation of the U.S. military between 1948 and 1965. In addition, the extraordinary progress made in eliminating all formal discrimination and a good deal of informal prejudice in promotions has resulted in the military, especially the army, becoming a virtual model of successful race relations for the civilian community. With more than 30 percent of the army's recruits and more than 10 percent of its officer corps Afro-American, the army stands out as an example of ethnic progress for American society. Of the present army, Charles C. Moskos and John Sibley Butler write, "It is an organization unmatched in its level of racial integration. It is an institution unmatched in its broad record of Afro-American achievement. It is a world in which the Afro-American heritage is part and parcel of the institutional culture. It is the only place in American life where whites are routinely bossed around by Afro-Americans."[9]

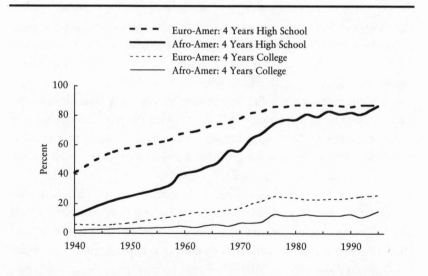

Figure 1. Percent of Persons 25–29 Years Old Who Have Completed Four Years of High School or Four Years of College. *Source:* Author's composition from Bureau of the Census, 1940 *Census of Population;* 1947 and 1952–1995 *March Current Population Survey* (Washington, D.C.: U.S. Census Bureau, Education and Social Stratification Branch, 1996).

Most of these developments were facilitated by another revolution in Afro-American life: the rapid growth in school enrollment and educational achievement at all levels. In 1940 there was a four-year gap in median years of schooling between Euro-Americans and Afro-Americans; by 1995 this gap had been reduced to a few months.[10] During the same period, as figure 1 shows, Afro-Americans in the ages 25 to 29 years almost eliminated the gap with Euro-Americans in the proportion completing high school, up from 12.3 percent to 86.5 percent, compared to the Euro-American improvement from 41.2 percent up to 87.4 percent. These dramatic improvements are not restricted to the youngest cohorts. Nearly three-quarters of all Afro-Americans over age 25 have had at least a high school education.

Nor is this improvement confined merely to years of school completed. Judging from the endless litany of criticisms of the public school system from both the left and the right, one would think that, whatever the increase in years of school completed, the effects on Afro-American educational achievement have been negligible. Critics such as Jonathan Kozol, for example, have issued dire warnings about the destructive impact of schooling on the minds of poor, especially Afro-American, children.[11] The educational statistics, however, tell a different story, as David Armor has pointed out.[12] Between 1970 and 1990 there was a dramatic narrowing of the gap between Afro-American and Euro-American 13-year-olds (mainly eighth-graders) in both reading and math achievement test scores, especially the former. Between 1971 and 1990 the reading achievement gap for this age group had been cut by almost half, from 39 to 20 points, nearly all of it coming from improvements in the Afro-American children's reading scores, the Euro-American scores remaining almost constant. In mathematics, while the Euro-American scores barely changed, going from 274 to 276 points between 1973 and 1990, there was a 21-point increase in the score of the Afro-American children, reducing the ethnic gap from 46 to 27 points.[13]

The record is far more mixed, and, overall very troubling, in two respects. One is that progress toward school integration may have stalled after a generation of positive change. The Harvard Project on School Desegregation recently warned that political decisions during the eighties, combined with recent Supreme Court rulings, have produced "clear signs that progress is coming undone and that the nation is headed backwards toward greater segregation of black students, particularly in the states with a history of de jure segregation."[14] This is a complex matter deserving close scrutiny. While there is certainly a problem—especially for Hispanic students—the significance of the evidence on recent trends in the resegregation of Afro-American students remains ambiguous. I will return to the subject at greater length in the concluding essay.

Of greater immediate concern are developments in higher education. After rapid increases during the 1970s in college completion among Afro-Americans, the numbers fell off during the eighties, especially among men. Afro-American women are now graduating from college at twice the rate of Afro-American men, and the gender differences in graduation rates are even greater for graduate and professional schools.[15] The long-term effect has been that while the proportion of Afro-Americans over 25 years of age completing college has grown from under 1.5 percent in 1940 to almost 13 percent in 1995, this is still barely over half of the Euro-American rate of 24 percent.

Even so, a tenfold increase in college completion is nothing to be sniffed at. Such great absolute progress constitutes a significant narrowing of the gap between the two groups, the Euro-American college completion rate having grown less than fivefold since the forties. Afro-Americans, from a condition of mass illiteracy fifty years ago, are now among the most educated groups of people in the world, with median years of schooling and college completion rates higher than those of most European nations. Although some readers may think this observation is a shocking overstatement, it is not. It is a fact. It only sounds like an overstatement when heard against the din of the liberal advocacy community's insistence that the miseducation of Afro-Americans is the major source of their present dilemmas.

This extraordinary growth in educational attainment largely accounts for another great change in the condition of Afro-Americans. The rise of a genuine Afro-American middle class in recent decades is cause for celebration, although no one is more inclined to belittle the fact than members of the Afro-American establishment itself.[16] What used to be called dismissively "the *Afro-American* middle class" meant those Afro-American persons who happened to be at the top of the bottom rung: Pullman porters, headwaiters, successful barbers and streetfront preachers, small-time funeral parlor owners and the like. Today the term *Afro-American middle class* means that segment of the *nation's* middle class that happens to be Afro-American, and it is no longer dependent on a segregated economy. What the economists James P. Smith and Finis R. Welch wrote in 1986 remains true today: "The real story of the last forty years has been the emergence of the black middle class, whose income gains have been real and substantial. The growth in the size of the black middle class was so spectacular that as a group it outnumbers the black poor. Finally, for the first time in American history, a sizable number of black men are economically better off than white middle-class America. During the last twenty years alone, the odds of a black man penetrating the ranks of the economic elite increased tenfold."[17]

These are without doubt the best of times for middle-class Afro-Americans, who now own more businesses, control a greater share of the national income, hold far more political offices, and lead more corporations than at any other period. The question of the size and stability of the Afro-American middle class has become a thorny one among social analysts.[18] There can be no definitive answer because so much depends on how one defines middle-class status. The most common measure is the median income of families. If we use a median family income of $35,000 as the cut-off point for middle-class status, then 36 percent of Afro-American families may be considered middle class.[19]

A better way of looking at the income data in order to ascertain middle-class status is to consider the mean income received by each fifth, or quintile, of all Afro-American households (see figure 2). In 1995, the upper two-fifths of Afro-American households had mean incomes of over $36,000. The fourth quintile of households had an average income of $36,710, while the highest fifth earned a mean income of $76,915. This was a striking improvement over the situation thirty years ago. In 1967, the comparable mean incomes for the two top quintiles, in constant (1995) dollars, were $27,554 and $52,933, respectively. Even more impressive has been the rise in the mean income of the top 5 percent of Afro-American households, which truly can be said to earn elite incomes: in 1995 this top 5 percent averaged $122,558 in household income, compared with $82,397 in 1967 (in 1995 dollars).[20]

Nearly all sociologists take into account educational and occupational factors when arriving at an estimate of the size of the middle class. My own calculations, using this approach, show that at least 35 percent of Afro-American adult, male workers are solidly middle class.[21] The percentage is roughly the same for adult female workers who, while they earn less than their male counterparts, are in white-collar occupations to a much greater extent.[22]

Liberal critics of this generally positive interpretation of middle-class developments like to bemoan what they consider the fragile economic base

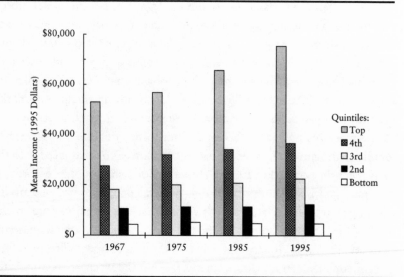

Figure 2. Mean Income of Each Quintile of Afro-American Households, 1967–1995. *Source:* Author's composition from U.S. Bureau of the Census, *Current Population Report, Series P-60* (Washington, D.C.: Income Statistics Branch/HHES Division, 1996), Table H-3.

of newly arrived Afro-Americans. Sharon M. Collins, in an informative study of Afro-American corporate executives, emphasizes "the dependency and the fragility" of this elite group of Afro-Americans, which she attributes to their "politically mediated opportunity structure." She warns that the size of the group faces erosion in the absence of a sympathetic political environment.[23] Apart from the fact that this is hardly a flattering view of the abilities of Afro-American executives, it flies in the face of clear evidence that their fortunes have not declined during periods of conservative Republican ascendancy.

Melvin L. Oliver and Thomas M. Shapiro have taken another tack in the relentless liberal insistence that Afro-Americans just cannot make it as a genuine middle class. They argue that the Afro-American middle class is all show and no substance, since its members rely overwhelmingly on income as their source of support, with few assets to back up their status. Afro-Americans, according to their calculations, own only 1.3 percent of the nation's financial assets, compared with 95 percent owned by Euro-Americans. They conclude pessimistically, "While income figures clearly show that progress was made in the post-civil rights era, the distribution of wealth paints a picture of two nations on diverging tracks labeled 'black progress' and 'no progress.'"[24]

The difference in asset ownership is important, but this conclusion is grossly overblown and, again, discredits the hard work, intelligence, and industriousness that middle-class Afro-Americans have put into acquiring the very real status and power they possess and the pride that they justly feel in their achievements. The problem that Oliver and Shapiro discuss—that of the extraordinary growth of income inequality in America since the mid-seventies—is a national rather than a racial issue. *All* middle-class Americans have been losing ground to the wealthiest 1 percent of families, who now own over 42 percent of all wealth, compared with the 22 percent they owned in 1975.[25] This is a good example of how a serious but nonracial issue is translated into a racial one, accompanied by the alarmist pseudoliberal mantra of "two nations." If two nations are emerging in America, they are the haves and the have-nots, a divide that cuts right across "race." Indeed, there is actually greater inequality, including asset inequality, among Afro-Americans than between Afro-Americans and Euro-Americans.[26]

Almost all new middle classes in the history of capitalism have had precarious economic starts, including Euro-Americans, most of whose families rose to middle-class status only after the Second World War. Therefore, a meaningful comparison of the asset base of Afro-American families with Euro-Americans would include information on Euro-Americans when they first started to become middle class.

But there is no reason to assume that Afro-Americans should follow the same paths into middle-class status as Euro-Americans did forty or more years ago. In the first place, the American economy has gone through fundamental structural changes, and the factors facilitating class mobility during the forties and fifties may no longer be available, or optimal, in our postindustrial era. For many, it may make more sense today to continually reinvest in the improvement of skills than to lock up funds in a mortgage. Second, it may well be that the Afro-American middle class has lifestyle preferences that direct it away from the asset accumulation tradition of Euro-American suburbanites. If this is the case, then such choices are entirely their business, and it is an impertinence for bourgeois liberals to bemoan them. In many parts of continental Western Europe, for example, the urban bourgeoisie rent rather than own their own homes, forgoing this major form of Euro-American asset accumulation in favor of a lifestyle that emphasizes concert going, eating out at gourmet restaurants, and enjoying longer annual holidays.

Taking a long-term perspective, the important thing to note is that the children of the newly emerged Afro-American middle class will be second- and third-generation burghers with all the confidence, educational resources and, most of all, cultural capital to find a more secure niche in the nation's economy. The evidence that this is already happening is everywhere, as the most cursory check of the class background of Afro-Americans at the nation's Ivy League colleges and major public universities will attest.

However, the impressive growth of the Afro-American middle class should not be used to mask the fact that, in comparative ethnic terms, the economic record is decidedly mixed. In 1995, the median income of all Afro-American families was $25,970, which was 60.8 percent of the Euro-American median family income of $42,646. This was only a 1.6 percent improvement on the ratio of 59.2 percent in 1967.[28] Figure 3 shows that, in spite of the considerable growth in income of the upper two-fifths of families—both in absolute terms and in relation to the two bottom fifths of Afro-American families—most of the modest changes relative to Euro-Americans were confined to the middle fifths of families. The top fifth of Afro-American families did not close the gap, earning 68 percent of what its Euro-American counterpart received in 1967 and 67 percent in 1995. The third or middle fifth of Afro-American families did the best in relative terms, moving up from 58 percent to 63 percent of their Euro-American counterparts. The bottom fifth of Afro-American

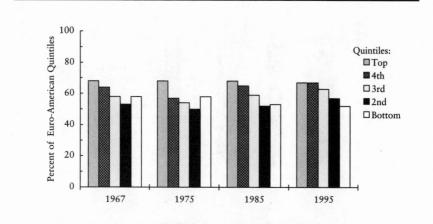

Figure 3. **Mean Income of Each Quintile of Afro-American Households as Percent of Euro-American Counterparts.** *Source:* Author's composition from U.S. Bureau of the Census, *Current Population Reports, Series P-60* (Washington, D.C.: Income Statistics Branch/HHES Division, 1996), Table H-3.

families did the worst: the ethnic gap with the bottom fifth of Euro-American families went from 58 percent in 1967 to 52 percent in 1995.

While these ethnic comparisons are important, we should be careful not to exaggerate them by concentrating too heavily on aggregate measurements. In America, and throughout the world, being middle class means having stable familial arrangements. One need make no judgment on the nature of such arrangements, whether they be East Indian extended families initiated by arranged marriages, Chinese clans, patriarchal Middle Eastern polygamous households, Icelandic common-law unions, California gay companionships, or standard married couple families. The important common feature is that they are usually enduring social units based on moderately stable unions in which at least two adults pool resources and skills to sustain a mutually desired lifestyle and to provide a structured, enriching environment for the reproduction and socialization of children who will become competent, middle-class adults. If we are to compare meaningfully the progress made by Afro-Americans in closing the gap with Euro-Americans, we should take into account this fundamental feature of middle-class life—otherwise, we are comparing sociological apples with pineapples.

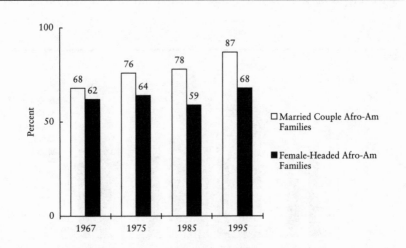

Figure 4. Marriage Matters: Afro-American Median Income by Family Type as Percent of Euro-American Counterparts. *Source:* Author's composition from Bureau of the Census, *Current Population Reports: Historical Income and Poverty Tables* (Washington, D.C.: Income Statistics Branch/HHES Division, 1996), Table F-7.

What do we find when such meaningful comparisons are made? The results are striking. As figure 4 shows, in sharp contrast to the failure to close the ethnic family income gap when all families are indiscriminately compared, we find that the median income of Afro-American families headed by a married couple was $41,307 in 1995, which was 87 percent of that earned by similar Euro-American families. This marked a stunning improvement in both absolute and relative terms for such Afro-American families that, in 1967, earned only 68 percent of their Euro-American counterparts.[28] We find the same impressive relative and absolute improvements when we compare individuals working full-time. The median earnings of Afro-American men working year-round and full-time went up from $20,056 in 1967 to $24,428 in constant (1995) dollars, jumping from 64 percent to 75 percent of Euro-American earnings.[29] And, in the most dramatic improvement of all, the year-round, full-time earnings of Afro-American women increased from $13,410 in 1967 to $20,665 in 1995—from 74.6 percent to 90 percent of Euro-American women's earnings.[30] Indeed, the most recent data bring even more extraordinary news about the progress of Afro-American women. For the first time in American history, a significant category of Afro-American workers now earns more than their Euro-American counterparts: as of March 1993, the nation's 1,025,000 Afro-American women who held a bachelor's degree or higher reported median annual earnings of $27,745, compared with earnings of $26,356 by Euro-American women with the same educational attainment.[31]

AND THE WORST OF TIMES

There can be no doubt that for a deplorably large minority of Afro-Americans life is tough—for some dismally so. However, the questions that concern us here go beyond whether a segment of the Afro-American population is facing hard times. First, just how hard a time are they facing? Second, what proportion of the Afro-American population faces conditions of chronic deprivation? And third, are conditions deteriorating, or are they improving, even if there is still a long way to go? If conditions are bad and getting worse, we have a crisis on our hands. But if they have been getting better and show signs of continuing to do so, it is clearly alarmist to label the situation catastrophic as so many have done. I cannot answer these questions at any length in an essay of this score. Fortunately, this is one area in which there has been a virtual mountain of research, plus easily accessible primary materials.

First, the bad news. A little over 29 percent of all Afro-American persons—some 9,873,000 souls—and slightly over a quarter of all Afro-American families (26.4 percent) were poor as of March 1996 (see figure 5). The comparative ethnic statistics are now familiar to anyone who pays even the most cursory attention to the news, since this tends to be the focus of the vast majority of public commentary on these figures. Afro-American individuals are 2.6 times more likely to be poor than Euro-Americans, and their families are slightly more than three times more vulnerable to poverty.

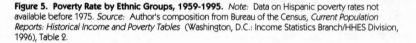

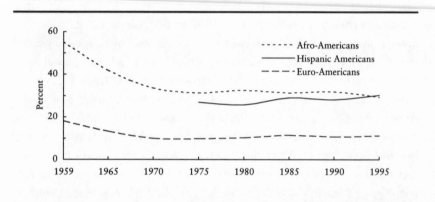

Figure 5. Poverty Rate by Ethnic Groups, 1959-1995. *Note:* Data on Hispanic poverty rates not available before 1975. *Source:* Author's composition from Bureau of the Census, *Current Population Reports: Historical Income and Poverty Tables* (Washington, D.C.: Income Statistics Branch/HHES Division, 1996), Table 2.

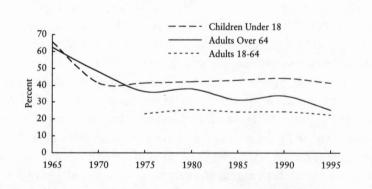

Figure 6. Percent of Afro-Americans in Poverty by Age Group. *Note:* Data unavailable on 18–64 age group prior to 1975. *Source:* Author's composition from Bureau of the Census, *March Current Population Survey* (Washington, D.C.: Poverty and Health Statistics Branch/HHES, 1996), Table 3.

Perhaps the most disheartening feature of the present situation is that children disproportionately bear the brunt of impoverishment. A disturbing trend, which began in 1975, continues apace: the poverty rate for children of all ethnic groups, but especially Afro-Americans, is higher than that for any other age group (see figure 6).[32] In 1995, a total of 4,552,000 Afro-American children, comprising 41.5 percent of Afro-American children under age 18 living in families, were poor. In our over-racialized mode of discourse, pundits are quick to point out that this rate is two and a half times that of Euro-American children, but it is just as important to note that the rate is almost twice that of Afro-Americans between ages 18 and 64, and over one and a half times that of the Afro-American population over 64 years of age.

Without doubt, the main reason for this high proportion of children in poverty is the fact that nearly 60 percent of all Afro-American children are in female-headed households, and 45 percent of female-headed households are in poverty. As figure 7 indicates, to look at the numbers from a different viewpoint, all but 6 percent of the nation's poor Afro-American children are in female-headed families, and, tragically, these families are increasing as a proportion of all Afro-American households. Figure 8 shows that married couple families have declined from nearly 70 percent of all Afro-American families in 1967 to 46 percent in 1995, the same percent as families now headed by single women.

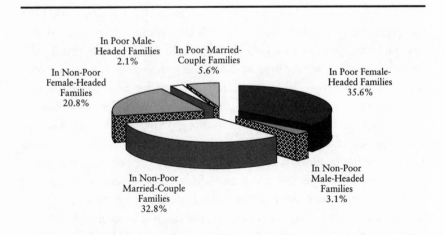

Figure 7. Distribution of Afro-American Children by Family Type and Poverty Status. *Source:* Author's composition from Bureau of the Census, *The Black Population in the United States, March 1995* (Washington, D.C., unpublished on-line data, 1996), Table 15.

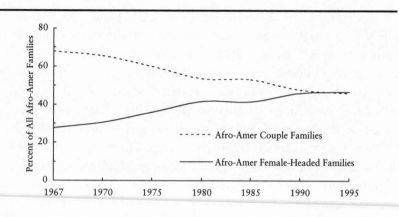

Figure 8. The Tragic Convergence in Afro-American Families: Percent Headed by Married Couples and by Single Women. *Source:* Author's composition from Bureau of the Census, *Current Population Reports: Historical Income and Poverty Tables* (Washington, D.C.: Income Statistics Branch/HHES Division, 1996), Table F-7.

This is clearly an unacceptable state of affairs. Nonetheless, what we want to know is this: has the situation been getting worse or better? Is progress being made or are there grounds for the pervasive pessimism of so many commentators? If we glance back at figure 5 we will see that, for Afro-Americans as a whole, the poverty rate has been going down, although the pace of change leaves much to be desired. Progress was impressive between 1959 and 1975, but between then and 1993 there was not only stagnation but some loss of ground. However, since 1993 the pace of improvement has picked up once more. After a remarkable decline in the poverty rate between 1995 and 1996, it now stands at a historic low. For the first time in the nation's history the rate for individuals has gone below 30 percent, and the rate for families—26.4 percent—is also at its lowest point. Figure 6, which looks at changes in terms of age, delivers some good news along with the bad news of stalled progress for children since the mid-seventies: this is the enormous progress made by elderly Afro-Americans, who, between the mid-sixties and the present, experienced a decline from 62.5 percent to the present level of 25.4 percent. As a nation we can do much better than to have one in four elderly Afro-Americans in poverty, but a decline in suffering from over three in five persons to only one in four is, by any standard, enormous progress.

It should also be noted that the official poverty rate masks important improvements by exclusively relying on cash payments as the measure. When a broadened definition is used, taking into account noncash benefits such as food stamps, the Afro-American poverty rate is at least another 4 to 6 points lower.[33]

The relatively high unemployment rate is often pointed to as the major culprit in explaining Afro-American poverty. High unemployment is a problem in its own right, as well as a possible explanation for the poverty and social problems of the lower classes. As figure 9 shows, Afro-Americans have always experienced unemployment levels more than double those of Euro-Americans. The rate now stands at 9.8 percent, exactly where it was in 1972, while the rate for Euro-Americans has gone down a full point to its lowest level in twenty-three years. For Afro-American youth seeking work, the figures are catastrophic: unemployment among them now stands at the Depression level of 31.2 percent—nearly two and a half times the Euro-American teenage rate—but in recent years it has gone as high as 40.6 percent.

The distinguished sociologist William Julius Wilson argues forcefully in his most recent book, based on years of research on the urban poor, "that the disappearance of work and the consequences of that disappearance for both social and cultural life are the central problems of the inner-city ghetto."[34] In earlier works Wilson, along with others, has argued that

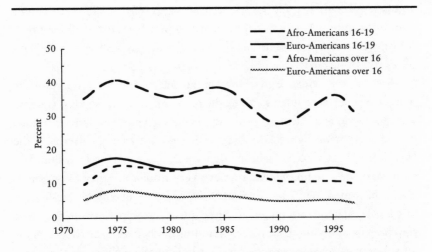

Figure 9. Unemployment Rates by Ethnic Group, 1972–1997. *Source:* Author's composition from Bureau of Labor Statistics, *Labor Force Statistics from the Current Population Survey* (Washington, D.C.: Bureau of Labor Statistics on-line data, 1997).

major structural and regional shifts in the nation's industrial base, international trade, and new technologies have created an enormous skill mismatch between the new jobs being generated and the qualifications of the least-educated young Afro-American males. These same forces have hastened the suburbanization of good jobs in metropolitan areas, creating a serious geographic mismatch for young Afro-Americans in the central cities, who find themselves living precisely where meaningful jobs are rapidly declining.[35]

Evidence is also increasing that the large influx of unskilled immigrants into the urban labor force has drastically reduced both the employment prospects and wages of young Afro-Americans still willing to work.[36] At the same time, as Harry J. Holzer notes, "opportunities in the illegal sector have grown relatively more attractive as regular earnings possibilities have diminished... [leading] large fractions of young black men to forgo employment altogether, many instead choosing illegal activities as an alternative income source."[37]

The high unemployment rate is certainly a problem, and figure 10 does lend some support to Wilson's argument: there is a short-term relationship between unemployment and poverty, and the long-term trajectories of both are also similar. But is Afro-American unemployment, especially in the central cities, due to the disappearance of jobs, as Wilson claims, and is it, in turn, the source of the multiple social problems that beset lower-class Afro-Americans? There are several problems with Wilson's argument. The first is that joblessness, per se, is only one of many causes of poverty among Afro-Americans. A little over 50 percent of all poor people worked at least part-time in 1995 but were simply unable to pull themselves out of poverty.[38]

Second, the evidence that unemployment is the major source of the more severe social problems among the Afro-American lower class is weak. The most serious of these problems is, of course, the rise in families headed by single women. Figure 10 indicates that the long-term patterns of the overall female-headed household rate (that is, those with and without children) and the unemployment rate are very different. Unemployment is about the same in 1997 as it was in 1970, while the overall female-headed rate has escalated from under 30 percent to over 46 percent. In the short run there is, if anything, an inverse relationship between the two rates for all subperiods except perhaps the first half of the eighties. If there is a relationship between poverty and the overall female-headed household rate, the unemployment rate is certainly not explaining it.

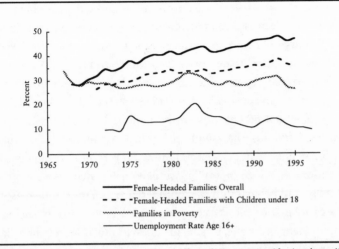

Female-Headed Families Overall
- - - -Female-Headed Families with Children under 18
〰〰〰Families in Poverty
Unemployment Rate Age 16+

Figure 10. Poverty, Female-Headed Families, and Unemployment among Afro-Americans, 1967–1997.
Source: Author's composition based on data from Bureau of the Census, Poverty and Health Statistics Branch/HHES Division, March Current Population Survey (unpublished on-line data extracted April 1997) and Bureau of Labor Statistics, Labor Force Statistics from the Current Population Survey (on-line data extracted May 1997).

The graph lines in figure 10 lead us to question whether there is, indeed, a relationship between female-headed families and poverty. Cross-sectional studies strongly suggest that there is, but the absence of an overall long-term relationship indicates that the relationship should be carefully specified.[39] Many female-headed families are, in fact, not poor, and as Rebecca M. Blank has recently reminded us, "the fact that many women choose divorce or single parenting over marriage is not necessarily a bad thing," especially if it means escaping physical and sexual abuse.[40] As out-of-wedlock childbearing becomes less negatively sanctioned in the society at large, an increasing number of nonpoor and even middle-class Afro-American women are becoming single mothers. This process has been hastened by the growing participation of women in the labor force.[41] The participation rate has always been relatively high among Afro-American women, and it has increased since the early seventies. Furthermore, Afro-American women have been doing relatively better than Afro-American men in the labor market—and for those with college degrees, absolutely better than Euro-American women—and have also benefited more than men from supplementary transfer payments.

The problem with female-headed households is not simply that there is a single parent. Although single parenting is always emotionally or economically challenging for both parent and child, a capable adult living in a stable environment who has adequate resources and a dependable network of friends and relatives is usually able to surmount the inherent risks. It is when single parenting coexists with catalytic factors such as impoverished, high-crime neighborhoods; low educational attainment and work skills; little or no earned income; attenuated social support networks; and an environment with a misogynistic, "cool-pose" street culture in which a large minority of sexual predators identify manhood with impregnation and irresponsible fathering that single parenting becomes a devastating social choice for women. The poorer and more dangerous a person's environment, the more marriage or stable companionship matters economically, emotionally, and behaviorally, for both women and men. One reason that the Mexican-American lower class has higher labor force participation and employment rates and in general does so much better than the Afro-American, even with the sometimes severe handicap of inadequate English among immigrants, is its far greater commitment to marriage in the face of adversity.

An additional problem with Afro-American single parenting is that, unlike in other ethnic groups, single adult Afro-American women have a higher birth rate than married women. While the birth rate for single adult Afro-American women ages 20 to 44 has declined since the sixties—from 115.4 births per 1,000 women in 1960 to 83.7 births in 1990—it has declined at a far slower pace than the birth rate for married Afro-American women, which fell from 163.2 to 77.6 during this same period. This contrasts sharply with other ethnic groups: married Euro-American adult women, for example, had a rate of 90.2 births per 1,000 women in 1990, which was more than two and a half times *greater* than the rate for single adult women.[42] When teen births are taken into account, the result is that in 1995 single women accounted for 70 percent of the Afro-American births, and, if present trends continue, they will soon be parenting over 90 percent of all Afro-American children. This is an internally generated disaster. As we have seen, poor Afro-American children are six times more likely to be in single-mother families than in married couple ones (see figure 7).

Another serious challenge to Wilson's argument is the increasing body of evidence that jobs, far from having disappeared from the nation's cities, have actually increased substantially, at both the skilled and unskilled levels. Over the past six years the American economy has had one of the highest growth rates since the sixties, generating a considerable number of new jobs. Roger Waldinger has shown that in New York, between Euro-

American departures from old lower-level occupations and the generation of new unskilled jobs, especially in the hotel sector, a tight labor market emerged at the bottom end of the occupational queue. However, young urban Afro-Americans declined to take advantage of the situation because of their aspirations for higher paying jobs, especially in the public sector—the federal and municipal civil service, the post office, mass transit, the municipal hospital and telephone company jobs that sustained the growing Afro-American middle class. Unfortunately, they lacked the educational attainment for public sector jobs, and the un-skilled openings in the private sector were quickly filled by immigrants, who then set up employment networks that effectively excluded Afro-Americans from reentering these niches.[43] Work, then, has not disappeared. Rather, what has vanished—from a small, but significant and increasingly troublesome minority of younger, urban Afro-Americans—is the willingness to accept the labor-intensive, "lousy" jobs available to the poorly educated, and the willingness of employers, including Afro-American entrepreneurs, to hire underqualified persons further burdened with poor soft skills. Interestingly, no one has more poignantly documented this dilemma than Wilson himself.[44]

Finally, there is the simple, stark fact that most Afro-American (and Euro-American) poor people are poor not because they are not working, but because the jobs they hold pay too small a wage to pull them out of poverty. Rebecca M. Blank sums up this predicament as follows:

> As a result of recent economic changes, escaping poverty through work alone is increasingly difficult. If earnings are the only source of income available to a family, few less-skilled single mothers earn enough to escape poverty; about three-quarters of less-skilled married men earn enough to assure that their family escapes poverty through earnings; and slightly less than two-thirds of single persons earn enough in the labor market to escape poverty. These numbers indicate that finding and holding a job is not an adequate strategy for many of today's poor families to escape poverty. Their earnings must be supplemented with other forms of public and private support.[45]

Let me turn now to the set of social problems that no doubt first come to mind whenever the problems of Afro-Americans, especially the urban lower class, are mentioned. The most important of these, which I have touched upon briefly already, is the growing rate of out-of-wedlock births, especially to teenagers who lack the social and financial means to support themselves, much less one or more children. The great popular confusion and misapprehension on this subject are partly due to its complexity, but also in good part due to its connection with sex—and Americans, for all their literacy and advancement, have a problem thinking clearly on this subject. While it is true that adolescents have become more sexually active since the sixties and seventies, they are having far fewer babies than previous generations. Attributable in part to the greater use of contraceptives, the number of births to teenagers has declined by over 34 percent between the mid-fifties and the mid-nineties.[46] Since 1975 the rate has actually gone down slightly for Afro-American teenagers, after having escalated during the second half of the eighties, and in 1995 it fell a full 8 percent.

In spite of this decline, it is correct to view the present rates as a major problem. Teenage childbearing, whatever its marital status, comes at greater costs within the context of postindustrial America than in earlier times. Preparation for competent adulthood requires not only more years of schooling but more years of acquiring the increasingly complex social and cultural capital essential for even moderately successful adulthood, and even more years of learning the demanding role of parenting a competent postindustrial child.

A second and even greater reason for the national concern is that paralleling this declining birthrate has been a rapid increase in the overall rate of out-of-wedlock births (see figure 11). In 1995 over three-fourths of all

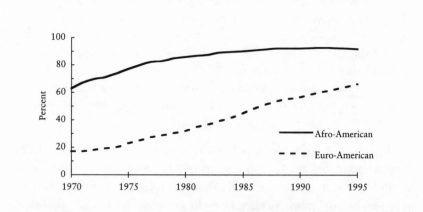

Figure 11. Percentage of All Births to Women Ages 15–19 Occurring out of Marriage by Ethnic Group, 1970–1995. *Source:* Author's composition from S. J. Ventura, "Births to Unmarried Mothers: United States, 1980–1992." National Center for Health Statistics, *Vital and Health Statistics,* Series 21, No. 53, 1995. *Monthly Vital Statistics Report,* 45:5 (December 1996): Table 1; 45:11(S) (June 1997): passim.

births to teens were out of wedlock. The percentage has been increasing rapidly among both Euro- and Afro-American teens. Among Afro-American teenage girls, the rate went up from an already high 68 percent in 1970 to the 1995 level of 92 percent. The consequences are extremely serious for both groups, but they may be greater for Afro-Americans. For the teenage mothers it means far greater risk of poverty, of remaining a single mother permanently, of curtailed educational attainment and poorer employment prospects, and of welfare dependency.[47]

In the early nineties, a revisionist group of social scientists argued that the consequences of teenage childbearing have been overstated: the observed differences in the fate of teen mothers and those who delayed childbearing until later are due, they argue, to differences in the family background of the teen child bearers ("mother's and father's education, number of siblings, parental family arrangements") rather than to teenage childbearing per se.[48] Later studies, however, have reconfirmed the well-documented, not to mention commonsensical, view that the effects of teen childbearing are considerable, even if not as catastrophic, for the mother, as previously thought.[49]

What defenders of teenage childbearing (and scholars who statistically downplay its effects) often fail to take into account are the costs to society and taxpayers, and, even more important, the consequences for the children born to mothers who are themselves still children. One reason that the costs to the mother may seem, from her individual perspective, to be minimal when she compares herself with teenagers who postpone childbearing, is that the major financial and social costs of this maternal precocity are passed to the nation's taxpayers, who foot the bill of greatly increased welfare costs incurred by these girls over the course of their lives. Conservative, baseline estimates show that teen mothering costs U.S. taxpayers at least $7 billion annually in social services and lost tax revenues, and as much as $15 billion when indirect costs are calculated. The ripple effect goes further: "The costs of society are twice the costs to taxpayers—an estimated $15 billion a year due to early childbearing itself, and up to $30 billion a year if all the risk factors amenable to policy influences were successfully eliminated."[50]

Among these other risk factors, the most serious are the consequences for the children of these teen mothers. Here is the real heart of the tragedy, and it has had a devastating effect on the Afro-American lower class. The evidence is overwhelming that the children of these children have far more deprived home environments and are at significantly greater risk of cognitive impairment; are far more subject to child abuse and run a greater likelihood of being placed in a foster home. Further, when their children, in turn, become teenagers, they are somewhat more likely to drop out of school and three times more likely to be incarcerated, and their daughters are significantly more likely to become teenage mothers themselves.[51]

Euro-Americans are increasingly seeing this problem with their own, mainly lower class, girls—as figure 11 makes clear. Afro-Americans, as we have seen, have lived with this social problem for generations. This growth in teen births since the seventies has exacerbated what has come to be known as the underclass problem. I mean by the underclass that small but dangerous segment of the Euro-American and Afro-American lower class made up of persons who are either unable or unwilling to live by the norms of working- or middle-class life in their own communities. Instead, they opt out of the labor force, surviving either through chronic welfare dependence or in the marginal and illegal economic sector. They are people with multiple social problems. The Afro-American underclass is largely confined to severely depressed, inner-city areas where they prey upon poor but working-class and nonunderclass residents. Members of the Euro-American underclass are scattered in suburban and rural pockets, but are increasingly found in certain smaller or midsized cities. One study found that 55 percent of the rural population with this complex of problems was Euro-American.[52]

Christopher Jencks has warned us of the dangers of talking about multiple social problems. He prefers to speak of different kinds of underclasses: the impoverished, the jobless male, the jobless female, the educational, the violent, and the reproductive underclasses.[53] This is one of those rare occasions on which I disagree with this eminent social analyst. First, there is no need for the term *underclass* when it is so used. Second, there is a great danger in this approach of including the entire poor population under one or another of these versions of the underclass when the underclass constitutes only a small fraction—at most 10 percent of the Afro-American poor, or a total of about 900,000 persons—and perhaps a smaller fraction of the Euro-American poor. As Rebecca Blank recently reemphasized, only a small minority of residents of even the most impoverished and crime-ridden neighborhoods engage in underclass activities, and the majority of the poor do not live in the ghettos upon which the underclass preys.[54]

But my main reason for not adopting Jencks's approach is that I am firmly convinced that a small, hard core of dangerous people with multiple social problems does in fact exist. What is more, they have been around from the late nineteenth century. Consider the following:

> In the city of Philadelphia the increasing number of bold and daring crimes committed by Negroes in the last ten years has focused the attention of the city on this subject. There is a widespread feeling that something is wrong with a race that is responsible for so much crime, and that strong remedies are called for. Judges on the bench have discussed the matter. Indeed, to the minds of many, this is the real Negro problem.[55]

This is not a conservative account of modern Philadelphia but a description of the underclass by W. E. B. Du Bois based on his sociological researches during the 1880s. Du Bois argued that the underclass of his day was long in the making, although there was a critical turn for the worse from the third decade of the nineteenth century. Laws had been repeatedly passed in Philadelphia during the eighteenth century to control the "tumultuous meetings and other disorderly doings" of the Afro-Americans, much to the "great Terror and Disquiet of the Inhabitants of this city."[56] Du Bois noted that between 1830 and 1850 the Afro-American, though "less than one-fourteenth of the population was responsible for nearly a third of the serious crimes committed."[57] He offered a sociological explanation of the escalating underclass crime problem of his day: "He [the Afro-American] had lately been freed from serfdom, he was the object of stinging oppression and ridicule, *and paths to advancement open to many were closed to him.* Consequently the class of the shiftless, aimless, idle, discouraged and disappointed was proportionately large." (Emphasis added.)[58]

By the time Du Bois published his findings in 1899, Afro-Americans had already been locked out of the manufacturing and craft jobs by the new immigrant groups and their racist labor leaders.[59] Following Du Bois's lead, the historian Roger Lane has traced the development of this original underclass in fine detail, attributing its rise and growth to the overtly racist exclusion of Afro-Americans from the nation's emerging industrial economy. He tells us that "with legitimate opportunities so often blocked from the city's Afro-American population, criminal activity was very important to it, helping to define and shape much of its culture and its relations with the wider world. Afro-American crime was distinctive in significant ways. And, sometimes, it paid."[60]

The underclass has remained a thorn in the side of Afro-American urban communities throughout the twentieth century. Until the early seventies it was not viewed as a national problem for the simple reason that crime within Afro-American communities was not considered worthy of Euro-American attention, Afro-Americans not being a part of what I earlier called the broader moral community. Beginning with the early seventies, two developments changed all this. On the one hand, the lower class and the more vulnerable lower end of the working class have suffered from the growing trend toward income inequality and decreased income for the lowest fifth of workers. This, combined with the rising expectations of lower-class Afro-Americans prompted by the successes of the civil rights movement, has made the marginal economy and its underclass entrepreneurs more seductive. People simply had to find a way to supplement their meager incomes. At the same time, there was another devastating development: the introduction of crack with its murderous consequences. This development, ironically, went along with slowly but significantly declining use of drugs. However, crack is distinctive in that women are especially vulnerable to it, particularly poor women burdened with many problems and low self-esteem. Increased drug dependence among women inevitably meant greater vulnerability to sexual predators, and with it an escalation of irresponsible and unintended pregnancies and births. The rise of single-woman families, in turn, generated further poverty and more vulnerable youth and young adults.

On the other hand, these developments were taking place at precisely the time when Afro-Americans were being embraced by the broader moral community. Afro-American crime now made the headlines and was no longer tucked away on the back pages in the traditional what-else-do-you-expect-of-*them* manner. Indeed, the pendulum may have swung full circle. The malign neglect of previous centuries may have become the malign obsession of the post–civil rights years.

Between the growth of the more sensational drug-related urban crimes and the growing embrace of Afro-Americans by the wider national community, the idea of the underclass was born. And while the underclass may not have grown much, if at all, in numbers, it has certainly become more deadly, taking its toll on the more vulnerable inner-city Afro-American communities. The situation it creates is one of social anarchy and moral nihilism, reflected in the horrible devaluation of human life. Kids and young adults kill for sneakers, leather jackets, cheap jewelry and drugs; worse, they kill for no other reason than having been "dissed" by a wrong look or misstatement. Linked to this social and moral crisis are all the other well-known pathologies. What the Children's Defense Fund wrote in 1992 in its annual report on the state of America's children is still true today:

The deadly combination of guns, gangs, drugs, poverty, and frightened, hopeless youths is turning many of our inner cities into Vietnams of destruction and despair and our neighborhoods and schools into corridors of fear. Prison walls are bulging with the 1.1 million inmates that make us the world's leading jailor. Yet, violence escalates. For thousands of inner city youths the American dream has become a choice between prison and death. In fact, prison has become a more positive option than home and neighborhood for many youths who see no hope, no safety, no jobs, and no future outside prison walls.[61]

What this cry of anguish fails to emphasize is the fratricidal nature of underclass criminality and the fact that the victimizers are almost all Afro-American. Afro-Americans constitute 25 percent of all arrestees in the United States, and 47 percent of all those arrested for violent crimes, nearly all against fellow Afro-Americans. Murder is the leading cause of death among Afro-American men ages 15 to 24, and Afro-Americans in general are six times more likely to be murdered than Euro-Americans.

Compounding this already bad situation is the complete failure of the government's "war on drugs" and its disproportionate impact on the young Afro-American population. A 1995 report of the Sentencing Project shows that on any given day almost one in three (32.2 percent) of Afro-American men between the ages of 20 and 29 is under some form of criminal justice supervision, in either prison or jail, or on probation or parole.[62] As shocking as this figure is, it actually underestimates the true situation, since it refers only to control rates for any given day. When the flow of persons coming under the control of the criminal justice system in the course of a year is considered, the rates escalate even further. A 1987 study of California, which calculated such rates, revealed that two-thirds of all Afro-American males between the ages of 18 and 29 had been placed under arrest at some time.[63] The arrest rate for violent crime among Afro-Americans remains disproportionately high—45 percent of all such crimes are committed by them—but has not changed over the past twenty years. What has skyrocketed is the arrest rate for drug offenses, which increased from 24 percent of all drug arrests in 1980 to 39 percent in 1993. And the situation is likely to get worse in coming years. As the Sentencing Project's Marc Mauer and Tracy Huling point out: "In addition to the steady twenty-year increase in criminal justice populations, the impact of current 'get tough' policies in particular suggest continuing increases in criminal justice control rates and increasing racially disparate impacts."[64]

The disproportionate impact of the "war on drugs" on Afro-American youth is especially unjust in light of the fact that drug use has been generally on the decline, especially since the mid-eighties. Not only has the "war" unnecessarily increased the incarceration rate, it may well have worsened the situation by increasing the price of drugs and glamorizing the parasites who dispense them. However, it is an error to generalize this failure to the entire justice system and dismiss it as racist, as so many advocates have done. There is, in fact, no evidence of any such bias. As Michael Tonry bluntly puts it, "The evidence seems clear that the main reason that black incarceration rates are substantially higher than those for whites is that black crime rates for imprisonable crimes are substantially higher than those for whites."[65]

This is all grim news, and it would be irresponsible to deny or underplay it. At the same time, it would be equally irresponsible to overplay it, and this, sadly, is the danger we now face. An unholy alliance of conservative, law-and-order hardliners, sensationalist media producers, and Afro-American "race" leaders all have vested interests in exaggerating the degree to which the underclass has infected both the broader Afro-American population and the nation at large.

The simple truth is that not only is the underclass, demographically, a small fraction of the urban poor and a nearly insignificant component of all Afro-Americans, but all the evidence points to the fact that their corrosive impact is, at last, diminishing. As every literate American except the producers of TV news and tabloid editors now knows, the nation's crime rate is in sharp decline. Between 1994 and 1995 the overall victimization rate fell 13 percent from the 1994 rate of 46.2 per 1,000 persons, the largest fall in the history of the U.S. Justice Department's victimization survey. This decline occurred across all categories of crime except motor vehicle theft. The declines were highest in violent crime and most noticeable among the poorest households. Significantly, the declines, especially in violent crime, were highest in urban areas most associated with the Afro-American underclass. Among Afro-Americans the aggravated assault rate fell by 24 percent between 1994 and 1995.[66]

We come, finally, to another area that is often cited as a major failure both in ethnic relations and in the amelioration of the Afro-American condition: the persistence of segregation and the rise of hypersegregation in many of the nation's large metropolitan areas, accompanied by the ghettoization of the urban poor. This development has been linked, paradoxically, to the very successful growth of the Afro-American middle class.[67]

Douglas Massey and Nancy Denton, in *American Apartheid,* are partly correct in describing the increasing physical separation of the Afro-American poor as "the forgotten factor in American race relations," but they exaggerate the significance of hypersegregation, and their insistence on labeling it "apartheid" is grossly misleading and unfair.[68] No one who has visited the slums of Johannesburg or Cape Town, or who is remotely knowledgeable about the execrable corruption and murderous brutality of the apartheid police force, or the complete abandonment of the rule of law in the fascist apartheid state, can take such comparisons seriously. At the same time, it is true that the promise of the civil rights acts of the sixties, which banned discrimination in housing and other areas of American life, is yet to be fulfilled.

In a more recently published work, Paul Jargowsky summarized the situation as follows:

> Nationally, about 11 million persons lived in urban ghettos in 1990. Seven out of eight were members of minority groups. About six million blacks—one in five—lived in ghettos in 1990, up 36 percent since 1980. On average, the "level of ghetto poverty," that is, the proportion of a metropolitan area's black population that lives in a ghetto, increased from 20.2 to 23.7 percent. The proportion of the black *poor* in metropolitan areas who live in ghettos increased even faster—from 37.2 to 45.4 percent—indicating an increasing isolation of the black poor from the black middle class.[69]

That the geographical isolation of the Afro-American poor has increased, there can be little doubt. But what does it mean? The situation, on closer inspection, turns out to be far more complex, and a good deal more hopeful, than these studies suggest. Indeed, more recent works make it clear that the assessment of integration solely on the basis of the spatial segregation of America's cities is extremely misleading.

In the first place, there is strong evidence that the attitudes of Euro-Americans toward living with Afro-Americans have become more liberal. Modest but significant declines in segregation were seen during the eighties, even using the old yardsticks of spatial segregation, especially in what Reynolds Farley and William Frey described as "young, southern and western metropolitan areas with significant recent housing construction."[70] Further, in their later study of hypersegregated Detroit, Farley and his associates found not only that Euro-Americans have become significantly more tolerant about living in moderately mixed neighborhoods, but that their motivations for not wanting to live in majority

43

Afro-American neighborhoods "did not invoke racial stereotypes," but instead were based on fears about declining real estate values, differing attitudes toward neighborhood living, and fear of increased crime.[71] These are *not* racist concerns: Afro-Americans, especially lower-class Afro-Americans, do have different views about the public uses of space, different tolerance levels for the public display of sounds, different norms of teenage sexuality, and a much higher rate of crime. Class-based, rather than purely racist, aversion to integration has been found to be true even of Mississippi. In their study of the demand for private education in that state, John R. Conlon and Mwangi S. Kimenyi concluded that Euro-American flight from the public schools was due more to prejudice against poor Afro-Americans and their behavior patterns than to Afro-Americans per se, although a degree of old-fashioned racism was certainly still present.[72]

These findings are reinforced by a Gallup survey in June 1997, which found that while half of all Afro-Americans now live in neighborhoods that are either half or nearly all Euro-American, 41 percent are still living in neighborhoods that are mostly or all Afro-American. The great majority of Euro-Americans, 77 percent, continue to live in neighborhoods that are mostly or all Euro-American. At the same time, attitudes toward mixed neighborhoods continue their trend toward greater tolerance: less than two in ten Euro-Americans say that they would move if Afro-Americans moved into their neighborhood "in great numbers" and only 1 percent said that they would move if an Afro-American moved next door.[73] Many people have expressed great skepticism about these attitudes, pointing to the still segregated living condition of 40 percent of Afro-Americans. These skeptics fail to distinguish between class-based and ethnic responses.

There is, however, another more important criticism of those scholars who overemphasize hypersegregation as the great failure of American ethnic relations. It is the fact that its spatial focus masks major changes in the direction of closer personal integration. In an important recent study, a team of sociologists led by Lee Sigelman demonstrated that even in hypersegregated Detroit considerable progress has been made in relations between Euro- and Afro-Americans. What they found was that integration at the workplace and other non-neighborhood contexts led to a substantial increase in interethnic contact, which, in turn, resulted in a surprising level of personal friendships. Earlier studies had found both Euro-Americans and Afro-Americans claiming a level of personal friendships with people from the other group that was wholly inconsistent with the dismal accounts of growing hypersegregation being reported by spatially oriented scholars. Sigelman himself had found in his national study, conducted in 1989, that 82 percent of Afro-Americans and 66 percent of Euro-Americans claimed to have genuine friends from the other ethnic group.[74] In the 1997 Gallup poll, 75 percent of Afro-Americans claimed that they had a "close friend" who was Euro-American and 59 percent of Euro-Americans claimed similar "close friendships" with Afro-Americans.[75]

Further, the Afro-American directors of the National Survey of Black Americans were amazed to discover that 57 percent of Afro-Americans claimed to have a good Euro-American friend, one to whom they felt they could really say anything they thought.[76] And even in hypersegregated Detroit, Sigelman and his associates were surprised to find that, in 1992, some 43 percent of Afro-Americans and 27 percent of Euro-Americans claimed to have had a "good friend" from the other ethnic group. The evidence is overwhelming that, as Sigelman and his associates put it, "a genuine change in the likelihood of interracial friendships has occurred since the mid-1970s."[77] But how do we reconcile this with the bad-news trends in hypersegregation?

Surprisingly, propinquity turned out to be a less important factor in interethnic friendships than is usually thought, which largely explains why the emphasis on spatial segregation is misplaced. Where Euro-Americans live does influence their friendship patterns with Afro-Americans, but this is not an important factor determining Afro-Americans' contacts with Euro-Americans. Where one works was a far more important factor, especially for Afro-Americans. Personal attributes and socioeconomic factors were also important: younger, more educated Euro- and Afro-Americans made more contact with each other, regardless of where they lived. Lower-class, less-educated Euro-Americans maintained their historic antipathy to Afro-Americans, although there is evidence of change even within this group. Casual contacts made at work and other places led to close interethnic friendships to a significant degree among male and female Euro-Americans and Afro-American women, but, interestingly, not with Afro-American men. Early childhood contacts were also important, especially for Euro-Americans. Sigelman and his colleagues concluded: "It appears that since the late 1960s, Detroit has become more integrated in fact as well as in law. Indeed, very few residents of the Detroit area…have no personal contact with members of the other race, and most have considerable casual contact. Moreover, in the hypersegregated Detroit area, where media reports of racial hostility appear almost every day, the fact that approximately one person in three has one or more close friends of the other race may be welcomed as unexpectedly good news. Thus, some may take heart from our findings, buoyed by what they consider the progress that has been made in recent decades."[78] We do.

It is striking that neither the Farley nor Sigelman research team drew an important inference that fairly shouts from their findings. It turns out that even in hypersegregated Detroit the vast majority of Euro-Americans claimed that they would feel comfortable living in a neighborhood that was a quarter Afro-American. Both research teams note that this ratio is the same as the ethnic composition of the Detroit metropolitan area. But what this, in turn, implies is that Euro-American attitudes now make possible the complete integration of the metropolis *if only Afro-Americans were willing to live in neighborhoods in which they were a quarter of the population.* This is not an unreasonable bargain. Euro-Americans are, after all, over 80 percent of the population, so there is some give on their part in their willingness to live in neighborhoods with less than their proportion of the population. At the same time, this attitudinal change permits Afro-Americans to live in mixed neighborhoods where the proportion of Afro-Americans is almost twice that found in the general population.

Furthermore, there is reason to believe that Euro-Americans mean what they say to pollsters on this matter. The Gautreaux program, conducted in the Chicago metropolitan area, another famously hypersegregated region, has produced persuasive evidence that if low-income Afro-Americans wish to live in working- and middle-class Euro-American neighborhoods—at about the same ratios indicated in the surveys discussed earlier—and are prepared to abide by the basic communal norms of these neighborhoods, they and their children are generally accepted.[79] Why won't most Afro-Americans accept these terms?

The answer, which liberal students of segregation repeatedly insist on sidestepping, is that persisting segregation is partly—and for most middle-class Afro-Americans, largely—a voluntary phenomenon.[80] As a strong believer in integration, I personally find this fact discouraging, but one simply has to face up to it. One important set of data that scholars who warn about increasing hypersegregation and its deleterious consequences tend to avoid commenting on are the responses of Afro-Americans to questions about their level of satisfaction with their housing condition. One would expect growing dissatisfaction in tandem with the growth of hypersegregation. To the contrary, Afro-American self-reported levels of satisfaction with their housing condition has been increasing substantially over the past quarter century, and the gap between Euro-American and Afro-American satisfaction levels has decreased dramatically. In 1973 only 45 percent of Afro-Americans expressed satisfaction with their housing compared with almost three-quarters of Euro-Americans; by 1997 almost three-quarters of Afro-Americans (74 percent) were satisfied with their housing, compared with 87 percent of Euro-Americans.[81] Satisfaction with one's housing must surely be the best indicator of satisfaction with one's neighborhood: the old and proven adage of the real estate industry, that the three most important things about housing are "location, location, location," is as much a sociological as a business truism.

There are no doubt important remaining levels of racist resistance to Afro-Americans and other minorities among some Euro-Americans— approximately 12 percent—necessitating the continuation of vigorously enforced antidiscrimination laws with stiff penalties. A study by the Urban Institute prepared for the U.S. Department of Housing and Urban Development in 1991 found that in the most serious form of housing discrimination—denial of access to available units—there was still a 13 percent probability of systematic discrimination. However, in the classic form of discrimination known as "steerage," where "minority homeowners are offered houses, but in systematically different neighborhoods than their white Anglo counterparts," the study found that discrimination severity was now "low."[82]

One may interpret these results in a favorable or unfavorable light, depending on the base of one's comparison and one's expectations about the pace of change. I am convinced by the sociological evidence, and from my own experience, that any Afro-American family that truly desires to live in an integrated, predominantly Euro-American neighborhood— which is not to say *any* predominantly Euro-American neighborhood—is capable of doing so. This is quite consistent with persisting ethnic resistance to living in neighborhoods with more than 30 percent Afro-Americans on the part of a majority of Euro-Americans as well as the resistance of a small minority of Euro-Americans (about 12 percent) to living in neighborhoods with any Afro-Americans.[83]

We now see that the students of segregation have been busily accumulating a statistically impeccable case against the segregation of America's urban spaces, especially that demographically invented construct known as "the census tract." In the process, they have completely missed the dramatic changes in the interactions among the real, live people who live in these "tracts." America's great cities may be hypersegregated, but this has not prevented Americans from impressively altering their traditional patterns of personal segregation. Not only have ethnic attitudes changed to a remarkable degree over the past forty years,[84] and especially so over the past quarter of a century, but Afro- and Euro-Americans are actualizing these changed attitudes in the impressive increases in the number of contacts they make with each other. Most surprising of all are the remarkable percentages of persons of both ethnic groups who report that they have close friends from the other ethnic group.

The portrait of relations between Afro-Americans and Euro-Americans recently reported by the Gallup Poll has taken the professional leaders and pundits on "race" in politics and the mass media completely by surprise. So committed are they to the "two-nations" and "racism forever" view of America—the media because it sells copy and increases ratings, the pundits and "race" leaders because it enhances their pundit and broker roles, the misguided liberal academics because they are intellectually terrorized by the fear that any report of a decline in racism exposes them to the charge of racism or of being a "Tom"—that they have all either dismissed the very polls on which, in other contexts, they slavishly rely, or dismissed the nation's respondents as a sample of liars. Nonetheless, the Gallup Poll's findings are consistent with what more detailed and unintimidated academic studies have been finding over the past fifteen years, that "a portrait of a separate America for blacks is no longer valid. Blacks in America today have relatively high levels of daily contact with whites across a variety of settings. Blacks live with, work with, send their kids to school with, and have close friends who are white."[85]

☐■

As we have seen, there is undoubtedly much to complain about. But on balance, there can be no doubt that the record of the past half century, especially the past thirty years, has been one of progress, in some cases considerable progress. The positive progress made toward social, political, and cultural inclusion has been phenomenal, reflected in the impressive growth of the middle class and the not insignificant penetration of the nation's upper class by Afro-Americans. Even in those areas where major problems remain, the long-term trends are in the direction of significant improvements. Contrary to the conventional wisdom, Afro-Americans (the vast majority of whom *do not* live in inner-city areas plagued by the underclass) are today safer than they have ever been, with sharply declining victimization rates in almost every category of crime. The rates of drug and alcohol addiction are lower than they have been in decades and declining constantly, in spite of the rhetoric and misdirection of the government's "war on drugs." Afro-Americans are experiencing the lowest poverty rate in the history of the group even when using the present narrowly defined official index of poverty. The current unemployment rate of 9.8 percent, while still unacceptably high, especially when compared to the Euro-American rate of 4 percent, is nonetheless down to the lowest point recorded since 1972.

The one area where things have gotten decidedly worse—the sharp increase in out-of-wedlock births, especially to teenagers—is completely within the power of Afro-Americans to change. This is not the result of poverty, not a cultural preference, and certainly not a rational choice, as some befuddled advocates and social analysts have inanely claimed. The best available evidence indicates that 79 percent of sexually active Afro-American teenagers who become pregnant report that the pregnancy was unintended.[86] Even here there have been improvements and recent signs of hope: as we have seen, the teenage birth rate (as distinct from the out-of-wedlock rate for those who do give birth) has been trending downward since the early seventies, and has declined sharply over the past three years.

Accompanying these dramatic improvements in the misery rates has been a startling decrease in the number of welfare cases since the peak year of 1994, a decline that began two full years before the federal welfare law enacted in late 1996 and therefore cannot be attributed to its restrictive policies. This decline has taken the entire academic and policy community by surprise, and there is, as yet, no good explanation for it. What it does suggest is that people on welfare have begun to take matters into their own hands and are demonstrating a preference for personal responsibility over chronic dependency.[87] The only people alarmed by this development are middle-class welfare advocates unable or unwilling to believe that the Afro-American poor can choose their own life courses and change their own lives.

In spite of these remarkable developments, the pain completely dominates the gain in the current rhetoric of race. Among Afro-American intellectuals the mood of pessimism and the assumption of an unyielding system of racist domination are sometimes laughable in their extremism. This, for example, is how Anthony J. Lemelle Jr., an associate professor of social science at Purdue University, sums up the present situation:

"The social fabric that includes the four major institutions of economic, political, cultural, and ideological structures forms the overdetermination of class exploitation and political repression under the hegemony of white supremacist logics. For most African Americans, the experience of everyday life is played on the landscape of the ghetto or internal colony, which is the backdrop of the 'microphysics of power.'"[88] Among Afro-American legal scholars, the leading new school of thought is the critical race theorists, who finally shattered the once strong coalition between the liberal civil rights scholars and the liberal civil liberties scholars.[89] Critical race theorists argue that "race" dominates our view of the world and that there is therefore no hope of genuine interethnic understanding between Afro- and Euro-Americans, much less integration. Indeed, integration is rejected as an ideal altogether. "Race," one of the leaders of this school recently told the *New York Times*, "has affected our perception of reality and our understanding of the world—in almost every way."[90]

The standard rhetoric of the great majority of Afro-American political leaders and opinion makers is one of unrelenting pessimism. Here is Derrick Z. Jackson, the *Boston Globe's* lead Afro-American columnist, pouring scorn on the enthusiastic national embrace of Tiger Woods after his phenomenal victory in the 1997 Masters golf tournament:

> America has not progressed beyond a carefully constructed acceptance of a relatively harmless, apolitical corps of black pro athletes who make up .00006 percent of the African-American population. It is carefully constructed because white America lets athletes run and shoot the ball while it maintains power.... If it is that tough for African-Americans to be promoted in sports, then you have a good hint of what is out there for the 99.99994 percent of African-Americans who are not pro athletes. At the very moment America praises [Jackie] Robinson and Woods for smashing barriers, it is building new walls that will leave most African-Americans segregated and shattered.[91]

Paradoxically, while some like Derrick Z. Jackson spread pessimism by writing hyperbole about resegregation, others have not only given up on integration, but think resegregation might not be such a bad idea. Thus, a group of Afro-American ministers in Guilford County, North Carolina, calling themselves the Pulpit Forum, along with a sixty-member citizens committee, have joined forces with Euro-American racist opponents of busing. Pastor Amos Quick wrote in the *Greensboro News and Record* in May 1997: "Separate but truly equal would not be so bad."[92]

Most extraordinary of all is that the greatest expressions of rage, not only about the poor but about themselves, come from the Afro-American middle class, the group whose growth and prosperity is perhaps the greatest success story in American ethnic relations over the past quarter of a century. "Among successful blacks," we are told by one of them, "the number who spend much of their energy fighting desperation is alarmingly high."[93]

To understand why the pain overwhelms the gains among Afro-Americans, and why a sense of crisis and hopeless despair characterizes discussion on the subject among all parties, Euro- and Afro-American, we must turn to another paradox, what I call the objective paradox of desegregation.

THE PARADOXES OF PERCEPTION AND EXPERIENCE

THE OBJECTIVE PARADOX OF DESEGREGATION

When Afro-Americans and Euro-Americans were segregated—physically, occupationally, and culturally—from each other, there was little opportunity for conflict and therefore relatively little real conflict. The two groups lived in largely separate worlds and when they did come in contact their interactions were highly structured by the perverse etiquette of "racial" relations. The system may have worked well in minimizing conflict, as long as both groups played by the rules, but it was clearly a pernicious arrangement for Afro-Americans since it condemned them to inferior status, excluding them from participation in the political life of their society and from nearly all the more desirable opportunities for economic advancement.

Desegregation meant partial access to the far superior facilities and opportunities previously open only to Euro-Americans; hence it entailed a great improvement in the condition and dignity of Afro-Americans. All of this should be terribly obvious but must be spelled out, because it is precisely this obvious improvement that is implicitly denied in the condemnation of the inevitable consequence of desegregation, namely, that as individuals in both groups meet more and more, the possibility for conflict is bound to increase.

Take two classic cases in point: the integration of the student body at the University of Michigan at Ann Arbor and the editorial staff of the *Washington Post*. Until as late as the early seventies, both were models of ethnic peace for one reason: there were hardly any Afro-Americans with whom to come in conflict at either institution, in spite of the large Afro-

American presence in Michigan and the nation's capital. As the numbers and proportion of Afro-American students increased dramatically at Michigan, the number and viciousness of ethnic incidents escalated. And although more nuanced and verbal, the experience of the *Washington Post* has been hardly less painful. In 1970 there were hardly any Afro-Americans in significant jobs at the *Post,* not even on its national staff in a city that is majority Afro-American. The newspaper then made a concerted effort to diversify its newsroom and was extraordinarily successful at the task. Over 18 percent of its professional staff was of minority origin by 1995.[94]

By any standard, this was real progress. But, inevitably, it was won at the cost of a great deal of friction. When the *New Republic* did a cover story that could easily have been called "The Ordeal of Integration at the *Post,*" it found tensions running high, although the *Post* insisted, in the controversy following the *New Republic*'s story, that the level of friction had been exaggerated. Whatever the actual degree of rancor, no one denied that there were conflicts, misunderstandings, and grievances. The leadership of the *Post* had been forewarned of these consequences by the diversity experts it had hired. But when its executive editor, Len Downie, echoing this expert view, said that in integration efforts "things get worse before they get better," he was selling himself, and the integration achievement of his newspaper, short. Rather, things appear to get worse, and are perceived as getting worse, *because* they are getting better. If the integration of two groups legally and socially separated for more than 350 years does not produce friction, it is the surest sign that no meaningful change has taken place.

These experiences, it cannot be too strongly emphasized, are real—often vicious—and, for the Afro-Americans as well as many aggrieved Euro-Americans, traumatic, as Ellis Cose and sociologists of the Afro-American middle class have amply demonstrated.[95] But they are side effects of progress, not signs of failure.

Nor is this seeming paradox confined to middle-class integration. A striking illustration of the paradox of integration comes from what is arguably one of the most imaginative and successful attempts to integrate lower-class Afro-Americans into previously Euro-American suburban communities. In the government-sponsored Chicago-area Gautreaux program, inner-city families were moved to both Euro-American suburban communities and more secure, working-class Afro-American city communities. Everyone expected some level of friction, given Chicago's reputation on interethnic relations. They were not disappointed. A carefully planned follow-up study found that children in the suburban schools were verbally harassed, with 52 percent reporting at least one incident of name-calling and 15 percent being physically threatened.[96] This was the news that made it to the press, always hungry for more and more "proof" that Afro-Americans and Euro-Americans can never get along successfully, the gorier the better. (The racist consequences of such bias notwithstanding, the mass media consider such reporting "liberal.") But the more crucial findings of the follow-up study destroyed so many misconceptions about "race" and class in America that the media have been stunned into silence, and even though the Gautreaux program is a real-life case for examining "racial" attitudes and behavior, rarely encountered in the social sciences, the project has been studiously shunned by sociologists and poverty analysts who are ardently committed to the "racism forever" view of American minority-majority relations.

First, when the suburban movers were compared to another group that had moved to the Afro-American city neighborhood, it was found that the suburban movers were four times less likely to drop out of school, more than twice as likely to attend college, almost twice as likely to be employed full-time when not in college, and four times more likely to be in better-paying jobs. As one would expect, they had three times as many Euro-American friends, but unexpectedly, they also had almost as many Afro-American friends as the city movers. Living in the suburbs thus does not cut Afro-Americans off from their "roots" or from friendships with other Afro-Americans, a finding consistent with those of other sociologists, discussed earlier, who find that propinquity is not a decisive factor in Afro-American friendship patterns.

Second, it turned out that youths who had moved to the Afro-American city community were almost as likely to be verbally harassed and *more* likely to be physically threatened. What the Gautreaux program powerfully brought to light is that class prejudice is alive and well among Afro-Americans. Afro-American apologists will no doubt argue that being harassed by a Euro-American is worse than being "dissed" and threatened by your own people. But from the voices of these youths, feeling hurt and being threatened is color-blind in its emotional impact.

One of the most important findings of the study of the Gautreaux experience perfectly illustrates the paradox of desegregation. The researchers found, as expected, that positive behaviors were associated with other positive ones: doing after-school activities, for example, was associated with cross-ethnic home visiting. What came as a complete surprise—but should amaze no student of the sociology of intergroup relations and conflict—was that "negative behaviors do not predict an absence of positive behaviors."[97] To the contrary, negative and positive behaviors often went together. Suburban movers who claimed that they had been threatened by Euro-Americans were more likely to have had meaningful friendship relations with them such as home visiting and after-school activities. So too were those who had been verbally abused, including being called racist names. About these counterintuitive associations, the researchers concluded: "They indicate that many of the same individuals who are being threatened and harassed by whites are also being accepted by whites, interacting with whites, going to each others' homes, and participating in school activities. That does not make the threats and name-calling pleasant, but it does make it easier for these youths to feel as though they are a part of these white suburban schools."[98]

Joining the mainstream is painful, as in the cases of middle-class students at formerly segregated universities and journalists at the *Washington Post* and other newsrooms around the nation. It isn't fair, and it may even make you "want to holler." But we cannot deny that the youths in the Gautreaux program were better off and that their relations with Euro-Americans had immeasurably improved. Nor can we deny that increasing the proportion of Afro-American students and journalists at the leading national institutions constitutes real progress—for the individuals and institutions involved and for the nation at large.

THE EXPERIENTIAL AND PERCEPTUAL
PARADOX OF "RACIAL" CHANGE

Put briefly, as the relations between the previously segregated groups change, becoming objectively better for Afro-Americans, they will be experienced by Afro-Americans as getting much worse even as they are genuinely seen by Euro-Americans to be improving. Both perceptions will be correct. And the fact that both are correct in arriving at opposite perceptions of what is going on will itself lead to further misunderstanding. How do we make sense of such a tangle?

What we have here is a serious mismatch in the experience and perception of ethnic change, compounded by a great deal of ignorance and misinformation concerning simple demographic and socioeconomic realities by Afro-Americans and Euro-Americans about the other group and about themselves. Most middle-class Euro-Americans feel, correctly, that things have changed for the better not only in the objective socioeconomic condition of Afro-Americans but in improved attitudes toward Afro-Americans. The typical Afro-American person experiences and perceives conditions and attitudes either as having not changed or worsened. Figure 12 shows just how far apart the two groups were in 1994 in terms of their perception of changes in the condition of Afro-Americans. Exactly two-thirds of Afro-Americans think that the condition of Afro-Americans has grown worse or remained the same (22 and 45 percent, respectively), whereas 58 percent of Euro-Americans think the Afro-American condition has improved. The Gallup poll conducted in June 1997 found little change in this perceptual gap: 62 percent of Afro-Americans think that the quality of life for Afro-Americans has either grown worse or remained the same, while 58 percent of Euro-Americans continue to believe that it has gotten better for Afro-Americans.[99] It is important to note that these are perceptions by Afro-Americans about the quality of life among other Afro-Americans across the nation. We get a completely different set of responses when Afro-Americans are asked how satisfied they are with their own standard of living: 74 percent express satisfaction with both their standard of living and the way things are going in their personal lives.[100]

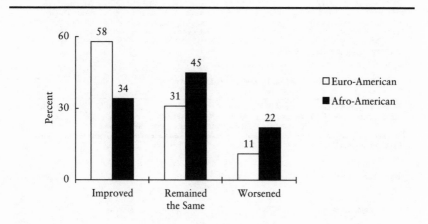

Figure 12. Different Perceptions of Ethnic Change by Ethnicity: Percent of Respondents Who Believe that in the Past Few Years Conditions for Afro-Americans Have Improved, Remained the Same, or Worsened. *Source:* Author's composition from the General Social Survey Data Base, 1994 (Chicago: National Opinion Research Center, 1995).

A recent joint study by the *Washington Post* and Harvard University in conjunction with the Kaiser Family Foundation revealed differences in perception of racial realities and change that are extraordinary, although a close examination of their results indicates that *both* Afro-Americans and Euro-Americans are badly misinformed about the other group *and* their own condition.[101] As table 1 shows, Euro-Americans, who make up between three-fourths and four-fifths of the U.S. population (depending on whether one counts Hispanic Euro-Americans, as one should in this case), imagine that they are slightly less than half of it while imagining Afro-Americans to be 24 percent of the population, almost twice their true proportion. But Afro-Americans, it turns out, are even more misinformed about their numbers. They imagine Euro-Americans to be only

Table 1. Perceived U.S. Population Composition by Ethnicity

What percentage of the U.S. population is . . .	Euro-American Responses	Afro-American Responses	Latino-American Responses	Asian-American Responses	Census Facts: 1995
Euro-American?	49.9%	45.5%	46.7%	54.8%	73.5%/ 83.0%
Afro-American?	23.8%	25.9%	22.7%	20.5%	12.6%
Latino-American?	14.7%	16.3%	20.7%	14.6%	10.4%
Asian-American?	10.8%	12.2%	10.8%	8.3%	3.6%

Note: Response percentages are averages of the estimates made by those polled. Latinos can be of any pan-ethnic group such as Euro-American, African-ancestry-Americans or Asian-American. The Euro-American population increases from 73.5 to 83 percent when Hispanic Euro-Americans are included.
Source: Adapted from the Washington Post/Kaiser Family Foundation/Harvard University Survey on Race, October 1995, Table 1.1; and U.S Census Bureau, Population Division, release PPL-57, U.S. Population Estimates, 1990-1996.

Table 2. Perceived U.S. Poverty Rates by Ethnicity

What percentage of each group is poor?	Euro-American Responses	Afro-American Responses	Latino-American Responses	Asian-American Responses	Census Facts: 1995
Euro-Americans	30.5%	27.9%	25.9%	24.2%	11.2%
Afro-Americans	37.6%	42.9%	41.9%	38.2%	29.3%
Latino-Americans	38.0%	38.5%	42.6%	36.8%	30.3%
Asian-Americans	24.1%	24.7%	27.8%	21.5%	14.0%

Note: Response percentages are averages of the estimates made by those polled. Latino-Americans can be of any pan-ethnic group.
Source: Adapted from the Washington Post/Kaiser Family Foundation/Harvard University Survey on Race, October 1995, and U.S. Census Bureau, "Historical Poverty Tables," Poverty and Health Statistics Branch/HHES Division, 1997.

45.5 percent of the total population and inflate their own proportion to 26 percent. In other words, the average Afro-American person goes around thinking that Euro-Americans are a minority group.

It is an indication of the level of pessimism that prevails in the nation that all ethnic groups exaggerate their poverty rates, especially Euro-Americans, who turn out to be the biggest whiners of all (see table 2). Although the actual Euro-American poverty rate was only 11.2 percent, the average Euro-American person imagined that 30.5 percent of all Euro-Americans were poor. Only 31 percent of Euro-Americans believe that Afro-Americans have less opportunity to live a middle-class life than they do, compared with 71 percent of Afro-Americans (see figure 13). Most extraordinary of all, 58 percent of Euro-Americans think that the average Afro-American is as well or better off in the jobs category than the average Euro-American person, and more than 40 percent think that Afro-Americans are as well or better off than Euro-Americans in their income and housing condition (see figure 14).

The other side of the coin is worth emphasizing, especially since unwarranted conclusions about the nature and level of racism in America have been drawn from this study. In view of the concentrated nature of poverty among Afro-Americans—in sharp contrast with the Euro-American poor, who tend to live scattered among the middle class—it is understandable that Afro-Americans exaggerate the degree of poverty among themselves. But harder to understand is why they so grossly exaggerate the level of Euro-American poverty, estimating it at 28 percent. This may reflect the kind of Euro-American people they typically come in contact with, or it may be a projection of their experience of the world.

Remarkably, fewer than 30 percent of Afro-Americans disagree with the view that Afro-Americans have less opportunity to live a middle-class life than Euro-Americans, and more than one in five Afro-Americans actually believes that Afro-Americans are as well or better off than Euro-Americans in jobs and housing. Presumably, these respondents are the well-established middle-class Afro-Americans who are merely projecting their own successful experience.

Complicating this situation even more, however, is a paradoxical result reported in many national surveys of Afro-American attitudes. While approximately two-thirds of Afro-Americans were of the opinion that Afro-Americans as a whole faced serious discrimination in wages and promotion to management occupations, less than 40 percent, when asked about their own lives, reported actually experiencing such discrimination.[102] In other words, the typical Afro-American person, while generally positive about his or her own situation, is highly negative about the condition of other Afro-Americans. This is a clear reflection of the pervasive, highly negative rhetoric of "race" in the nation that is relentlessly broadcast by the mass media, which thrive on bad news. As we will see below, there is a similar problem among Euro-Americans.

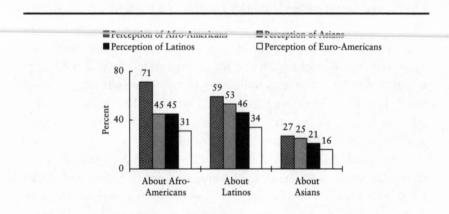

Figure 13. Percent of Respondents Who Believe that Afro-Americans, Asians, and Latinos Have Less Opportunity to Live a Middle-Class Life than Euro-Americans. *Note:* Response percentages are averages of estimates made by those polled. Percentages do not add up to 100 because other groups' responses are not shown. *Source:* Adapted from the Washington Post/Kaiser Family Foundation/Harvard University Survey on Race, October 1995, Figure 7A.

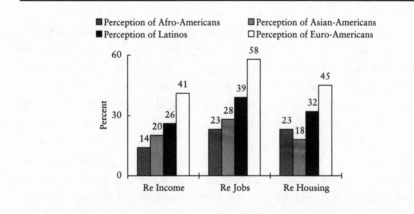

Figure 14. Percent of Respondents Who Think the Average Afro-American Is As Well or Better Off than the Average Euro-American in Terms of Income, Jobs, and Housing. *Source:* Adapted from the Washington Post/Kaiser Family Foundation/Harvard University Survey on Race, October 1995, Figure 7B.

These misperceptions, by themselves, explain a good deal of the confusion and resentment over "race" in the nation. If the average Euro-American person seriously believes that Euro-Americans have become a demographic minority—in spite of the fact that non-Hispanic Euro-Americans alone constitute 74 percent of the population and Euro-Americans of all ethnic groups make up 83 percent—it is easy to see how this breeds all sorts of resentments. The group whose ancestors carved this nation out of the wilderness, they no doubt rage, has now been outnumbered by others. Worse, while others benefit from their minority status, Euro-Americans are being unfairly treated like the dominant majority they no longer are. Further, since the average Euro-American person thinks that over 30 percent of Euro-Americans are poor—which is almost the actual figure for the percentage of Afro-Americans who are poor—it is obvious that the attention given the Afro-American poor will be begrudged. One begins to understand the susceptibility of the Euro-American electorate to reactionary rhetoric about "welfare queens" and lazy, undeserving Afro-American poor people, since a much smaller fraction of Euro-Americans are on welfare. And the vulnerability to anti–affirmative action rhetoric is also better understood in light of the incredible belief of 58 percent of Euro-Americans that Afro-Americans are doing as well or better than the average Euro-American person in terms of jobs.

But the misperceptions of Afro-Americans are nearly as serious, and also begin to explain a good deal of their resentments, in spite of all the progress made in recent decades. If the average Afro-American goes around thinking that Euro-Americans are a minority of only 45 percent of the population, the fact that Euro-Americans appear to dominate all the major institutions of the nation must be a source of constant rage. And if it is the typical view among Afro-Americans that they constitute fully 26 percent of the nation's population, then affirmative action programs that aim toward the hiring of Afro-Americans in numbers that reflect their actual national proportion of 13 percent are going to be perceived as unfair, even if they achieve their goals. It also means that in all areas of representative politics Afro-Americans are going to expect far more than what their numbers dictate. This is perhaps mitigated by the fact that all other groups exaggerate the proportions of Afro-Americans more than any other out-group—which can be taken as a tribute to the enormous Afro-American cultural presence in America but is countered by the fact that all other minority groups imagine their own proportions to be twice what they actually are.

Finally, these demographic misperceptions by Afro-Americans may well explain the disturbing growth of nationalist politics and chauvinistic economic fantasies among them. A program of separatist economic development makes no sense for a minority group of 13 percent, but it begins to seem plausible if one imagines one's group to be more than a quarter of the world's most powerful economy. This inflated demographic conception of the group also partly explains why so many young Afro-Americans, including Afro-American university students, imagine that they can make a success of life in America without making any effort to achieve a closer understanding of the subcultural emphases and habits of the dominant middle-class Euro-American majority.

What accounts for these serious misapprehensions and "racial" perceptual gaps? Part of the explanation is obviously just ignorance and misinformation, as the *Washington Post*–Harvard report goes on to show. However, the perceptual gap is not simply a result of misinformation. To a significant degree, people are honestly reporting on their own experience in their answers. Afro-Americans and Euro-Americans experience ethnicity and racism from different perspectives and contexts, which partly explains why they may truthfully arrive at radically divergent perceptions of the problem. To comprehend what is going on, let's look more closely at the Afro-American situation.

The experience of racism by Afro-Americans is the result of four factors: the relative demographic proportions of the two groups, the geographic location of Afro-Americans in relation to liberal and racist Euro-Americans, the frequency of contact with racists, and the intensity of the expression of racism by Euro-Americans who are racists.

In May 1997, there were 33,856,000 Afro-Americans in the United States, or 12.7 percent of the total population of 267,177,000 persons. Euro-Americans, including Hispanic Euro-Americans, numbered 220,976,000 persons, or 82.7 percent of the total. This means that Afro-Americans are outnumbered 6.5 to 1 by Euro-Americans. This simple demographic fact has enormous social significance that often goes unnoticed, one reason no doubt being the misperceptions of Afro-Americans and Euro-Americans about their true demographic numbers and proportions.

Numerous polls have shown that there has been tremendous change in Euro-American "racial" attitudes toward Afro-Americans over the past thirty-odd years.[103] For example, the number of Euro-Americans who hold racist beliefs in favor of laws against intermarriage declined from 62 percent in 1963 to 34 percent in 1982, then down to 14 percent in 1994.

Similarly, Euro-Americans openly in favor of racial segregation of neighborhoods declined from 36 percent in 1982 to 15 percent in 1994.[104] Obviously, these responses must be taken with a grain of salt. Observational and in-depth interview studies such as those of Joe Feagin and Bob Blauner strongly suggest that the proportion of genuine racists in the Euro-American population is substantially higher than these figures indicate.[105]

All things considered, it is reasonable to estimate that about a quarter of the Euro-American population harbors at least mildly racist feelings toward Afro-Americans and that one in five is a hard-core racist. This is not inconsistent with polls showing higher percentages of favorable views. Ethnic attitudes are not monotonic. However one may wish to quibble over the meaning of attitude surveys and other data, this is real progress, an enormous change from the fifties and sixties, when the great majority of Euro-Americans were openly racists, measured by whatever means. Nonetheless, when roughly a quarter of all Euro-Americans are racists, it still remains the case that for every two Afro-American persons there are three Euro-American racists. In spite of all the progress among Euro-Americans, this is still an outrageous situation for any Afro-American.

It is very likely that the majority of Afro-Americans are less likely to come in contact with the most tolerant group of Euro-Americans on a regular basis for simple socioeconomic reasons. More educated, more prosperous, and more suburban, the tolerant majority tend to live exactly where Afro-Americans are least likely to be found: in the expensive suburbs. On the other hand, it is the least educated and most prejudiced Euro-Americans who tend to be in closest proximity to Afro-Americans.[106]

Further, the behavior of the most liberal group of Euro-Americans and their attempts, or those of their representatives, to improve the conditions of Afro-Americans often tend to intensify racist feelings among those Euro-Americans most likely to come in contact with Afro-Americans. The cost of racial change is disproportionately borne by Euro-Americans traditionally most hostile to Afro-Americans. Afro-American improvement is invariably perceived as competition in the traditionally protected economic preserves of working-class Euro-Americans. Hence, not only do racist Euro-Americans continue to outnumber Afro-Americans, but the greater intensity and frequency of their racist behavior create a "racial" climate that is realistically experienced by Afro-Americans as worse, or no better, than in earlier decades.

Of special concern here is the behavior of law enforcement agencies. The typical big-city police officer is the Euro-American with whom the typical lower- and working-class Afro-American is most likely to come in contact. Unfortunately, Euro-American police officers tend to come, socially, from precisely the working-class urban communities most likely to be hostile to Afro-Americans. There is some evidence that racial prejudice is "the norm" among Euro-American police, although some analysts question whether such prejudice necessarily translates into discriminatory behavior.[107] At the same time, their profession brings them into contact with the most lawless members of the Afro-American community, continuously reinforcing their prejudices.

The result is that all Afro-Americans are held in suspicion by the typical Euro-American police officer and treated in a manner that threatens their dignity and most basic rights. In some urban communities this amounts to life under a virtual police state for many law-abiding working-class and poor Afro-Americans. The basketball star Dennis Rodman recounts in his 1996 autobiography that his mother had to give up the Mercedes-Benz he had given her as a present because she was stopped and harassed so frequently by Euro-American policemen.[108] Middle-class status makes some difference, but only in well-defined social situations. It can sometimes even be a disadvantage. During the O. J. Simpson criminal trial, the tapes of LAPD detective Mark Furhman speaking with an aspiring screenwriter revealed what every bourgeois Afro-American person already knew: that in unprotected contexts—driving on the highway, visiting a Euro-American suburban friend, or getting caught in some minor traffic or other infraction—Afro-Americans are likely to find themselves targeted by Euro-American police officers and detectives who resent their success and take malignant pleasure in harassing them, especially if they are in mixed relationships. All this is in direct contrast to the experience of the typical Euro-American person, who views the police officer either as a friend or acquaintance from the neighborhood or as a protector and guardian of the public peace.

The experience of Massachusetts is typical. By all objective criteria it is one of the most ethnically liberal states in America. Not only did it elect, in 1966, the first Afro-American U.S. senator since reconstruction, but its two current senators are among the most liberal and pro–Afro-American members of Congress. And yet, among Afro-Americans of all classes, the Boston area has the unenviable reputation of being one of the most racist parts of the country, and many Afro-Americans still refuse to move to the area because of its racist image. The fears of Afro-Americans are legitimate, but so is the bewilderment of Euro-Americans in middle-class Boston or in neighboring cities such as Cambridge (arguably one of the most ethnically liberal cities in the nation) when informed by Afro-American colleagues that they would rather go back South than settle anywhere near the Boston area, including Cambridge.

The sad truth is that even as the number of tolerant Euro-Americans rapidly increased between the sixties and seventies, the amount of contact between Afro-Americans and racist working-class Euro-Americans also increased, as did the vehemence of the racism of these Euro-Americans, expressed most notoriously in the antibusing violence of South Boston.

The antibusing turmoil of the 1970s is now history—even Afro-Americans are now generally opposed to busing—but the bedevilment of race relations by the combined impact of the demographic discrepancy and increased hostility of the declining number of racist Euro-Americans continues. Consider the quiet village of Whitinsville in central Massachusetts, where four Euro-American youths were charged with stapling racist fliers in front of an interracial couple's home in 1995. Nearly all of the 14,000 Euro-American residents expressed shock and outrage at this incident, one selectman regretting that "we got so civilized we can't grab these guys by the neck and boot them out of town."

But what distressed the Euro-American residents even more was the insistence of the fewer than thirty Afro-American families that the experience of ethnic hatred was typical of their daily life in Whitinsville. This was "just another day in Whitinsville," one young Afro-American woman told a Boston Globe reporter: "Everyone seemed so shocked, but I am not shocked, nor are any of my friends. This is something I deal with on a daily basis." The Euro-Americans all felt this was terribly unfair. One lifelong resident got to the heart of the matter when he said helplessly, "She may experience that in her life in town. I obviously do not, and I don't see any evidence of it."

That's just the tragic point. As one of the Afro-Americans acknowledged, the "good people" of the area were clearly in the great majority. But the fact remains that for the Afro-American families, daily life in pastoral, overwhelmingly tolerant central Massachusetts means running the gauntlet of racist taunts and a genuine fear of being harmed by a tiny fraction of bigoted Euro-Americans.

The hostile reaction of a small proportion of Euro-Americans can do worse than impair the experiences of a large proportion of Afro-Americans. Given the adversarial and litigious nature of the culture and the tendency of the media to highlight the exceptional and negative, a small but active number of Euro-Americans can disproportionately influence the perception of all Euro-Americans, with consequences deleterious to Afro-Americans. The present political hostility to affirmative action is a perfect case in point.

Only a small proportion of Euro-Americans—7 percent, it turns out—claim to have been personally injured in any way by affirmative action.[109] However, the whole point of affirmative action is to bring Afro-Americans into greater contact with Euro-Americans at the workplace and other sites where they were traditionally excluded. Aggrieved Euro-Americans who feel they have been passed over in preference for Afro-Americans react with unusual intensity to this experience, coloring the views of many Euro-Americans who are in no way influenced by the policy. The result is the so-called "angry white" syndrome: increased hostility toward what is perceived as unreasonable Afro-American demands, and the conviction that the vast majority of Euro-Americans are being hurt—78 percent of Euro-Americans think so—when, in fact, only 7 percent can actually attest to such injuries from their own experience.[110]

THE OUTRAGE OF LIBERATION

The experiential and perceptual mismatch I have just described is exacerbated further by yet another paradox of changing ethnic relations, what I call the outrage of liberation. A formerly oppressed group's sense of outrage at what has been done to them increases the more equal they become with their former oppressors. This is, in part, simply a case of relative deprivation. It is also partly a result of having a greater voice—more literate and vocal leadership, more access to the media, and so on.

But it also reflects the formerly deprived group's increased sense of dignity and, ironically, its embrace of the formerly oppressive Other within its moral universe. The slave, the sharecropping serf, the Afro-American person living under Jim Crow laws administered by vicious Euro-American policemen and prejudiced judges—all were obliged, for reasons of sheer survival, to accommodate somehow to the system. One form of accommodation was to expect and demand less from the discriminating group. To do so was in no way to diminish one's contempt, even hatred and loathing, for the racist oppressors. Indeed, one's lowered expectations may even have been a sign of contempt.

In the discourse on racism, it has often been observed that one of its worst consequences is the denial of the Afro-American person's humanity. What often goes unnoticed is the other side of this twisted coin: that racism left most Afro-Americans persuaded that Euro-Americans were less than human. Technically clever, yes; powerful, well armed, and prolific, to be sure; but without an ounce of basic human decency. No one whose community of memory was etched with the vision of lynched, barbecued ancestors, no Afro-American person who has seen the flash of greedy, obsessive hatred in the fish-blue stare of a cracker's cocked eyes could help but question his inherent humanness. Most Afro-Americans, whatever their outward style of interaction with Euro-Americans, genuinely believed, as did the mother of Henry Louis Gates, that most Euro-Americans were inherently filthy and evil, or that, as the poet Sterling Brown once wrote, there was no place in heaven for "Whuffolks... being so onery," that indeed, for most of them "hell would be good enough—if big enough."[111]

Integration, however partially, began to change all that. By disalienating the Other, the members of each group came, however reluctantly, to accept each other's humanness. But that acceptance comes at a price: for Euro-Americans, it is the growing sense of disbelief at what the nightly news brings in relentless detail from the inner cities. For Afro-Americans, it is the sense of outrage that someone truly human could have done what the evidence of over three and a half centuries makes painfully clear. Like a woman chased and held down in a pitch dark night who discovers, first to her relief, then to her disbelief, that the stranger recoiling from her in the horror of recognition had been her own brother, the moral embrace of integration is a liberation with a doubletake of outrage verging on incomprehension.

THE PARADOXES OF IDEOLOGY AND INTERPRETATION

THE PARADOX OF ANTIRACIST RACISM

A good part of the present turmoil in American ethnic relations—both the problem itself and the attempt to explain it—springs from the failure of Afro-American leaders to recognize the limits of one important, but risky and necessarily transitional, strategy in the struggle for ethnic equality. That strategy is itself a paradox, first described by Jean Paul Sartre with the gripping phrase "anti-racist racism."[112]

What Sartre was getting at is the fact that any group that has experienced centuries of racial hatred and oppression has, of necessity, to go through a period of self-liberation in which it draws attention to, and even celebrates, the very thing that was used against it. Afro-Americans had no choice but to emphasize their Afro-Americanness in mobilizing against the iniquities of a system that discriminated against them because they were Afro-American. And after centuries of being brainwashed by every symbol and medium of the dominant culture into a sense of their own inferiority and unattractiveness, it was inevitable that Afro-Americans go through a process of psychological liberation that entailed not just the denial of their worthlessness but some emphasis on the positive worth of being Afro-American.

What was true on the psychological level held equally on the economic and political fronts. Some recognition of "race" had to inform policies aimed at alleviating centuries of racial injuries. It is disingenuous in the extreme to argue—as Euro-American and Afro-American conservatives do—that because the ideal of the civil rights movement, and of all persons of ethnic good will, is a color-blind world, any policy that takes account of African ancestry betrays this ideal.

Fire, as the old saying goes, can sometimes only be fought with fire. The Afro-American identity movements and some form of affirmative action were the inevitable social fires that had to be ignited in the fight against the centuries-long holocaust of Euro-American racism.

We are approaching the limits of the antiracist strategy in politics, but, tragically, Afro-American leaders now seem trapped by the fire they started. The results are disastrous for the mass of Afro-American people. Afro-American identity rhetoric and race-conscious politics not only have negative educational consequences but play straight into the hands of the most reactionary political forces in society.

The phase of the movement when only Afro-Americans could be trusted to represent Afro-American interests has long passed, as the recent experience of Georgia shows. In a compact that was as reactionary as it was stupid, Afro-American leaders agreed to the gerrymandering of their state in full knowledge that the price of two more guaranteed Afro-American congressmembers was a sweep of the entire state by the Republicans. In five years, as a result of this compact, Georgia moved from a congressional delegation of nine Democrats (one of them Afro-American) and one Republican to three Afro-American Democrats and eight Euro-American Republicans.

Needless to say, the three Afro-American congressmembers from Georgia ended up twiddling their thumbs in the ineffectual Afro-American caucus of a minority party while their eight Euro-American Republican bedfellows joined in the dismantlement of every policy dear to their Afro-American constituents. The only Afro-Americans to gain from this counterproductive fire fighting are the three Afro-American congressmembers, their families, and aides. An incremental increase in the Afro-American middle class has been bought at the expense of the mass of Afro-American constituents.

This sad contradiction has now been thoroughly documented by David Lublin in a work called, appropriately, *The Paradox of Representation*. On the basis of elections to Congress between 1972 and 1994, Lublin shows clearly that where the election of an Afro-American leader does not take precedence over the representation of Afro-American interests, even a small proportion of Afro-American voters can powerfully influence the elected leaders of both parties—whatever their ethnic ancestry—to vote in a manner that advances the interests of Afro-Americans and the less privileged. On the other hand, the practice of specially concentrating electors into minority districts so as to ensure the election of a minority representative almost always makes all the other voting districts of such a gerrymandered state not only more conservative, but more self-consciously hostile to the interests of the Afro-American minorities in their midst.[113]

Perhaps the greatest irony of this whole sorry episode in Afro-American and liberal racialization of the polity was the outcry that greeted the Supreme Court's very wise decision to outlaw the practice. Afro-American leadership, led most vociferously by the Congressional Black Caucus, denounced the Supreme Court's decision as a racist throwback to Jim Crow days. However, when the same Afro-American candidates ran in non-gerrymandered districts with majority Euro-American electors in the 1996 elections, *every single one was re-elected*. Once again, ordinary Americans—both Euro-Americans and Afro-Americans—turned out to be far more progressive than the Euro-American pundits and Afro-American leadership gave them credit for. And, as with the Gautreaux program, the liberal and Afro-American leadership has maintained an embarrassed, almost palpable silence over this utterly unexpected outcome.

The chauvinist strategy also harms attempts to improve the educational performance of lower-class Afro-American students and may even have begun to adversely affect those of the middle classes. Knowledge, tragically, has been racialized. Academic success—except in Afrocentric subjects—is sneered at, even condemned as a form of selling out to Euro-American culture. Bright Afro-American schoolchildren, as Signithia Fordham and John U. Ogbu showed in 1986, must either mute their success by being good athletes or playing the clown, or else simply "dumb themselves down."[114]

Afro-American students attending predominantly Euro-American colleges and universities also inflict grave educational harm on themselves by their commitment to resegregation. The problem is not that Afro-Americans congregate with each other, since Jews, Asians, and other ethnic students do the same. Rather, the problem is the tendency to confine their personal and extracurricular relations almost exclusively to Afro-American organizations and informal groups.

Many of these students have grown up in all–Afro-American communities and, in all likelihood, intend to live in predominantly Afro-American communities after graduation. They seem not to appreciate that college and professional schools offer them an opportunity to get to know Euro-Americans and other minorities on a personal basis. Such relationships are not only vital for the social capital, enhanced "emotional intelligence," and learning skills acquired, but are essential if and when Afro-Americans are to assume supervisory positions over Euro-Americans later on. A manager who speaks a different social and body language from the people he supervises—who knows and cares little for the intimate details of personal relations, the myriad unverbalized gestures, signs, face cues, masking techniques, and other interaction rituals of everyday life among non–Afro-Americans—is a manager doomed to failure. Afro-American students who fraternize on intimate terms only with other Afro-Americans are forfeiting the opportunity to acquire this essential social knowledge and the implicit rules that guide the vital social games that Euro-Americans and other groups play, rules that are often very different from those informing the distinctive interaction games of Afro-American folks.

THE PARADOX OF THE "ONE-DROP" RULE

Commitment to the risky strategy of antiracist racism partly explains another ethnic paradox, although sheer cultural and political inertia and elite self-interest may be as important in understanding it. This is the persistence of what once went by the name of the "one-drop" rule. America is unusual among Western Hemisphere societies in its traditional commitment to a binary conception of race. Despite the fact that the vast majority of non–Euro-American persons of African ancestry are mixed, all persons with the proverbial "one drop" of African ancestry are classified as "black."[115]

This unusual mode of racial classification has a vicious ideological history rooted in the notion of "racial" purity and in the racist horror of miscegenation. Traditionally, it was used as a major ideological bulwark of legalized segregation, and was at the heart of the "white" supremacist opposition to any form of integration. There is no gainsaying the fact that this conception of "race" historically rationalized the most pernicious legal, social, and political injustices against Afro-Americans.

An important aspect of contemporary ethnic change is the fact that this binary conception of "race" is under siege, for reasons I will mention shortly. The paradox is that the two groups of Americans now most committed to its survival are "white" supremacists and most Afro-American intellectual and political leaders!

First, we should note the social factors undermining the one-drop rule. One was the integrationist ideal of the early phase of the civil rights movement. By definition, this struggle called into question the one-drop "purist" rule. Integrating schools meant accepting the prospect of mixed dating, the ultimate anathema of "white" supremacists. The direct assault on antimiscegenation laws, culminating in their prohibition by the Supreme Court, implicitly attacked the one-drop rule.

Of even greater importance, however, have been the demographic and cultural changes resulting from the current wave of immigration with the inflow of mainly brown-skinned Latin Americans and Asians. Previous immigrants played by the binary rule as soon as they landed on these shores: those who were visibly brown, such as West Indians, were assimilated into the Afro-American population whether they wished to be or not (and most did not, coming from societies in which minute, socially meaningful distinctions of color were the norm). Those who were visibly or vaguely "white" eagerly sought membership within the Caucasian chalk circle and were usually welcomed as long as they could prove no trace of African "blood." Indeed, "whiteness," or rather non-"blackness," became a powerful unifying force in the integration of immigrants who previously never imagined that they had anything so important in common. Swarthy Sicilians and Arabs now found themselves one with blond Northern Europeans, Irish Catholics with English Protestants, formerly persecuted Jews with Gentiles, refugees from Communist Eastern Europe and Cuba with Western Europeans—all were united in the great "white republic" of America by virtue simply of not being tainted by one drop of the despised Afro-American blood. The demonization of blackness in the one-drop rule not only served the interests of "white" supremacists but was a major unifying force in the rise of this great democracy of the non-blacks.[116]

This pernicious system of racial ideology worked only as long as there were no ambiguous third "races" to muddy the binary construction. Native Americans were not only too small in numbers but also, cut off on reservations, out of sight and out of mind. All this was to change with the massive inflow of brown people. The sheer strength of their numbers was enough to bring the binary conception of "race" into question. In addition, the new wave of immigrants refused to play by the binary game. Unlike previous Latin immigrants, recently arrived Latinos insist that they are neither "white" nor "black." And Asians not only look different but are usually sufficiently proud of their distinctive somatic type not to want to play the binary game either. East Indians are the main exceptions.

In recent years, there has also been a significant increase in children of mixed Afro-American and Euro-American parentage.[117] Although still small proportionately, their absolute numbers have been growing phenomenally. The census found 1.5 million mixed marriages in 1990, with 2 million children claiming mixed ancestry. They are also disproportionately middle and upper class and are concentrated in the major metropolitan centers. They have recently broken ranks with the established Afro-American leadership in insisting on being classified for what they are: mixed. In July 1996 they held a Multiracial Solidarity March in Washington to register their demand for a census category recognizing their mixed heritage.

All these developments have had a profound impact on the nation's traditional conception of ethnic norms and ideals. The traditionally staid Census Bureau has now become what one report calls a "political hotbed" as numerous groups challenge the five official racial and ethnic categories in use since 1977.[118] The most cursory review of recent media images and of intermarriage rates clearly indicates that the nation's traditional Western European somatic norm is being replaced by a mixed or "morphed" type that is a blend of darker-skinned and lighter-skinned peoples. Shadowing this development has been a similar change in the physical-beauty ideal from its traditional Nordic image to one that reflects a mix. Euro-Americans increasingly risk skin cancer and the plastic surgeon's knife to acquire darker skin and larger, more trans-Saharan lips. And whatever Afrocentrists or multiculturalists may say, the huge proportion of their incomes that Afro-Americans devote to processing and lengthening their hair indicates an appearance ideal that is neither European nor African but something in-between, more like Tiger Woods, the ultimate hybrid prodigy in whom America sees its somatic future.

In the face of all this, it is odd that the orthodox line among Afro-American leaders is now a firm commitment to the one-drop rule. The extent to which Afro-American leaders will go to defend what was once a cardinal principle of "white" supremacy is best illustrated by the position of the National Association of Black Social Workers on "transracial" adoption. Not only is the group adamantly opposed to such adoption on the grounds that it constitutes what the social workers claim to be a form of "genocide," but many of their spokespeople imply that it is better for an Afro-American child to suffer the hardship and impoverishment of multiple foster families and state wardship than to be subjected to adoption by Euro-American middle-class parents. Astonishingly, both the Congressional Black Caucus and a number of liberal Euro-American politicians have been intimidated into accepting this blatantly racist and cruel dogma. It is one of the many ironies and paradoxes of modern American ethnic politics that it took a Republican-controlled Congress to legislate against it.

Afro-Americans offer two main reasons in defense of the one-drop rule. One is the Afrocentrist position that it is good to preserve the Africanness of the Afro-American population. "Blackness" is to be celebrated as a virtue in itself. While Afrocentrists are at least honest enough to openly acknowledge this, many more established Afro-Americans are uncomfortable with the idea for the simple reason that it is merely the Afro-American version of the Euro-American purist position.

More commonly heard is the political defense of the one-drop rule: the fact that a recognition of the mixed segment of the Afro-American population will dilute the demographic and political base of Afro-Americans. There is something amiss, even circular, in this argument. If mixed persons chose to identify with other non–Euro-Americans politically—as many of them insist they do—there is nothing to fear, since they will continue to join forces with all such non–Euro-Americans. But if their insistence on a separate identification entails separate political interests, it is undemocratic and possibly illegal to force them to continue doing so. I strongly suspect that most ordinary Afro-Americans would just as soon say "good riddance" to any group of light-skinned non–Euro-Americans wishing to dissociate themselves from an "Afro-American" identity, a point made with some emphasis in Spike Lee's *School Daze*.

Ironically, a study conducted by the Census Bureau in 1995 on this subject indicated that, should the "multiracial" category be included, Afro-American leadership has nothing to fear concerning the dilution of their political base. While 1.5 percent of the surveyed population identified themselves as "multiracial," the proportion identifying themselves as Afro-American was not affected by the introduction of the multiracial option in the list of "racial" categories.[119]

THE PARADOX OF LIBERAL RACIALIZATION IN ACADEMIC AND PUBLIC DISCOURSE

A strange contradiction has emerged in liberal discourse and studies of "race" in America. It is somewhat related to the one-drop paradox, but is more insidious and pervades all scholarship and popular writings on intergroup relations. Having demolished and condemned as racist the idea that observed group differences have any objective, biological foundation, the liberal intellectual community has revived the "race" concept as an essential category of human experience with as much ontological validity as the discarded racist notion of biologically distinct groups.

The paradox lies hidden in the seemingly innocent distinction between "race" and ethnicity. Almost all social scientists, social commentators, and journalists, not to mention ordinary Americans, now routinely use the terms *race* and *ethnicity* as if they referred to different, if related, social things. My question is, why do we need the term *race* at all? What explains its nonredundancy in the phrase "race and ethnic relations"? Trying to understand why social scientists, in particular, insist on making this distinction leads us into a Pandora's box of liberal contradictions and unwitting racism.

The standard liberal explanation is that "race," while not meaningful biologically, is nonetheless important because people believe it to be important, and this has severe consequences in "multiracial" societies such as our own. The problem with this explanation is that the same holds true for "ethnic" differences and prejudices. Why then distinguish between the terms *racial* and *ethnic?* The conventional response is that ethnic distinctions and prejudices, while admittedly similar in their believed-in and self-fulfilling nature, nonetheless differ from "racial" distinctions and beliefs because they refer not to observed and believed-in "physical" differences, but to observed and believed-in cultural ones. The object of a false belief, then, is what justifies the distinction even among speakers who recognize and reject its falseness. "Racial" beliefs, the argument goes, are based on observed differences that, while not biologically salient, are outwardly real and somehow immutable, and this differentiates interactions and beliefs pertaining to racial differences from those pertaining to ethnic differences. Afro-Americans, we often hear, cannot hide or conceal their "blackness," whereas in Irish-WASP or Jewish-Gentile relations such visible markers are absent. Furthermore, "racial" relations are also held to be more intense, conflict ridden, and horrible in their consequences for the believed-to-be inferior "race."

Is any of this true? On the one hand, as the psychoanalyst Michael Vannoy Adams recently noted, "People differ much more culturally than they do naturally. And there is no necessary connection between psychical differences and physical differences. The reason that natural categories like color are so useless (except to racists, for whom they are all too useful) is that they convey very little, if any, information about significant psychical differences. In this respect, the colors white and black—as in the white-black opposition that racists employ—are especially uninformative."[120] There is abundant anecdotal and scientific evidence to support Adams's view. Robert A. Hahn, an epidemiologist at the Centers for Disease Control and Prevention, told a *New Yorker* reporter that after analyzing infant deaths over a two-year period a discrepancy was found in the "race" of the infant identified on its birth certificate with the "race" given on its death certificate in "an astounding number of cases." Hahn was led to question the implicitly biological understanding of "race" he had been working with. "We have to ask, 'What do these categories mean?' We are not talking about race in the way that geneticists might use the term.... It's closer to self-perceived membership in a population—which is essentially what ethnicity is."[121] Hahn almost got it right: nearly all respectable geneticists have abandoned the idea of different human races.

On the other hand, even where no outward physical differences appear to exist, people have no problem inventing them. Consider the horror of Nazism and the Jewish Holocaust. The Nazis, and indeed nearly all Germans (and other Europeans), considered the Jews to be a biologically different race, and this had horrendous self-fulfilling consequences. But to non-Europeans nearly all German Jews looked very much like Gentile Germans. What, then, was Nazism? Ethnic prejudice and genocide, or racial prejudice and genocide? Does it matter? Are we to believe that the Jews in Germany were a racial group (sociologically speaking) but in America an ethnic group?

The simple truth of the matter is that however similar people may look to outsiders, those who believe that there are differences tend to have very little difficulty identifying the believed-in different group and to see gross physical differences that outsiders find it hard to identify. Indeed, the comparative data on intergroup relations strongly suggest that wherever people believe that there are important differences between them, they tend to interpret these differences as biologically grounded.

In medieval Europe, descriptions of serfs almost always portrayed them as a distinct, physically different race, so much so that even accidentally referring to a nonserf as a serf was an offense serious enough to justify homicide. Descriptions of Scandinavian slaves in the Icelandic sagas suggest that they were physically different even though the vast majority of the slaves are known to have been fellow Scandinavians and Celts.[122] From their earliest contact with the Irish, the English and Scots have considered them a different "race." A Scottish antiquarian, John Pinkerton, wrote in 1797 that the Irish Celts were "savages, have been savages since the world began, and will be forever savages; mere radical savages, not yet advanced even to the state of barbarism."[123] At the height of the Victorian period the image and perception of the Irish actually worsened. Encouraged by the new theory of social Darwinism, the Irish image was "simianized" in both newspaper cartoons and scientific writings of the day, and as L. Perry Curtis Jr. explains: "The simianization of Paddy in the 1860s... emanated from the convergence of deep, powerful emotions about the nature of man, the security of property, and the preservation of privilege."[124] The Victorian English, however, were equally prone to racializing their own underclass, what they called the casual "residuum" as distinct from the respectable working class.[125] During the 1880s, when fear of the "residuum" heightened, a new theory of hereditary urban degeneracy consigned them to the category of a race apart that not only looked, smelled, talked, and behaved differently, but was destined for extinction since it was, in the words of the influential theorist of imperialism C. F. G. Masterman, "the relics of a departing race."[126]

Such racialized perceptions of what American social scientists insist on distinguishing as mere ethnic differences persist today all over Europe and other parts of the world. In what was formerly Yugoslavia, the genocidal mutual slaughter of Serbs, Croats, and Bosnians is referred to as "ethnic cleansing." But to these peoples, so culturally and physically similar to outsiders, the idea that there is something different in their mass rapes and killings justifying the use of the term "ethnic cleansing" rather than "racial cleansing" must seem like a bad sociological joke.

Nor is this confined to Europeans. The Caribbean is notorious for the sharp physical distinctions people make within populations that, to Americans, seem to be nearly all "black." Haiti is a good case in point. The typical lighter-skinned middle- and upper-class Haitian considers the typical poor dark-skinned peasant or shantytown dweller a physically different order of humanity, and thinks no more of him as a human being than the typical American "white" supremacist thinks of the typical Afro-American person in the ghetto. Is the Haitian problem an ethnic problem? A racial problem? A class problem?

American social scientists need not go beyond their own borders to appreciate the meaninglessness of the race/ethnicity distinction. We easily forget that up until as late as the beginning of the Second World War, Jews in the United States were considered a separate "race" by all "real white" Americans. Karen Brodkin Sacks, who grew up in postwar years when the Jews rapidly won their "whiteness" and middle-class status, confesses that she is still surprised at the recency of her "racial" identity. However, her parents, "first-generation U.S.-born Eastern European Jews, are not surprised," since they grew up in an America where "scientific racism sanctified the notion that real Americans were white and real whites came from northwest Europe." Sacks thinks that becoming suburban middle-class through taking advantage of the massive postwar affirmative action programs of the federal government—the GI Bill, the FHA and VA mortgages—was the Jewish route to "whiteness." But she is not sure: "Did money whiten?" she asks, intriguingly, "Or did being incorporated in an expanded version of whiteness open up the economic doors to a middle-class status?"[127]

The situation is less ambiguous with that other previously nonwhite group, the Irish Americans. As is well known, no "white" person in his right mind considered the Irish "white" up to as late as the 1920s. Indeed, as late as the last quarter of the nineteenth century, being called an Irishman was as great an insult as being called a nigger. The Irish "Catholic race" was stereotyped here, as in Victorian England, as simian, bestial, lazy, and riotous in both scientific and popular writings until the early decades of this century. In their hard-fought, self-conscious struggle for the status of "whiteness," the Irish, unlike the Jews and later "ethnics," used political power. And, as the historian David Roediger adds, "The imperative to define themselves as white came from the particular 'public and psychological wages' whiteness offered."[128] Afro-Americans, of course, were to remain the one group denied these "wages." Indeed, their believed-in immutable "racial" difference is today the last remaining source of value for the positional good that is "whiteness."

Not only do people find it easy to make "racial" or believed-in, socially meaningful physical distinctions where none seem to exist (to outsiders), but they have an equally powerful capacity not to make these distinctions, even when they seem strikingly obvious to outsiders. The classic case in point here is one we have discussed already: America's one-drop rule. The Afro-American population is somatically extremely varied. Nonetheless, we categorize and perceive of them as a single type in our binary system of racial beliefs. If Afro-Americans and Euro-Americans find it so easy not to see differences where outward differences are so manifestly present, there is no reason to believe that they lack the capacity to see no differences between the groups categorized as "Afro-American" and "white." That they recognize differences is clearly a matter of cultural and political beliefs and of an identity that is, like all others, part chosen and part imposed.

What, then, is the basis of the distinction between the "racial" and the "ethnic"? We must conclude that making this distinction is itself a belief, a distinctively American belief, an essential part of American racist ideology. The distinction, we now see, plays a crucial role in maintaining the binary conception of "race" that prevails in America, and remains the foundation of racist and purist dividing lines between Americans. This is its only linguistic function. It conceptually bedevils the meaning of integration.

So the question we must now ask is this: If the history of relations between peoples has been, as the distinguished American anthropologist Virginia Dominguez correctly puts it, "the continuous historical pattern of determining race by man-made law rather than by processes of nature,"[129] why on earth are American social scientists (presumably the most liberal group in the nation) actively promoting a purist conception of "race"?

Could it be that these emperors of liberalism really have no clothes? Do these mainly Euro-American social scientists find the "racial" identity of "whiteness" so deeply gratifying, so essential a part of their understanding of themselves as true-blue Americans, that they unwittingly promote a distinction that is implicitly racist? Why is it not enough to be simply Jewish-American, Anglo-American, Irish-American, or, if one so chooses, just plain American? Why the added need for "white-Jewish American," "white-Anglo-American"...unless there remains the age-old American desire to define being truly American as not being that essential contradistinctive definition of oneself as "white": namely, "black." And have Afro-American social scientists and intellectuals so rejected the ideal of integration and so mistakenly committed themselves to a racialized identity that they are prepared to reinforce this racist distinction? Why is it not enough to be simply, and gloriously, Afro-American or, if one so chooses, just plain American, which anyway is already a good deal Afro-American?

We must resolve this paradox if we are serious about achieving the ideal of integration, and we can do so simply by dropping the distinction and all that it implies. All this requires is a little clear thinking. The distinction between "race" and ethnicity is only meaningful if we wish to reinforce the racist belief that Euro-Americans and Afro-Americans are, indeed, biologically and immutably different. The distinction invigorates the salience of "race" in our private and public life. And by legitimizing the binary conception of "race," the distinction perpetuates, to the detriment of Afro-Americans (the self-serving disagreements of their political leadership notwithstanding), the nastiest dogma from our painful ethnic past.

THE PARADOX OF AFRO-AMERICAN SCHOLARSHIP

From all that I have already said, it should be clear that if ever a group needed rigorous and honest scholarship to make sense of its complex, tortured past, to illuminate its social problems, and to clarify debates over public policy, Afro-Americans most certainly do. But sadly, recent scholarship on the group is where we find some of the most confounding paradoxes and ideological contradictions.

Take, first, the strange situation that has emerged over the past quarter century in the study and interpretation of the Afro-American past. Up to the end of the sixties, there was general agreement among all scholars concerning major events in Afro-American history and their consequences. Slavery, in which Afro-Americans spent two-thirds of their existence in this country, was interpreted for what it patently was: a viciously exploitative institution that severely handicapped Afro-Americans, especially in the way it eroded vital social institutions such as the family and marital relations and in the way it excluded Afro-Americans from the dominant social organizations and thus denied them the chance to learn patterns of behavior fundamental for survival in the emerging industrial society.

If ever there was a victim, the American slave, like slaves elsewhere in the Americas and the world, was most certainly one. Slavery and the postjuridical slavery that was Jim Crow are what make the Afro-American experience unique in America. The impact of these institutions was devastating, and it continues today—which, in the long duration of social history and the development of human institutions, is but a moment away from these tragedies. Every Afro-American, regardless of his or her ideology and independence, has a right not only to invoke this past, but an obligation never to forget it. This was the position of all the classic Afro-American historians and historical sociologists from W. E. B. Du Bois to John Hope Franklin, as well as activist intellectuals such as Malcolm X.[130] One would have thought, then, that of all the experiences of Afro-Americans, the devastating social impact of the slave and Jim Crow past would have figured most prominently among Afro-American scholars and advocates.

There were two main reasons why it did not. One was the laudable goal of interpreting the Afro-American past in terms that emphasized the positive and creative in Afro-American social and cultural life, and that presented Afro-Americans as people who were agents of their own past rather than merely passive creatures. With such an objective I completely agree. This was in keeping with the best of the Afro-American tradition of historical scholarship, and in the hands of scholars such as the historian John Blassingame it was admirably realized.

But the revisionist scholarship soon got completely out of hand. Emphasizing the fact that Afro-Americans developed their own communities and subculture soon became confused with the denial of all negative impact of slavery. People falsely believed that a focus on slavery lent support to the view that something was wrong with Afro-American behavior and cultural inheritance, and that these "pathologies" explained Afro-American inequality. In other words, the traditional interpretation of Afro-American history as a chronicle not only of success but of social and psychological damage was rejected because it amounted to blaming the victim. Revisionist scholars, beginning in the 1960s and continuing into the eighties and nineties—with the strong support of Euro-American scholars such as Herbert Gutman and Eugene Genovese—want it both ways. They want all the moral capital and compensation that is due the victim, but they reject the notion that the victim was in any way injured or scathed by this victimization.

The second reason for the denial of the destructive impact of the past is the false pride bred by chauvinism. Afro-American bourgeois chauvinists yearn for a past as glorious and unblemished as those mythologized pasts of other ethnic groups. To achieve this, not only is the impact of the slave past denied; worse, even the West African past with its rich cultural traditions is belittled in favor of a preposterous return to the Pharaonic and Islamic pasts with which the Afro-American has no lineage. One cannot help feeling that the source of this denial is shame about having been enslaved and, sadly, shame and ignorance about the West African cultures, stemming from a slavish embrace of the worst aspects of Euro-American chauvinistic historiography.

Chauvinism always makes for bad or neglected history, and Afro-Americans are not alone in this. We have all heard of the "luck of the Irish," the horrendous bad luck of five centuries of English depredation notwithstanding, and it is no accident that it is rare to find courses on modern Irish history anywhere in the United States. Better no history than a history that cannot be viewed with "smiling eyes." When the damage of the slave and sharecropping past is not simply being denied altogether by crude Afrocentrists leapfrogging the Atlantic, the Sahara, and the previous five thousand years, it is being revised by Afro-American historians and their Euro-American allies into a tradition of revolutionary protest, familial resilience, and communal solidarity that pretty nearly writes the slave master and the psychosocial horrors of the system completely out of the story. Fortunately, this essentially male revisionist literature has recently come under the withering counterattack of a new wave of sensible, feminist scholars. [131]

Running parallel with this feel-good revision of Afro-American history during the seventies and eighties was the revisionist sociology and psychology of contemporary Afro-American life. Up to the end of the sixties, nearly all sociologists and psychologists were alert to the ways in which racial discrimination, rural poverty, and urban segregation adversely influenced Afro-American social organization and denied Afro-Americans the social capital essential for competence in an advanced industrial society. Scholars such as the sociologists E. Franklin Frazier and Lee Rainwater, the psychologist Kenneth Clark, the social psychologist Thomas Pettigrew, and the urban anthropologists Elliot Liebow and Ulf Hannerz—all with impeccable liberal or radical credentials—had no hesitation in identifying the ways in which Afro-American inequality resulted both directly from persisting racism and segregation and indirectly from Afro-American behavior patterns which emerged, tragically, from maladaptations over time to their hostile environment. None of these scholars blamed Afro-Americans for these maladaptations. They were scrupulous in identifying the socioeconomic and external historical causes of these self-victimizing behaviors and attitudes, all insisting that they were not immutable but could be changed with the right social policies.

Nonetheless, with the rise of the chauvinist and black identity movements in the early seventies came a two-pronged assault on all previous studies, especially of Afro-American family life. First was the notion that no Euro-American scholar had the right to study contemporary Afro-American issues, and second was the hackneyed argument that to specify the pathologies of self-victimization was to blame the victim. The result was a disastrous period in the sociology and psychology of Afro-Americans, lasting from the early seventies to the late eighties, in which Euro-American scholars largely abandoned the field and most of the remaining Afro-American scholars toed the party line. That line went something like this: "There is nothing problematic about the Afro-American family or gender and marital relations, and any explanations in terms of behavioral or cultural patterns are inherently suspect." Afro-American scholars who refused to conform were slandered as "Toms" or dismissed as "black conservatives" who had sold out, regardless of whether their criticisms of the academic party line came from the left or the right. Even William Julius Wilson came under suspicion for daring to suggest that postindustrial structural forces were more important than simple direct racism in explaining the plight of the underclass.[132] The study of poverty during this period almost became the monopoly of economists, with unfortunate consequences for our understanding of the social sources of poverty.[133]

The culmination of this deplorable episode in academic censorship was the paradoxical emergence of the view among Afro-American academics, led by the Afro-American sociologist Andrew Billingsley,[134] and their few remaining, frightened Euro-American colleagues, that the Afro-American family was "strong" and "resilient," precisely when teenage pregnancies, paternal abandonment, and impoverished single mothering were rising to alarming levels and more than half of all Afro-American babies were being born into dysfunctional, chronically poor households. Astonishingly, in the midst of this social disaster, any scholar who failed to signal conformity to the "no problem" dogma by neglecting to drop the buzzwords of "resilience" and "strength" when talking about the Afro-American family was dismissed as a racist if Euro-American or a self-hating Tom if Afro-American. Rarely in the history of the social sciences has there been such ostrich-like and cowardly behavior among scholars.

Happily, social scientists have, at last, begun to come to their senses. A new wave of scholarship since the late eighties—again, significantly, mainly from women—is boldly returning to honest studies of Afro-American life.

Perhaps the greatest irony in all this is the fact that ordinary Afro-Americans have always maintained that the root source of their problems is the dislocation of their families. Scholars of Afro-American life have been completely out of touch not only with the realities of the Afro-American family, but with the sensible and honest appraisal of their own condition by the vast majority of Afro-Americans. This was forcefully brought home in the 1995 *Washington Post*–Harvard University survey. When a sample of Americans was asked whether the breakup of the Afro-American family was one of the four main reasons for the economic and social problems of the group, fully 62 percent of Afro-Americans agreed that this was a major factor, a higher agreement rate than in any other group.

CONCLUSION

Some forty years ago, this nation set itself a great and long overdue task: to rid itself of the centuries of racist discrimination against Afro-Americans. A decade later that goal merged with another: to undo the institutional and other consequences of centuries of discrimination through a concerted effort to improve the socioeconomic condition of all Afro-Americans.

I have tried to show in this essay that, while we still have a good way to go, and while we may even have stagnated in a few areas, the effort has been, on the whole, successful. The essence of this change can be summed up as a move toward greater integration of our society—not merely in neighborhoods, but in the economic, social, cultural, political, and moral life of the nation.

Afro-Americans, from a status of semiliterate social outcasts as late as the early fifties, have now become an integral part of American civilization and are so recognized both within the nation and outside it. Middle- and working-class Afro-Americans can now take pride in their personal achievements as full civic participants in their society and in their many collective contributions to what is now the world's only superpower.

We have seen that Afro-Americans and Euro-Americans have both radically altered their attitudes toward individuals of the other group. The number and proportion of avowed racists among Euro-Americans, while not insignificant, are a mere fraction of what they once were and declining steadily. Afro-Americans and Euro-Americans are still too spatially separated from each other. Whatever the reasons for the only modest improvements made in this area—class differences and prejudices, ethnocentric choices, or persisting ethnic prejudice—residential segregation remains a poor mark on an otherwise laudable card of progress. But even here, as we have seen, Americans have rendered geographical segregation a less severe failure by the many ways in which they have made contacts and close friendships across ethnic neighborhood boundaries.

This generally successful move toward greater integration, if still far from complete, has, of necessity, been painful. Indeed, for many it has been something of an ordeal. Nonetheless, all of the evidence suggests that most ordinary Americans have proven themselves extraordinary in their willingness to suffer the pain of ethnic change. Often they do so in sharp contrast to the established leaders of both groups, who seek either to exploit public anxieties or to pessimistically proclaim failure for their own political ends. They do so in merciful ignorance of the strange bedfellowship between revisionist scholars on the right who proclaim all government programs since the sixties dismal failures and equally revisionist scholars on the left who endlessly mourn "the dream deferred" in an America that is irredeemably racist. They persist in the face of a mass media that relentlessly plays on their basest fears for profit while crying crocodile tears of liberalism.[135]

They do so because the truth has finally dawned on all but the most ethnically myopic that Afro-Americans are among the most American of Americans. They do so because it is the right thing to do. They do so because they know that integration, however difficult the journey, is the only way to go, and what's more, that they are already well on their way. They do so because, as a nation, there can be no turning back.

Most Afro-Americans share, or would like to share, America's and the Western world's core value of autonomy, which embraces the twin moral imperatives of personal responsibility and self-determination. When Afro-Americans claim that they want to control their own destiny, to control and be responsible for themselves and their communities, they are echoing this pivotal element of America's civic culture.

At the most conservative estimate, this desire holds for about 60 percent of the population—the vast majority of that resilient core of hardworking, God-fearing men and women of the working and middle classes who have triumphed over racial and class discrimination to become models of self-determining Americans.

For the remaining large minority of Afro-Americans, however, the story is different. Among established Afro-American political leaders and a growing number of young college graduates—and among the poor and troubled bottom quarter of the population for whom they speak—there has been a near complete surrender, in their politics, ideology, and intellectual discourses, to deterministic explanations and moral justifications. The crisis I plan to discuss applies to this marriage of socioeconomic determinism between the leaders, vocal professionals, and majority of intellectuals who make up the top 15 percent and the misled bottom quarter of the Afro-American social hierarchy.

There are good reasons for this moral surrender to deterministic advocacy. Up to a point, political determinism—the belief that all our problems can be attributed to the socioeconomic environment—has worked well in the struggle for equality. As is well known, the landmark case *Brown v. Board of Education* and President Johnson's Great Society programs drew heavily on deterministic social science arguments, rather than the morally more desirable but pragmatically less appealing argument that these were the right things to do.

The deterministic charge of racism can also explain every moral failing, as the most cursory review of any day's newspaper will illustrate. Thus, when the Afro-American California congressman Walter R. Tucker, an ordained minister, was convicted of extortion and tax evasion, he reportedly complained, like the convicted congressional representatives Mel Reynolds and Charles Diggs before him, that "he was a victim of Government prosecutors who he said were bent on imprisoning Afro-American officeholders like himself."[1] More recently, the Reverend Henry J. Lyons, president of the nation's largest Afro-American denomination—the National Baptist Convention—blamed racism for the media's focus on his extravagant living and his flagrantly adulterous liaison with a church officer that drove his distraught wife to an alleged act of arson. And Sergeant Major Gene McKinney, the nation's highest-ranking enlisted officer, has blamed racism for the charges of sexual harassment, adultery, and obstruction of justice against him.

Sometimes "the system," rather than direct racism, gets the blame. The *Boston Globe* is typical of the nation's liberal newspapers in its willingness to blame the system while passing no judgment on the murderous and self-destructive behavior of the underclass persons it writes about. Thus, in a front-page story that described the horrible details of nine-year-old Michelle Walton's murder by being crushed to death after suffering a life of "chronic" sexual and other abuse from her natural and foster parents, the paper lamented that "the *system* that failed the frail schoolgirl during her lifetime may do no better by her in death" (emphasis added).

Perhaps the most egregious use of the system as an excuse for barbaric behavior was the explanation offered by Mike Tyson for biting off a piece of the ear of Evander Holyfield during their heavyweight title fight. "I grew up on the streets," he pleaded in a television broadcast. "I fought my way out." This was not an isolated expression of desperation. In spite of his enormous success in his field and his vast fortune, Tyson has made an art of whining. Five days before the fight he told a group of reporters,

"I've been taken advantage of all my life. I've been used, I've been dehumanized, I've been humiliated, and I've been betrayed."[2] Talk about the whine of a privileged class. Nothing better illustrates my point that the great majority of Afro-Americans reject this embrace of determinism by their leaders and "role models" than the reaction of the poor but stalwart residents of the Brooklyn neighborhood in which Tyson grew up. Speaking on Tyson's explanation of his behavior, Rosemarie Washington, a 43-year-old resident who lived near Tyson's boyhood house, epitomized the commitment to personal responsibility and rejection of determinism that sustained Afro-Americans during their long ordeal of slavery and racist persecution: "It doesn't explain it to me. It doesn't matter where you grew up. As you grow older, you grow out of those things. You don't hold your childhood and carry it into your adulthood."[3]

Blaming racism or the racist system and its consequences for everything has not only been good politics, it has had the full weight of the social sciences behind it. The first thing the freshman social science student interested in the "race" problem learns is how to relentlessly control away all variables until the only one of any significance remaining is personal or institutional racism. So thoroughly have modern social determinists done their job that the major problem in the social sciences today with regard to Afro-Americans is not why the bottom 25 percent fails, but why the miracle of working- and middle-class successes persists among them. Social science is at a complete loss to explain the two-thirds of Afro-American people leading normal, uncursed lives, very much a part of the American mainstream. They simply don't fit into the conventional wisdom of the "two nations" determinists.

In Andrew Hacker's *Two Nations,* which quickly became the locus classicus of the determinist view of all Afro-Americans upon its publication in 1992, we are given this second-person portrait of the Afro-American everyman daily toiling under the Sisyphean burden of "blackness." In addition to the agony of knowing that you are not wanted here and that the land of your ancestors is held in contempt,

> there will be the perplexing—and equally painful—task of having to explain to your children why they will not be treated as other Americans: that they will never be altogether accepted, that they will always be regarded warily, if not with suspicion or hostility. When they ask whether this happens because of anything they have done, you must find ways of conveying that, no, it is not because of any fault of their own. Further, for reasons you can barely explain yourself, you must tell them that much of the world has decided that you are not and cannot be their

equals; that this world wishes to keep you apart, a caste it will neither absorb nor assimilate.[4]

Oh God! And this is barely the start of the daily pile of agonies. As an Afro-American person, you soon learn, according to Hacker, that you are "a carrier of contaminations" shunned by all Euro-American neighbors. When in the presence of Euro-Americans, you are humiliated by the fact that they expect you to "smile" and be "upbeat" to salve their guilty consciences for the horrible way they have treated you. But you are also haunted by the fact that even when you are not among Euro-Americans "you are forever in their conversations." Turning on the television for some relief, you find more agony. Either you are being neglected or caricatured, or you see, very rarely, a dignified person such as a Toni Morrison and resent them because "'black' is missing" from their on-screen behavior. "At the same time," adds the liberal professor Hacker, "you feel frustration and disgust when white America appropriates your music, your styles, indeed your speech and sexuality." And that's not all. You think of your children at school and you are sick to your stomach at the thought that nothing they are learning there will be of relevance to their experience as black persons, that apart "from brief allusions to a Sojourner Truth or Benjamin Banneker, your people appear as passive victims and faceless individuals." They will never experience the identity-enhancing joys of Euro-American children who "can be led to see how the travails of Shakespeare's heroes shed light on the human condition." Instead they bear the agony of verbal abuse. That word. That curse. Oh horror of horrors, that "knife with a whetted edge," the word *nigger* with which any white person can destroy you, since it sums up your "vulnerability to humiliation."

"Then there are the accusations of inconsistency..." and on and on it goes, for another six pages to be exact, in which the great liberal determinist lists the litany of abuses—endless slights, chronic insensitivities, restricted opportunities, caste-like avoidances, and intellectual contempt—that are the "racial" cross borne each day by each and every Afro-American, no matter how wealthy or successful he or she may seem to be. Even a Colin Powell must know in his heart of hearts that even though he may have headed the greatest military machine in the history of the world, he is still only a nigger in the eyes of the land he has so loyally served. There is no way out of the daily, grinding agony of "blackness." No escaping the totality of racist determination. And if anyone doubts this portrait of pitiless gloom and hopeless desolation that is the daily woe of all Afro-Americans, Hacker has literally hundreds of up-to-date tables and figures to prove it.

No wonder determinism has hardened into a strongly enforced orthodoxy. Any Afro-American person who dares to question the deterministic dogma is immediately dismissed as a self-hating Tom and reactionary; any Euro-American person rash enough to do so gets flattened with the twin charges of racism and "blaming the victim."

Either that or he is simply ignored, which was the fate suffered by Mitchell Duneier, the author of one of the finest recent ethnographies on ordinary working-class Afro-Americans. The kind of people portrayed by Duneier are so different from the caricature drawn by Hacker that one might be excused for thinking that the two men are writing about populations on either side of the globe. This is the real world of working-class Afro-Americans as Duneier saw them, relying not on statistical tables but on participant observation for his information:

> By living in accordance with principles such as pride, civility, sincerity, and discretion, these men confirm for themselves—rather than proving to others—that they possess some of the most important human virtues. Thus they make evident the extraordinary strength of their sense of self and their ease with their own selves. In each of these qualities one recognizes a different aspect of the fixed conception of self-worth that inheres in these men. Quiet satisfaction, pride, inner strength, and a genuine expressiveness without effusiveness here coalesce in a type of masculinity that is certainly more widespread in reality than in current accounts of the black male in the mass media and in sociology.[5]

This, too, is the kind of working- and middle-class Afro-American with whom I am familiar, and whose special charms and virtues quickly persuaded me to become an Afro-American, a choice that, according to Hacker, no sane person would want to make.

Ironically, the social sciences are thoroughly implicated not only in the promotion of Afro-American determinism. From one branch of these studies—the social psychology of self-esteem—we get the best evidence of both how extensive and disastrously ingrained the problem has become and the degree to which social scientists are themselves implicated in the problem they study.

Self-esteem, as the great Harvard social philosopher John Rawls forcefully argues, is "perhaps the most important primary good" for any human society. His definition of self-respect ("self-esteem" and "self-respect" are used synonymously) is a near perfect description of what I mean by personal autonomy: "It includes a person's sense of his own value, his secure conviction that his conception of his good, his plan of life, is worth carrying out. And second, self-respect implies a confidence in one's ability, so far as it is within one's power, to fulfill one's intentions." Self-respect is a "primary good," Rawls argues, because "without it nothing may seem worth doing, or if some things have value for us, we lack the will to strive for them." When Rawls adds that the parties in the "imagined primal contractual state or original position would wish to avoid at almost any cost the social conditions that undermine self-respect," this is just his philosophical way of saying that self-esteem is a fundamental social-psychological and moral prerequisite for any viable social order.[6] Rawls's conception closely resembles what social psychologists call global self-esteem, the central feature of which, according to Morris Rosenberg and his associates, is "self-acceptance or self-respect," and it is generally considered to be "a fundamental human motive."[7]

Consider, then, the findings of social psychologists who have extensively studied the problem of self-esteem among Afro-Americans.[8] These studies indicate that up to about the early 1960s Afro-Americans had relatively low levels of personal and ethnic self-esteem. Two explanations were put forth: Afro-Americans' sense of personal failure due to their commitment to the ethic of personal responsibility, and their sense of "racial" inferiority due to the disadvantaged condition of Afro-Americans and the low opinions held of them by the dominant Euro-American group and its media—opinions which Afro- Americans all too frequently internalized.[9] All this was to change dramatically during the sixties and seventies as a result of the civil rights movement and its socioeconomic and political achievements.

First, the good news from the social psychologists. Over the last thirty or so years, there has been a remarkable increase in the level of personal self-esteem among Afro-Americans of all classes, accompanied by an equally strong growth in ethnic self-esteem. Nearly all Afro-Americans now feel no sense of "racial" inferiority whatsoever when comparing themselves with Euro-Americans or any other ethnic group. And in reference to personal (individual) self-esteem, not only do Afro-Americans of all classes have a healthy sense of self-esteem, but numerous studies suggest that, especially among the working and lower classes, Afro-Americans often score higher than their Euro-American counterparts on tests measuring self-esteem.[10] All wonderful developments. Whatever is preventing lower-class Afro-Americans from succeeding in their society, overwhelming evidence from social psychologists—both Afro-American and Euro-

American—suggests that a crippling lack of a sense of their own personal worth is most definitely not a factor.

When these studies explore more deeply the reasons for the growth in lower-class Afro-American self-esteem, we get to the bad news. And it is really bad. What studies from the mid-seventies repeatedly found among lower-class Afro-Americans (although, significantly, not among the middle class) were "higher levels of self-regard but lower feelings of personal efficacy."[11] In probing the nature of self-esteem, social psychologists distinguish between a sense of internal control, which is the perception that one is responsible for one's successes and failures, or that "reward is contingent on individual behavior," and a sense of external control, which is "the notion that rewards are controlled by external forces."[12] Most social psychologists assume, as does Rawls, that a strong sense of self-esteem based on the notion of internal control is psychologically healthy and socially necessary. But it is this very assumption that has been abandoned by lower-class Afro-Americans and many of the Afro-American and liberal Euro-American psychologists who study them.

Almost all psychologists who study self-esteem among lower-class Afro-Americans have reported the close association of high self-esteem and low sense of internal control. But where many Euro-American social psychologists find this association problematic, it has now become almost the party line among Afro-American psychologists and Euro-American liberal scholars who toe the advocacy line to interpret this association not as alarming but as "normative and healthy." In this view, "feelings of external control may thus represent not a passive belief in chance or fate but instead system-blame, which indicates a healthy sensitivity to the real world."[13]

Certainly, it is healthy to have a realistic grasp of the way in which one's socioeconomic world constrains one's opportunities. Abundant experimental and survey evidence from social psychology shows that Afro-Americans, like all disadvantaged groups, protect their ethnic and global self-esteem "by selectively devaluing those domains in which the outgroup is advantaged and selectively valuing those domains in which their in-group has advantages" and "by ignoring or devaluing problematic areas of functioning."[14] Something is surely wrong, however, when one completely divorces one's regard for oneself from one's capacity to make choices, to carry out one's wishes, to exercise control over one's life.

What is bothersome here is not that lower-class Afro-Americans no longer feel bad about themselves because they have come to blame the system instead of themselves for their condition. We all tend to do that. Rather, it's the sense of positive self-regard they get from their commitment to blaming the system. Not feeling bad about oneself—the absence of low self-esteem—is not the same as feeling good about oneself—the positive presence of high self-esteem. Self-esteem is not a binary quality, with individuals swinging between polarities of bad and good. It is a continuum that includes a midpoint between low and high self-esteem wherein one regards oneself neutrally, that is, not feeling lousy about oneself, but also knowing that there is nothing about the way one is feeling about oneself to write home about.

That neutral state is a vitally important point of psychological reconnaissance and rest, for it is there that people usually pause to take stock of themselves and, if necessary, prod themselves into action. A sense of low self-worth is always something to be avoided, but it is possible to feel too good about oneself, especially in the absence of desired outcomes. A threat to our self-esteem can function as a positive force in motivating us to take control of our lives. Among Euro-Americans self-esteem seems to develop interactively with the individual's degree of effective control of his or her environment. Students who perform poorly lose self-esteem, which spurs them to perform better to ensure the outcomes that will restore their pride.[15]

Afro-American students, however, researchers have found, have high global self-esteem, regardless of whether they are performing poorly or not. The work of Morris Rosenberg and his associates partly explains the seeming paradox that "specific self-esteem is most relevant to *behavior,* whereas global self-esteem is most relevant to *psychological well-being.*" It is possible to feel good about oneself generally (healthy global self-esteem), while having low esteem of one's self, or "low self-efficacy," about a particular area of competence.[16] The social psychologist Claude Steele takes this idea a step further. He argues that poor academic performance threatens not just the specific self-esteem of Afro-Americans—as it does that of Euro-Americans—but also their more general or global self-esteem due to their fear that this might seem to confirm ethnic stereotypes about them. Instead of redoubling their efforts to regain their specific self-esteem relating to academics, they seek to protect their global self-esteem by applying the well-tried psychological coping strategies of disengagement: they disidentify with the academic domain. This works well in maintaining their global psychological well-being, Steele argues, but it has disastrous consequences for academic performance. Steele notes that this process of disidentification hardly exists in the early school years—there is little difference between Euro-Americans and Afro-Americans at the eighth-grade level—but increases as students make their way through the school system.[17]

But there is an even greater problem. Several social psychologists have found that "blaming the system" has become more than a substitute for fate, and that it actually accounts for the high self-esteem found among lower-class Afro-Americans. In other words, not only have lower-class Afro-Americans come to dissociate a sense of personal control from their feelings of self-respect, but they have associated their sense of being a victim of the system with feeling good about themselves. "System-blame," we are told, is an integral part of lower class sub-culture.[18] Theirs is a world in which all sense of responsibility for failings has been abolished and in which the highly developed sense of being determined by external forces acts as a security blanket, a source not of shame but of pride. Self-esteem has been stood spectacularly on its head. Lower-class Afro-Americans, with the full support of their leaders and professional psychologists, have come to respect themselves because they have no autonomy. The parties in Rawls's hypothesized Original Position, thinking about the construction of a fair social world, have been stopped dead in their tracks. However liberal they may be, when faced with Afro-American people and advocates like these, they will have no choice but to segregate themselves if they are to rationally conceive and construct a world.

At this point, the social scientists, political leaders, and theorists defending the situation I have just described may well ask: what's so morally wrong with determinism, anyway? It is acknowledged even by the most extreme of moral indeterminists that we live in some kind of causal order, so why should we not be consistent and live by a moral determinist creed, as several distinguished psychological determinists have forcefully argued?[19] These questions must be taken seriously. Moral and psychological autonomy and self-determination are so taken for granted by most Americans that there is a danger of neglecting the intellectual need to defend them. As we do freedom, we may cherish something so much that we forget the reasons we believe in it. I was dismayed to discover from my survey on Americans' notions of freedom, conducted in the early nineties, that nearly all Americans become tongue-tied when asked to give a few good reasons for their love of this ideal, and the same, I suspect, goes for our belief in autonomy and self-determination.

In the remainder of this essay I will therefore attempt to do two things. First, I will offer the best arguments I know against determinism and, by negation, in favor of self-determination. Second, I will examine the ways in which Afro-Americans have successfully achieved self-determination, in spite of the overwhelming pressures in the opposite direction coming from their environment, from racist determinists of the right who see them as victims of their genetic destiny, from liberal and other determinists of the left who see them as victims of their socioeconomic surroundings, and from conservative determinists of the center, who see them as victims of culture.

AGAINST DETERMINISM: THE PHILOSOPHICAL ISSUES

The philosophical problem is ancient, as is the best solution available to us. When the West's first philosophers and proto-social scientists, the Sophists, and their contemporaries, the tragic dramatists, dared to raise questions about the tyranny of fate, they immediately posed the most profound question of moral freedom and autonomy.[20] The ordered cosmos of the preclassical city-state, in which mankind's best hope lay in acting nobly in the face of the inscrutable tyranny of the gods, began to unravel even with the later Aeschylus, who, in his earlier plays, had so faithfully inscribed the fatalistic tradition. When, in *Prometheus Bound,* the wimpish Hermes, who remains fully committed to the traditional notion of divine determinism, is dismissed by the enchained but defiant Prometheus as "the lackey [the Uncle Tom?] of the Gods," we know immediately that we have moved to a wholly new, and troubled, moral terrain. Even so, Prometheus, for all his defiance, has to accept that "craft is weaker than necessity."

Sophocles takes us a step deeper into the problem. Oedipus, in *Oedipus at Colonus,* even though ending his life like an old African slave on a cruel Southern plantation—a stranger in a strange land, ugly, alienated, and despised—nonetheless spurns his outer chains of blindness, guilt, and destitution with the defiant assertion of his inner freedom. There is always choice, if only the ability to choose where one will die: "In this land among strangers he died where he chose to die," sacralizing the ground upon which he fell, free, free at last, and blessed.

Curiously, the elitist philosophers of the classical period, most notably Plato and Aristotle, perhaps because of their elitism, entirely sidestepped the issue of freedom of the will. It was the Stoics who took it up again and, in many ways, defined the problem in terms that were to dominate Western thought and morality right down to modern times, although they failed to offer a satisfactory answer. Indeed, they passed down to us a sublime contradiction that is a near perfect paradigm of the Afro-American moral dilemma.

On the one hand, their love of logic, which they identified with the divine, dictated an uncompromising determinism: everything we do is the consequence of some cause. All of nature, including the social universe, was an uninterrupted causal chain. Fate was identified with the law of universal causation and, with God, was considered the primal and everlasting cause.

And yet, no group of men more cherished and insisted on the possibility of human freedom, even though it remained the privilege only of the wise. Freedom, an autonomist way of life, is always in our power, even when we are slaves, as the former slave and philosopher Epictetus insisted with a forbearance that some in his own audience occasionally found insufferable. This is not the place to examine Epictetus's claims or Chrysippus's intricate, often clever, as often obscure, but in the end unpersuasive philosophical attempts to reconcile determinism with freedom.[21]

The idea that, in acting rationally, we are doing not only what was foreordained by a rational cosmos, but also doing freely what we want and will to do, even if, at any given moment, we foolishly imagine otherwise, is the ancient precursor of modern rational choice and neoclassical economic philosophy. The metaphysics of the "unseen hand" or the "spontaneous order"—the perfect market that harmonizes our individual rational choices or, if one prefers, imposes an unintended design on our socially blind selfish acts—has merely replaced the more attractive Stoic metaphysics of the individual sage living in harmony with the divine, rational cosmos. The Stoics at least allowed that only a few acted truly rationally and would have been dumbfounded by the identification of selfish greed with rationality.

Although it is still not sufficiently recognized, it was the founder of Epicureanism who has provided us with what remains the best philosophical defense of the idea of moral freedom and personal autonomy.[22] Epicurus's starting point is the elegant demonstration of a contradiction at the heart of determinism: "The man who says that all events are necessitated has no ground for criticizing the man who says that not all events are necessitated. For according to him this is a necessitated event." This is the kind of paradox in which the Greeks delighted, but it does not sit well with the modern mind; as the English would say, it is rather too clever by half.

More powerful and convincing is what I have called Epicurus's argument of sociological pragmatism, and it anticipates nearly everything Kant—who dominates modern thought on this subject—has to say. Basically, Epicurus's argument is that if there were no freedom of will we could hold no one responsible for their actions, and without such an indeterminist ethic society would not be possible. The determinist must, at the very least, determine a world of indeterminist persons if there is to be any social world at all.

This pragmatic sociological argument is then shown to be simply a special case of the more general logical argument through an infinite regress critique. The fact that indeterminism or autonomy is sociologically necessitated does not vitiate the self-contradiction of determinism. The determinist finds himself, at the very point where he seems to have triumphed, in a self-refuting regress in which he can never prove that *everything* is necessitated because, at the very least, Epicurus argues, "he debates this very question on the assumption that his opponent is himself responsible for talking nonsense." In other words, the very discourse of the defense of determinism assumes its contradiction.

Epicurus has another very attractive, although less intellectually forceful, argument for indeterminism, one that should have special appeal to Afro-Americans. He argues that it is natural to assume personal responsibility and act freely. That naturalness, however, is not to be confused with mere animal spontaneity. A caged bird has no choice but to endlessly flap its wings against the bars of its cage in its vain attempt to get away. Its desire for release is necessitated, and hence it is not real freedom but pure spontaneity. It is a peculiarity of human beings that only we are capable of nonspontaneity, of falsehood, of what Sartre would, with much un-Epicurean fuss, call "bad faith." But for precisely this reason, our freedom is a chosen one, a human choice, and hence we are most distinctly human when we act freely and deliberately, liberating ourselves from the bars of bad faith and false conventions behind which only we are capable of imprisoning ourselves.

When the poets Paul Laurence Dunbar and Maya Angelou say that they know why the caged bird sings, they may be saying that a caged bird singing is demonstrating a nonspontaneity, an unnaturalness—contrasting sharply with the more natural tendency to beat its wings "till its blood is red on the cruel bars"—that seems human. It suggests the possibility of a willed negation of its unnatural singing, a willing that is itself the essence of human freedom and that Afro-Americans, more than any other group of Americans, know, or should know, all about.[23]

Kant's theory of freedom is largely a modernization of these Epicurean arguments. In his *Groundwork of the Metaphysic of Morals,* he argued that freedom must be presupposed as a property of the will of all rational beings. Such a presupposition, however, stands in stark contradiction to the dictates of pure reason, which assert a natural, sensible world subject to the laws of causality and natural necessity and therefore admitting of no freedom. Kant's "practical" solution to the problem was to make a "rough" distinction between the "sensible" and the "intelligible" worlds, and then to argue that human beings can consider themselves from two points of view: as sensible entities subject to the laws of nature (including society) and as uniquely free creatures acting in an intelligible world independent of nature, one with laws that "are not empirical but have their ground in reason alone." He argues further: "To the idea of freedom there is inseparably attached the concept of autonomy and to this in turn the universal principle of morality—a principle which in Idea forms the ground for all the actions of rational beings, just as the law of nature does for all appearances."

In the final analysis, Kant readily admitted—and here he differs radically from Epicurus, who would have made no such concession—that "we shall never be able to comprehend how freedom is possible," but while logically incomprehensible it is morally and socially necessary.[24]

PROBLEMS OF AFRO-AMERICAN DETERMINISM

The major criticism of moral autonomy and self-determination, indeed the only one worth mentioning, is the seemingly persuasive argument that it appears to blame the victim for the crimes committed against him. But this familiar argument comes at great moral costs.

By its very nature, a deterministic framework accepts and accentuates the moral superiority of the victimizer. As long as one is in the position where one has to appeal to the moral sense and mercy of another person, one remains, almost by definition, morally compromised. The victim's cry for help and mercy concedes the nobility of the oppressor: Why should the man who has enslaved and exploited you respond to your cry unless, far from being an immoral tyrant, he has more than a spark of magnanimity?

Furthermore, to constantly explain away one's failure as being produced by one's environment, or worse, as the doing of another "race" or class, either directly or through the system it controls, is to reduce oneself to the level of an object, and further to prolong one's dependency on that other group or environment. On the objectifying consequences of determinism, I think the philosopher Sidney Hook has said the last word:

> Sickness, accident, or incapacity aside, one feels lessened as a human being if one's actions are always excused or explained away on the ground that despite appearances one is really not responsible for them. It means being treated like an object, an infant, or someone out of his mind. Our dignity as rational human beings sometimes leads us to protest, when a zealous friend seeks to extenuate our conduct on the ground that we were not responsible (we didn't know or intend what we were doing, etc.), that we really *are* responsible and that we are prepared to take the consequences of our responsibility. As bad as the priggishness of the self-righteous is the whine of the self-pitying.[25]

It makes no sense to claim that the crime of Euro-Americans is greater than that of Afro-Americans against each other and against Euro-American victims. To excuse one's actions on deterministic grounds while condemning similar actions on the part of one's oppressor on morally autonomous grounds is irrational and ethically unacceptable.

Further, determinism logically undermines all attempts to seize the initiative in asserting pride in one's genuine achievements. One cannot dismiss the undesirable aspects of Afro-American life on deterministic grounds and then proceed to exalt and take pride in the desirable areas of Afro-American culture on autonomous grounds. If Afro-American problems are the consequences of Euro-American social, economic, and cultural oppression, the same holds for the Afro-American cultural experience. If one is not responsible for one's problems, one can claim no credit for one's achievements, either individually or collectively. If the crimes of a Willie Horton and the disproportionate number of Afro-American rapists and murderers have nothing to do with Afro-American culture and are no reasons for shame, then we can take no pride, individually or collectively, in the novels of a Toni Morrison or the music of a John Coltrane.

But perhaps the biggest contradiction that determinism creates for Afro-Americans is the fact that it also relieves racist Euro-Americans of responsibility for their racism and discrimination against Afro-Americans. If Afro-American failures and criminality are the result of conditioning, then surely so are Euro-Americans'. A man brought up by Euro-American supremacist parents in a chronically racist culture can no more help himself in his vehement hatred of Afro-Americans than the Afro-American underclass can help themselves in their seeming inability to cope. The cry of the victim, then, is doubly futile: not only does it demean the victim by attributing all agency to the victimizer, but in assuming and legitimizing a wholly determinist social and moral universe, it explains away the injustice of the victimizer.

Anything is better than this. By one means or another Afro-Americans have had to find ways out of the deterministic trap. By what means have they done so? How have the 60 to 70 percent of successfully coping Afro-Americans made the leap from determinism to autonomy?

THE PATHS TO PERSONAL AUTONOMY

There have been at least three means of transformation for Afro-Americans: through declaration, through brotherhood, and through rebellion.

MORAL DECLARATION

The first way of assuming personal and moral responsibility is simply to declare that one has done so. This form of assumption is usually more delusory than real, although it is possible for a few to talk themselves into a state of responsibility. If one declares often enough that one is responsible, one might persuade oneself of the statement and, even better, persuade others who, because of their new expectations, reinforce or condition one's responses into a morally autonomous mode of being.

Many Afro-Americans have chosen precisely this path to moral transformation. It is reflected, for example, in the frequency with which Afro-Americans insist on the fact that they are "proud" or that they are "free," in stark contradiction to the actual situation or to their own statements on other occasions. The liberal segment of the Euro-American community has played along with this declaratory strategy.

A good example of an Afro-American leader's attempt at such a moral transformation is Jesse Jackson's use of the call-and-response strategy of Afro-American preachers, exhorting his audience at a youth conference in Atlanta in 1978 to repeat the following litany:

I am
Somebody
Down with dope
Up with hope
My mind
Is a pearl
I can learn anything
In the world
Nobody
Will save us

From us,
For us,
But us.[26]

The problem with the assumption of responsibility through declaration is the fact that the claim often lacks any substance, and surrounding it there is always a disquieting air of unreality and contradiction. Too often it is precisely those who have least to be proud of who are heard proclaiming their pride and independence. This, incidentally, is a very American tendency, and it is not confined to Afro-Americans or even the poor.

Americans, Euro-American and Afro-American alike, rarely hang their heads in shame anymore, even when caught red-handed in the most flagrant acts of immorality. It is common to see the once mighty, such as televangelist Jim Bakker and financier Michael Milken, smiling proudly as they are led off to prison for their crimes—just as common as seeing Afro-American ex-convicts and ex-junkies such as Marion Barry or charlatans such as Al Sharpton declaring themselves proud and ready to lead their fellow Afro-Americans. Keeping one's head up during the worst of times is a good personal strategy; it prevents depression and defeatism, which is psychologically healthy. But Americans have come in recent times to glorify the absence of demoralization as a virtue and, worse, to confuse pride with shamelessness. There is nothing virtuous about having survived a prison term or drug addiction, however high one may have held one's head throughout the ordeal.

Another, very American, reason for the overreliance on declaration as a strategy of moral transformation is the confusion of redemption with pride. This confusion has deep roots in the nation's Puritan and fundamentalist religious heritage, and to the degree that Afro-Americans are disproportionately fundamentalist in their upbringing, they are prone to this confusion. It is an article of faith that redemption is good for the soul. Acknowledging one's sins and paying one's debts to society are also good. But they are good only as means toward a better life and as paving the way for the achievement of virtuous goals; or, as an earlier generation of moralists might have said, they are right acts rather than good ones. They are not, in themselves, good ends, either in the religious or the secular world. Thus, the fact that Marion Barry paid his dues for the horrible way he betrayed his trust to his constituents and his wife by serving time and by rehabilitating himself from his cocaine addiction may justify his proclamation that he is now clean and redeemed, but it says nothing about his merits as a leader—certainly no more than what his track record as a leader dictates—and it offers no basis for pride. Redemption wipes the slate clean. It says nothing about what is to be written next. The assumption of responsibility by declaration is possible if the will is there; more often than not, however, it amounts to nothing more than sheer compensatory talk.

ETHNIC BROTHERHOOD

The second path to personal autonomy among Afro-Americans has been the medium of brotherhood. Increased ethnic consciousness and solidarity have been the major achievements of Afro-American activists in recent years. The Million Man March was a dramatic illustration of this strategy. But, as the march itself indicated, many Afro-American intellectuals, as well as activists and their mass followers, seem to use the term *self-determination* almost exclusively in the sense of collective or national liberation. Thus, the civil rights activist James Forman, in his book on self-determination among Afro-Americans, is solely concerned with the term as a "political concept," exemplified by efforts to forge a separate Afro-American state in the "black belt" counties of America.[27] And the historian V. P. Franklin, in his book *Black Self-Determination,* assumes throughout that the term refers to the collective culture and efforts of Afro-Americans. His concern is with "self-determination for politically and economically oppressed groups that define themselves as a people or 'nation.'" What he has in mind, he tells us in his preface, are collective struggles such as those of the PLO in the Middle East, of SWAPO in South West Africa, of the Irish Republican Army in Northern Ireland, all of which are, for him, "movements that have as their primary objective self-determination for a culturally distinct group."[28] To be sure, Franklin considers the personal aspect of self-determination, but only in regard to the development of what he calls a "distinct core black culture." Rarely does he concern himself with the term in its meaning of personal, individual autonomy. Indeed, he often equates the individualistic use of the term with an "integrationist approach," which is opposed to the nationalist, culturalist notion of self-determination that he favors.

Apart from its political aspect, the moral consequences of this strategy are worth considering, for solidarity carries with it, unmistakably, a measure of responsibility. This is the concern for and the commitment to other members of one's group. Though largely social, this commitment, this responsibility for others, does possess a moral quality. "Am I my brother's (and sister's) keeper?" is, as everyone knows, an intensely moral question. And the commitment of Afro-Americans to the view that they ought, in certain important respects, to be their brothers' keepers, is in part a moral commitment. Brotherhood implies loyalty, oneness, trust, care, and a sense of involvement with and responsibility for all other members of one's brotherhood, beginning with one's immediate kinsmen. It implies that one holds oneself responsible for everything, both good and evil, possessed by the group. Brotherhood, especially when allied to affliction, "recruits" responsibility as well as hope.

However, it is important to note that brotherhood is only a medium of transformation into true moral responsibility; it is not that responsibility itself. For oppressed minorities and colonized peoples, it is an essential first step, a paving of the way for the pursuit of personal autonomy. Numerous studies by psychologists have shown that, among Afro-Americans and other groups, a sense of collective deprivation—what is sometimes called fraternal deprivation—is a more important source of militancy than individual feelings of relative deprivation. During the sixties, it was found that "the individual's perception that others share his fate may cause him to blame the system rather than himself," to develop a strong ethnic self-esteem, and to engage in militant behavior that "replaces the 'old' role of subservience with a 'new' role of activism and positive group image."[29]

For some, especially the leaders of collective liberation movements, there can be no doubt that the act of liberation is itself personally transformative. But alas, this is rarely true of the mass of people engaged in such movements. Significantly, psychologists have found that ethnic and personal esteem can, and often do, vary independently of each other both within and between groups, although there was some tendency during the sixties for the two to reinforce each other among Afro-Americans.[30]

Perhaps the biggest problem with brotherhood as a strategy of self-reclamation is that it is too collective in its orientation. Self-transformation is, in the final analysis, a personal act. During the activist period of group solidarity, all those who participate are engaged in what is at one and the same time collective and personal self-determination. The activist phase of the civil rights movement was a classic case in point, as the many moving testimonies of Afro-American citizens who risked their lives for the goals of the movement make clear. Diane Nash, a student from Chicago attending Fisk University in Nashville, described this transformative experience this way:

> After we had started sitting in, we were surprised and delighted to hear reports of other cities joining in the sit-ins. And I think we started feel-

ing the power of the idea whose time had come. Before we did the things that we did, we had no inkling that the movement would become as widespread as it did.... The movement had a way of reaching inside you and bringing out things that even you didn't know were there. Such as courage. When it was time to go to jail, I was much too busy to be afraid.[31]

The same was no doubt true of thousands of other Afro-American and Euro-American participants in this great movement, as it was during the decolonization phase of the transformation to national independence all over Asia and Africa during the fifties and sixties.

But sadly, it is often a different story after the activist phase is over. As the tragic cases of Africa and most of Asia demonstrate, no sooner is national self-determination realized than the new leadership savagely denies the mass of people any chance of personal freedom and autonomy, using both political repression and kleptocratic rule. Group involvement and collective responsibility as a member of a group are not only possible without personal responsibility, but they may, tragically, undermine personal responsibility even during the activist phase.

Commitment to the autonomy and strength of the group often entails a submission of one's identity to that of the group. Collective freedom, collective power, and collective responsibility are all bought at the expense of the individual's complete suspension of, or submission to, the will of the group and its leaders. Isn't this, after all, the basic tragedy of Nazism? Repeated studies have shown that German Nazis during the era of their ascent and control of state power never felt more free and empowered. When Hermann Goering gave Hitler a birthday gift of an honorary sword before thousands of cheering followers at the Zirkus Krone in 1923, he tendered it with the words: "To the beloved leader of the German movement for freedom, in the conviction shared by hundreds of thousands of the most loyal Germans."[32] It was no exaggeration. One of these followers, an old railroad worker, explained later that "National Socialism, with its promise of community and blood, barring all class struggle, attracted me profoundly."[33] But we now know what was the true nature of that feeling of freedom, empowerment, and egalitarian blood-brotherhood. The free and responsible group, especially the strong, revitalized nationalist movement, too often requires unfree and submissive individuals, so blinded by the goodness and collective "freedom" and destiny of the group that they can become what Daniel Goldhagen has called the "willing executioners" serving genocidal leaders.[34]

Mention of Nazism brings me to yet another danger in the use of brotherhood or forms of ethnic solidarity as a strategy for achieving personal autonomy: it legitimizes this tendency among other groups, especially extremist segments of the Euro-American majority. Take, for example, the troubling revival of "white supremacist" and other neo-Nazi groups in America. These groups have not only found comfort in Afro-American chauvinism, but in many cases they have directly modeled themselves on Afro-American organizations and even appropriated Afro-American brotherhood and consciousness-raising rhetoric. One of the most virulent of such groups is the National Association for the Advancement of White People. In the 1996 presidential campaign, as extremists came out of the woodwork in support of Patrick Buchanan's candidacy, we heard rhetoric that sounded alarmingly like a "whitened" version of Afro-American solidarity talk. Thus Samuel Francis, whom the *New York Times* described as an informal Buchanan campaign adviser and former columnist and editorialist for the *Washington Times*, told a gathering of anti-immigrant nativists in Atlanta: "Whites must reassert our identity and our solidarity, and we must do so in explicitly racial terms through the articulation of racial consciousness as whites."[35] Sound familiar?

The Million Man March exhibited all the advantages and dangers of this form of empowerment. It was impossible not to be moved by nearly one million Afro-American men declaring themselves renewed individuals and initiating their renewal through brotherhood. Even so emphatic a believer in personal self-determination as the centrist economist Glenn Loury found himself, to his own surprise, "becoming misty" as he watched the brothers in their orderly, moving mass statement: "The march had not even begun, and already powerful sentiments, long buried inside me, were being resurrected. I knew then that I was in trouble."[36] Indeed.

It was impossible to forget that the Nation of Islam, which organized this event, places the group above the individual, achieves the healing of Afro-American manhood through the submission of Afro-American womanhood, and is not above the use of murder and violence in imposing collective obligations over personal rights, as the not-to-be-forgotten case of Malcolm X makes clear.

If we replace the term *black* with *white,* the rhetoric of Louis Farrakhan is often identical with that of Samuel Francis and David Duke. As I said earlier, Euro-American and Afro-American advocates of "racial brotherhood" now freely borrow each other's rhetoric; indeed, they sometimes even fraternize with each other, a bizarre bedfellowship that goes back to

Marcus Garvey, who led the first mass nationalist movement of Afro-Americans during the early twenties and invited Ku Klux Klan leaders to speak at his marches, arguing that they were "better friends of the race" than liberal or other Euro-Americans.

Like declaration, then, brotherhood, whatever its social and political merits and necessity as a starting point for liberation, is a limited and always potentially dangerous medium of moral transformation; it works for a few people but is not an acceptable path for the great majority. And in legitimizing fascist tendencies in the society, it unleashes forces that could prove dangerous for all minorities, Euro-American and Afro-American.

MORAL REBELLION

The third form of transformation is, simply put, moral rebellion. This is the activation of that part of one's being which instinctively resists indignity, which, in the noble phrase of Camus, "declares a limit" on dehumanization and objectification.[37] Unlike public rebellions, such as the civil rights movement or acts of civil disobedience, moral rebellion is achieved through purely personal effort.

There are several ways in which the morally oppressed person resists privately: through cultural appropriation, spiritual redemption, and existential rebellion.

Cultural Appropriation

Rebellion through appropriation is one of the most sublime forms of irony, for here what the oppressed does is to rebel by arrogating the culture and lifestyle of the oppressor. After all, what better role model of an autonomous group is there than that of a ruling elite? And what better way to acquire an elite's sense of purpose and moral responsibility, its aristocratic belief that the world is manipulable, than simply to enculturate its style?

This may seem to many an outrageous proposition. Yet the fact remains that countless members of oppressed groups have chosen precisely this path to moral transformation. The assimilated Jew of pre-Hitler Germany and of modern Britain, the *assimilé* of the French colonies of Asia and Africa, the "black Englishman" of Africa and the Caribbean, and the often castigated "Afro-Saxons" of the United States are cases in point. But the technique is not the monopoly of oppressed minority groups; it is practiced as frequently by members of exploited classes, the classic case being the English cockney who goes the well-trodden ascending route of grammar school, Oxford, and the Labor aristocracy. Because of the ethnic factor, however, the technique of cultural appropriation has always been condemned by Afro-American activists and intellectuals, even those intellectuals who, without acknowledging it, have in fact used precisely this technique.

An Afro-American man who appropriates the lifestyle of the elite betrays, it is claimed, not only his class but his "race." This criticism, however, has been grossly exaggerated. Certainly, a risk of betrayal is always involved in employing this strategy, and many who have chosen this path have fallen prey to these risks; nothing could be more pathetic than the shallow "black Englishman" or Frenchman or the English cockney upstart with upper-class airs who has nothing to offer but his acquired pretensions. As someone who has lived many years in England and the Caribbean, I know these obnoxious poseurs only too well. But it is quite possible to use this technique without in any way betraying oneself or one's origins. Indeed, the experience can be a radicalizing one, and Afro-American history is replete with cultural usurpers who have been strong defenders of and workers for the cause of Afro-American progress.

What, after all, was W. E. B. Du Bois but an Afro-Saxon? Can anyone intimately acquainted with his life and works doubt this? Nor did he ever try to conceal the fact: His aristocratic bearing is attested by all who knew him. He admired Thomas Carlyle, the nineteenth-century British elitist; and his call for the promotion of a vanguard elite of Afro-American people as a precondition of progress was in keeping with his aristocratic view of change, in sharp contrast to Booker T. Washington's bottom-up, artisanal approach.

What, too, was Frantz Fanon but a thoroughly French assimilé, right down to his very French left-wing rhetoric of liberatory violence? Or, to take an example from an even earlier era, what was Frederick Douglass but a cultural appropriator, Euro-American wife and all? Yet all these men have made undeniable contributions to the progress of Afro-American people. The great Marxist West Indian intellectual C. L. R. James is not only a fine specimen of this genre of men, but is interesting for openly acknowledging the fact.[38] In his classic autobiography, James tells us that his assimilation and passion for the very British game of cricket—a passion shared by all West Indian intellectuals, in addition to the West Indian masses—was the avenue by means of which he came to assimilate British intellectual culture, the radical wing of which he was to master and use against it in his successful anticolonial struggle.

Only believers in a crude form of ethnic nationalism, as totally obsessed with pigmentation as are Euro-American racists, have completely clouded the issue. The cultural appropriator may sometimes be a political conservative or a traitor to his group politically, or he may be a revolutionary, but whatever the public political stand, on the private level the arrogation of the oppressor's culture and style is always an act of personal rebellion. It is the rejection of the vicious circle, of the irrevocable whine of deterministic justification, and a forceful acquisition, through individual cultural conquest, of dignity and the ethic of personal responsibility.

The main drawback of this technique, apart from the admitted sociopolitical risks of group betrayal, is the fact that it is enormously demanding both emotionally and intellectually. It is much easier to wage war, start riots, and throw bombs than to engage in this particular form of rebellion. For this reason cultural appropriation is, and always has been, most successfully pursued by the more intellectually oriented members of the oppressed group—what Du Bois, in a statement most of his current admirers would rather forget, correctly called "the talented tenth."[39]

Spiritual Redemption

The second type of personal rebellion is by means of religion, drawing upon the redemptive power of faith. Afro-Americans have most extensively used this medium of moral transformation. It is a remarkable fact that, of the vast numbers of social analyses and commentaries on the Afro-American church, few, if any, have pointed out what is perhaps the central function of Christianity for its Afro-American adherents—the opportunity for the realization of personal responsibility that the Protestant version of the creed offers.

Fundamentalist Christianity, by placing the blame for sin and failure squarely on the individual, and by offering the hope of heaven through personal salvation for which the individual, and the individual alone, is responsible, presented Afro-Americans with an autonomous oasis of dignity and personal worth in what was often otherwise a desert of deterministic objectification. For the majority of lower-class, poorly educated Afro-Americans, the Christian creed has been the only escape from the twin grip of racist biologic determinism and liberal environmental determinism.

But fundamentalist spiritual redemption, like cultural appropriation, has its dangers, although these are almost all social rather than moral. The dangers are well known—Marx's "opiate," religion, displaces aggression, channels group action in the direction of fantasy, and offers an outlet for the organizational and political skills of group leaders. This may all be true, but it is equally true that on the social level religion offered the only meaningful nationwide organizational base for Afro-Americans at a time when such a base was desperately needed.

This is no place, however, to discuss the sociological merits and defects of the Afro-American church.[40] My main reason for raising the issue is to indicate that the church's role is too often discussed in either purely sociological or purely theological terms. Both approaches, I think, have missed its major contribution to the Afro-American experience—namely, its role as a medium of moral transformation. It is the autonomous ethic of the Afro-American church that has kept the brakes on a complete moral objectification of the group. When an Afro-American militant seems to contradict his own avowed deterministic moral stand by suddenly declaring that he is in fact free, or by resenting the moral patronage of someone who attempts too vigorously to explain and excuse him, this contradiction, this sudden, unwitting flash of a sense of moral responsibility is, as often as not, simply the expression of a half-forgotten fundamentalist past.

In his church, the Afro-American person is every bit a rebel—not only in the style and content of his particular interpretation of Christian practices, but in his transformation from whining determinist to almost self-righteous autonomist. Every Afro-American church member in the course of his or her religious practices independently comes to the conclusion that Kierkegaard articulated over a century ago:

> O, thou sufferer, whosoever thou art, if only thou wilt listen! People generally think that it is the world, the environment, external relationships which stand in one's way, in the way of one's good fortune and peace and joy, and at bottom it is always man himself who is too closely attached to the world, to the environment, to circumstances, to external relationships so that he is not able to come to himself, come to rest, to have hope. He is constantly too much turned outward instead of being turned inward. Hence, everything he says is true only as an illusion of the senses.[41]

Quite apart from its function as an opiate, another major disadvantage of fundamentalist religion is that it has a limited scope as a medium of moral transformation. The transformation wrought by this religion only marginally and sporadically permeates the secular *moral* life, in sharp contrast with its impact on the secular *social* and *political* world of Afro-Americans. In all religions, of course, there is a tension between the World and the Spirit, between the intrusion of the secular world into the sacred, and the sacred into the secular. Societies solve this problem through a variety of compromises—through the domination of the secular by the sacred, as in many Catholic and Muslim societies; through the domination of the sacred by the secular, as in several northwest European societies and traditional Chinese society; through a creative compromise in which there is a functional separation between the two on the social and political levels, but marked interpenetration on the cultural level, as in the Protestant ethic of nineteenth-century American society and in modern Judaism; or, finally, through a moral separation of the sacred and the secular even where the church plays an active political role.

Afro-American Protestantism, very much like its Euro-American fundamentalist counterpart, exhibits mainly the last kind of compromise. In spite of the strong social role of the church in the lives of Afro-Americans, there has always been a marked distinction between what personally belongs to Caesar and what belongs to God, a distinction that is well illustrated in James Baldwin's novel *Go Tell It on the Mountain* and, rather sadly, in the adulterous behavior of the Reverend Martin Luther King Jr. and many other activist Afro-American ministers.

The result has been that only a small proportion of Afro-Americans have benefited in all areas of their lives from the moral transformation of their religious experience. The Afro-American church has been good for the attainment of collective goals and for personal solace and the achievement of spiritual autonomy, but it has had only limited impact on the secular, personal lives of lower-class Afro-Americans.

It is hard to understand why this is so or even exactly what is going on morally and spiritually. The moral dictates of Afro-American fundamentalism are forcefully and unambiguously hammered home in every service: fornication, adultery, the bearing of illegitimate children, teenage sexuality, personal violence, and drug and alcohol addiction are all relentlessly condemned in every sermon as sins incurring everlasting punishments and damnation in hell. The Afro-American lower classes attend religious services more frequently than any other group of Americans; they listen and acknowledge these sins with an intensity unmatched by any other group of American Christians; according to a recent survey by the University of Chicago's National Opinion Research Center, they pray more frequently and more fervently for these sins than any other group of Americans. And yet, in spite of all this churching and praying they continue to commit these acts (these sins) with greater frequency than all other Americans. What happens between the sermon and the bed? How could so great a divide exist between a fervently believed-in creed and the behavior of its adherents?

Somehow, the religion succeeds in getting the individual to acknowledge his or her acts and to take full responsibility for them and for their wrongness, to plead forgiveness from God, and in frequent public testimony to solicit the forgiveness and support of fellow church members. All this is good for an ethic of personal responsibility. But personal autonomy goes beyond mere acknowledgement and assumption of responsibility for one's acts, especially one's sinful or wrong acts. Personal autonomy requires the individual to take action to change his or her behavior, not to commit the sin again. And it is here that the Afro-American church (like its Euro-American fundamentalist counterpart) fails miserably.

It is a hopeless, tragic puzzle. Poverty and racism are most emphatically not the answer. To a degree, one must attribute this failure to the Afro-American preacher who too often betrays his trust by committing the very sins he condemns from the pulpit, often with the most vulnerable followers he claims to shepherd. But the explanation must be more complex than this. Unfortunately, those who study the Afro-American church find the subject too sensitive or embarrassing to examine.

Existential Rebellion

The third type of personal rebellion is the purest of all, since it has no catalyst, no medium except its own occurrence. It is properly called "existential rebellion" because this is precisely the sort of thing that Camus, though he himself would have eschewed the term, discussed so eloquently in his great philosophical work *The Rebel.*[42]

Camus's treatise was in nearly all respects an intensely moral work. Yet, surprisingly, in spite of a careful typology of rebellious types, he failed to explicate, as a variant of his pure-type existential rebel, the moral rebel. Throughout his work, Camus uses the rebel slave as a paradigm of the existential rebel; and in the same way that a slave who has conformed all his life suddenly says "no," for absolutely no other reason than the purely moral fact that sooner or later an inherent sense of dignity demands to be released—Frederick Douglass's account being the classic real-life instance of this[43]—so it is that some members of modern lower-class Afro-American communities sometimes, out of the sheer need to exist in dignity and as human beings, forcefully transform themselves into morally responsible people.

Rebellion, Camus suggests, performs the same role in the daily life of the existential rebel as the Cartesian *cogito* does in the realm of thought: "I rebel—therefore we exist." One may, at the risk of being pretentious, expand the above aphorism in Afro-American terms as follows: "I rebel morally—therefore our humanity exists."

Whatever the philosophical foundations of this most extraordinary of moral transformations, it is a fact that many Afro-Americans have experienced it. There is no other way to explain the not inconsiderable number of successful Afro-Americans. I remarked earlier that social science has engaged in explanatory overkill in analyzing Afro-American failure, and that there are surprisingly few attempts at explaining Afro-American success. I suspect that few social scientists will take up the challenge, for there is no way in which the vast majority of these successes can be explained, either environmentally or genetically.

Yet the fact remains that two-thirds of Afro-American men and women, on the average no better endowed genetically than fellow Afro-Americans they have left behind in the ghettos, nonetheless succeed. Though many come from environments with the same sorry list of broken homes, crime-plagued neighborhoods, drug-infested streets, inadequate schools, and racist Euro-American authority figures, they nonetheless succeed. How are we to explain them? We cannot. They defy explanation precisely because they alone account for their success; they made their success, and they made it, first, through a rebellion against their deterministic moral environment, and then, having gained their humanity, through the much easier rebellion against their social and economic environments.

It is no accident that it is from the popular ethics of another former-ly persecuted group that we find one of the best practical definitions of existential rebellion. Alfred Jospe interprets the Jewish notion of *hutzpah* in terms very similar to Camus's existential rebellion. He defines it as "a spirit of creative defiance," and his elaboration nearly perfectly explains what I mean by existential rebellion:

> Hutzpah as I conceive it—is the rejection of peace between man and nature. It is the drive to touch, to build, to transform, to change the physical world as well as man's inner world. It is a spirit of rebellion that is unable to make its peace with that which is for the sake of that which ought to be. It is a spirit of defiance which refuses to acquiesce in the status quo and is ready to defy the forces of man, of nature, of history—yes, even of God—in order to reach out for something better, more complete, closer to the realization of hope and ideal.[44]

Clearly, existential rebellion has two critical elements, inextricably fused together. One is its negative quality, the refusal to accept the inner and outer status quo, the refusal to make peace with "that which is for the sake of that which ought to be." But this negation affirms something positive—what Jospe refers to as "the drive to touch, to build, to transform, to change the physical world as well as man's inner world." What is heartening about Afro-Americans today is that, both as individuals and as a group, they have largely achieved the negative aspect of existential rebellion. There can be no doubt that nearly all Afro-American people now refuse to acquiesce in their present status, and through their fundamentalist creed most Afro-Americans believe in the passive side of moral autonomy, namely, the willingness to acknowledge and take responsibility for their acts, in spite of the deterministic rhetoric of their elite leaders.

What is lacking and now badly needed among the Afro-American bottom quarter and established leadership are, first, an inward extension of this rebellion and, by means of this moral empowerment, an achievement of the positive side of rebellion and autonomy, the affirmation of true dignity in the unaided "drive to touch, to build."

BUT NOT ALONE: THE SOCIAL OBLIGATIONS OF MORAL AUTONOMY

Nothing I have just said should be taken to mean or imply in any way that socially impoverished Afro-Americans should struggle without help in their search for security and personal autonomy. A commitment to moral autonomy does not mean a surrender to selfishness and isolation in our social policies, nor does it mean abandonment of the exploited, the impoverished, and those who suffer discrimination to the mercies of "the unseen hand" or the patronizing charities of the prosperous.

The ethic of moral autonomy carries a fundamental and inescapable imperative: it is truly possible only in a world in which everyone else is morally autonomous. If the person with whom I am interacting either refuses or wholly lacks the means to behave autonomously—either in the passive sense of assuming responsibility for his or her actions after the fact, or in the active sense of taking responsibility beforehand—then all morally based sociality begins to break down. I can no longer assume that there is this minimal common ground between us; I cannot anticipate the person's moral reactions; I cannot assume that the person even accepts my moral autonomy or my willingness to take responsibility for my own views and behavior. If people are not prepared to assume their own moral being, I am reckless to think for a moment that they will consider mine.

If I encounter a man on a dark street who finds no reason to respect his own moral worth, I am in serious trouble. Not simply my ability to interact humanly, but my very life might be at stake. He might think so little of me as a precious moral creature, and of the life I value so much, that he might shoot me down just to get the fancy leather coat I have just bought; he might pull me from my BMW and run me over in his getaway; he might even take my life for something as trifling as the new pair of Nike sneakers in which I'm jogging.

These are not idle academic speculations. Things like this have been known to happen on the streets of America. Every day, and not just in the dark.

So the question arises: how do we guarantee our own autonomy while necessarily, imperatively, promoting the autonomy of others, without falling between a rock of self-contradiction in attempting to promote autonomy deterministically and a hard place of self-defeating selfishness and brutal isolation? The next essay addresses this question.

3 THE MORAL CRISIS OF
CONSERVATIVE "RACIAL" ADVOCACY

How can we promote autonomy and self-determination without falling prey to selfishness and the abandonment of those in need? How can we reduce dependency and shiftlessness without increasing human misery? How can a commitment to an ameliorative government and a return to the American revolutionary ideal of active citizenship in a virtuous, caring republic be reconciled with the amoral materialism of the capitalist marketplace?

We may approach these issues by way of Kant's distinction between the sensible and the intelligible worlds and the accounts required of each. For any sensible account of our world, a deterministic approach is necessary. But to explain our world in sensible terms is not to make it morally intelligible or to justify it in any way. Conservatives too often neglect the first part of this Kantian dictum, while Afro-American leaders and others seeking change for the disadvantaged are often too ready to neglect the second.

When then British prime minister Margaret Thatcher announced to the world, "There is no such thing as Society. There are individual men and women and there are families,"[1] she was stating in the shrillest terms possible the conservative denial of the brutally obvious fact that the social universe, like its physical counterpart, is a sensible, causal order. When defenders of underclass criminality and irresponsible parenting hide one more time behind the refrain, "It's racism that did it," they are likewise denying the fundamental prerequisite of personal responsibility for any intelligible form of human sociality. The former defends a one-sided, undersocialized conception of human beings, the latter advocates an equally one-sided, oversocialized view of human behavior and society.

The problem, however, is more complex than this, for the issue at stake is not simply that of finding a middle course between an oversocialized and an undersocialized view of human action. We get to the heart of the matter when we recognize two basic limitations in Kant's distinction between the intelligible and the sensible, limitations that persist in the thinking of his conservative inheritors. The first limitation concerns the nature and levels of human agency; the second, which will take us directly back to the Afro-American crisis, concerns the specification of those areas of a person's life over which he or she can reasonably be said to have no control.

First, Kant, like all modern conservatives, erroneously assumed that the problem of agency applies only to the individual level of human action. Thatcher's outburst is the extreme modern statement of this error. The truth, however, is that human agency exists on several levels, of which the individual is one, albeit the most fundamental. Not only do human beings act responsibly, and morally, as individuals, they act jointly as collective agents. The family is such an agent. The community is another. The state or its governmental arm is yet another. Nor is such agency confined to nonformal or noneconomic activities. Collective agency is an essential part of the capitalist system. Indeed, the most important example of such agency is the firm, that organizational foundation of capitalism.

And it is here that we come upon the most basic contradiction in the ideology of conservative capitalists, both lay conservatives and the practitioners of the discipline that intellectually undergirds capitalism, neoclassical economics. For, while dogmatically maintaining that only individuals are moral agents, conservatives, like all the rest of us, hold firms to be legally and morally responsible agents. If I suffer some injury as a result of the action of the firm known as AT&T, I do not seek remedy from the individual who happens to be the head of AT&T; I seek remedy from the collective entity known as AT&T. What's more, corporate agents are recognized not only in cases of tort, but in numerous cases where corporations feel that there are undue constraints on their freedom of action. Tax deductions and direct subsidies to corporations amount to a recognition of the moral (sometimes called "welfare") rights and entitlements of these collective agents. Nowhere is the distinction between individual and collective agency more fully acknowledged than in our tax system's insistence on taxing twice people who operate businesses: as individual agents and as corporate agents. Conservatives, of course, have always complained about this. But their complaints have gone unheeded precisely because the vast majority of people in modern capitalist societies, including nearly all moderate conservatives, accept the validity of the claim that corporate agency exists and that people in the role of corporate representative and in the role of individual must be treated differently.

Implicit in this recognition is another of vital moral significance: people in their roles as corporate, or representative, agents are expected to behave differently in their relations with people from the way they behave as individuals in relations with these same people. This leads me to the second important limitation of the neo-Kantian moral tradition—its refusal to recognize what may be called representational interactions. In a modern complex society, we are obliged to interact with people in the two distinct ways just noted—as individuals in face-to-face interactions and as representatives in corporate, communal, civic, and governmental roles.

Nothing attests more to the astonishing political genius of that greatest of American revolutionary leaders, James Madison, than his recognition of the fact that large constituencies were a prerequisite of a stable modern democracy precisely because they were large and, unlike Athens or colonial Virginia, did not permit face-to-face interactions between the representative and his constituents. To be sure, Madison shrewdly realized that the myth of face-to-face, small-scale democracy was necessary. We continue to maintain that myth today in the belief that so-called "retail" democracy is still possible, especially in places such as Iowa and New Hampshire, a belief devastatingly undermined by the plutocratic candidacy of Steve Forbes in the 1996 presidential primary.

What are the implications of the distinction between face-to-face and representational interactions for American ethnic relations? First, in our face-to-face interactions, Afro-American and Euro-American people should treat each other exactly alike: as responsible moral agents. We do not need any special set of sensitivities in our interactions with people from different ethnic backgrounds. Any attempt to observe such sensitivities will be folly, for it will lead one down a path of either patronizing contempt or relativistic moral and social chaos. The danger in face-to-face interactions for Afro-Americans comes not from conservatives but from liberals, for it is they who will attempt to sociologize and relativize such interactions—in other words, to apply a patronizingly oversocialized view of human relations in their attempt to be nice, seemingly nonracist, and fair. The nonracist conservative position is the only morally acceptable and sociologically workable one in face-to-face interethnic relations. By insisting on judging and relating to an Afro-American person in exactly the same way that one judges and relates to fellow Euro-Americans, including one's own kinsmen, the conservative acknowledges the inherent individual, face-to-face equality of the Afro-American person. Nothing else works, morally or socially.

Representational relations are a different matter. The representative, be he Euro-American or Afro-American, must take into account deterministic factors—in Kantian terms, he must consider the sensible, causal social order—in his dealings with Afro-American (and Euro-American) constituents. It is not just the fact that the representative of a large democracy deals mainly with interest groups and constituencies that enjoins the representative to behave differently—although this is an important factor—but that the representative, qua representative, is called upon to give primacy to the social, collective dimension of life in his or her dealings with constituents. The fundamental flaw in conservative thinking is the refusal to acknowledge the peculiar demands of representational behavior and collective life. Insisting that the representative should treat individuals exactly the same as in face-to-face interactions is perverse, hypocritical, and downright obtuse, in light of the treatment of corporate constituencies.

American conservative representative leaders are in hopeless intellectual disarray on this matter. Not only is the socioeconomic system that they cherish founded on the principle of corporate responsibility and action, but conservatives, more than any other group, are prone to appeal to collective ideals and agency when it suits them. Which group of people urges their fellow Americans to be patriotic and gets most upset when protesters exercise their First Amendment right to burn the flag? And what is patriotism if not the most extreme commitment to a belief in a supraindividual entity called the nation? Which group of Americans wants us all to pursue a common national culture with a single common set of virtues and ideals grounded on a common set of religious beliefs? Which group of Americans wants the government to abandon the libertarian underpinnings of capitalism—the fundamental capitalist tenet that individuals should be left to make their own choices as long as they do not interfere with the liberty of others—and intrude on the most private aspects of people's lives by controlling their reproductive choices and by censoring the books they read, the art they view, and the Web sites they surf to on the Internet?

It is not my objective here to launch into a general criticism of conservative American thought and behavior. My concern is to drive home the two points introduced so far: the first being that the notion of human agency exists on levels beyond the individual, and that no group of people, by their corporate actions, demonstrates this more than conservative Americans, whatever their professional intellectuals may say. The second point is that representative agents are corporate actors who must take account of the social environment—what constrains and destabilizes and what makes for cohesiveness—in their dealings with the individuals they represent. One of the great moral and intellectual failures of neoclassical economics is its grudging acknowledgment and general neglect of these collective problems.[2] The representative behaves autonomously not by dodging behind the insane myth that there is no such thing as society, or collective agency, but by boldly facing up to the reality of the social environment and attempting to change it in ways that optimize the public good.

Even if the conservative representative rejects the notion of collective agency (and, admittedly, there are many liberals who also do) and insists that only individuals are agents, he is still required to acknowledge one important aspect of individual agency that is not normally—and should not be for reasons of practical judgment—invoked in face-to-face interactions. This is the fact that individual agency is itself "profoundly social or collective," as the social historian William Sewell Jr. has elegantly argued. "Agency entails an ability to coordinate one's actions with others and against others, to form collective projects, to persuade, to coerce, and to monitor the simultaneous effects of one's own and others' activities," he writes. "Moreover, the extent of the agency exercised by individual persons depends profoundly on their positions in collective organizations. ... Personal agency is, therefore, laden with collectively produced differences of power and implicated in collective struggles and resistances."[3]

The representative agent's main role is to consider all those areas directly impinging on individual lives over which the individual has limited or no control—in other words, those constraints that inhibit the exercise of agency. These, I am arguing, are twofold: first is the problem of those agents that are themselves collective or corporate, against which all individuals, rich and poor, weak and powerful, must be protected by the corporate agency that is the leadership of the democratic state.[4] The individual needs a neutral collective agent, his representative, to do it for him. A pernicious aspect of conservative discourse in modern capitalist society is the deliberate refusal to even recognize a need for this role. By either denying or equating corporate and individual agency, it is assumed that individual consumers are the same kind of agents as the corporations from whom they buy their goods and services. Thus, when the full corporate weight of the health care industry was used to defeat the attempt at a national health plan through massive advertising and lobbying, it was blithely asserted that the industry was simply exercising its right to free expression and democratic representation, just like any other citizen. And for the better part of this century, the tobacco industry successfully exercised its individual rights, like any other ordinary citizen, to persuade the nation to become addicted to its life-threatening products, to lobby its government to subsidize the production of its narcotic, and to win its cases against individual plaintiffs in court.

The second focus of the representative is the systemic forces—what Kant had in mind when he spoke of the "sensible" world—that adversely affect individuals' control over their lives. American conservatives have always believed that there are major areas of the market economy that fail and that only bold, government action and regulation can correct: the enormous subsidies to farmers, the antitrust laws, the regulation of the stock market, and environmental laws are only a few cases in point. I am proposing nothing more radical than extending the rationale for such action to the Afro-American and Euro-American underclasses and other underprivileged groups.

Three proposed areas of extension will be discussed here. First, there are constraints on individual agency that may be called Acts of Man, the counterpart to Acts of God. These are the wholly unanticipated disasters that individuals are forced to confront as a result of some sudden devastating change in their environment brought about by the acts of powerful individuals and corporate agents. A good example is the closing of a firm upon which an entire community depends, not only throwing the majority of able-bodied people out of work, but undercutting the entire material, cultural, and moral basis of the community.

If one accepts that the state has a moral obligation to intervene in cases of Acts of God, it is hard to see why it does not in cases of such willful devastation by Acts of Man. With God, at the very least, we have the comfort of knowing that He acts in mysterious ways his wonders to perform; we are either being punished for our past sins or being tested and guided by tough divine love into becoming better people. With Acts of Man there is no such comfort and no such design. We blasphemously insult God when we intervene to correct His acts while neglecting those of man. I'm quite serious. This discourse is addressed to a largely Christian nation, and my conversation considers its religious dictates with all seriousness.

Working- and lower-class Afro-Americans, as the works of William Julius Wilson demonstrate, have disproportionately suffered from those Acts of Man which, to use the language of social science, are due to the structural transformation of the American economy from a goods-producing, industrial one to a service-oriented and high technology–based postindustrial system.[5]

The second proposed extension of universally accepted principles of intervention comes from our treatment of the environment, our recognition that there can be only a collective response to acts of degradation. The most die-hard antistatist accepts that, over time, severe damage is done to our environment by individuals and collectivities that can only be remedied by the state since the market provides no way for self-interested individuals to profit by correcting or preventing these degradations.

It makes sense, on the level of representational agency, to see the horrendous social and physical blight of the inner cities and the nihilistic violence and other behaviors of the Afro-American and Euro-American underclasses in these terms: as Acts of Degradation to the social and cultural environment. Chronic poverty and unemployment; overcrowded, ethnically segregated or rural ghettos; and drug-infested, crime-ridden streets all create a chain of degradation with dire consequences for all members of the society. The degraded masses cannot be escaped in a mass democracy, however great their hypersegregation. The great cities of the nation with their rich cultural heritage (a heritage that is disproportionately Afro-American) are under siege; no street is safe, and everyone experiences anxiety even when living in suburbs far from the madding, violent urban mob, as the mass murders committed by Colin Ferguson on a Long Island commuter train made horribly clear. Whole regions of the nation's economy may be threatened by this degradation, in exactly the same way that a minority of polluters (or bad apples of any type) may threaten whole industries. A tragic case in point was the spate of mindless killings in south Florida that threatened the tourist industry upon which the entire region depends.

Even greater than the costs to the economic environment, however, have been those incurred by the cultural environment. A mass democracy thrives on a mass culture. But the mass media and popular culture industry sets its standards by the least common denominator. When these happen to be the most degraded members of the nation, everyone suffers by the degradation of tastes and cultural standards.

Purely punitive responses not only do not halt the erosion; we know from a wealth of studies that they worsen it. The vast expansion in the number of prisons now being built may make people feel more secure, but it is a grim illusion. Prisons, as every criminologist knows, are ideal sites for spreading and deepening the cultural and social debasement they are supposed to cure.

We no longer respond to the degradation of the physical environment by asserting that only the individual exists and that the best the state agency can do is punish polluters after they have ruined our habitat. Instead, we have agreed-upon rules and regulations that protect the environment for the collective good. Along similar lines, I propose more drastic preventive action by a self-determining, autonomous state to undo the social and cultural blight and protect the social and cultural environment from further degradation.

This is a minimalist argument that appeals both to the most selfish of motives and to the need to protect the collective cultural environment of the national community. The argument, it is interesting to note, has an ancient analogue. The Athenians, during the period of the classical city-state, had large numbers of slaves, nearly all of whom they despised as barbarians—persons who, even when freed, could never become a part of the citizen body. Slaves were "two-footed stock," whose evidence could only be relied on if given under torture. And yet, surprisingly, the Athenians punished the murder of slaves with the death penalty. They explained this seeming contradiction with the argument that the capital punishment of the slave's killer had little to do with any love for the slave, and everything to do with the degradation of the community at large. The slave's murder was seen as an act of "impiety" against the cherished community by the wanton shedding of blood, which offended the communal gods even as it coarsened the city's moral tone. It is a lean, mean argument, for all its talk of piety, but if it is the only one that the American moral market will take, as I sadly suspect, then I'll truck it.

We should stop the impious degradation of human life by abolishing the death penalty and by shifting our emphasis in the treatment of nonviolent crime to prevention and rehabilitation rather than incarceration. When our leaders fail to take effective action in dealing with crime—such as their reluctance to sponsor drug rehabilitation programs and to change the iniquitous disparity in drug sentencing—because they are more concerned with the political consequences of their actions and how "tough" they appear to be on crime, our entire political culture has been degraded. The spate of murders of rap artists, especially Tupac Shakur, and the subsequent revelations about the violent and criminal behavior of Marion (Suge) Knight, the head of Death Row Records, including intimidation of executives of major entertainment companies, indicates the extent to which both our popular culture and corporate life have been debased.[6]

To these Acts of Man and Acts of Degradation we may add a third extension that only the representative actor mobilizing the agents of state can deal with: call it Acts of History. By this I refer to the accumulated patterns of discrimination over long periods of time against particular groups of people that create not only generalized disabilities of a collective nature but also generalized advantages to those who benefit from the discrimination. These Acts of History are what, together, are often referred to as institutional discrimination.

Such Acts of History might include other forms of cumulative discrimination such as class exploitation, which Afro-Americans shared with the Euro-American working classes and underclasses. Only Afro-Americans, however, spent two-thirds of their history under a system of slavery; only they suffered the peculiar indignities and disabilities of chronic, nationally pervasive racism; and only they experienced the pain, anguish, and legal disabilities of Jim Crow laws. Most important of all, only they were systematically shut out of the emerging industrial revolution at the end of the nineteenth century, preventing them from developing those critical patterns of behavior and cultural tools necessary for keeping in phase with the nation's changing economy.[7] While these Acts of History may no longer exist or are on the decline, there can be no doubt that their accumulated impact persists. The impact takes various forms: the advantages that accrued to other groups as a result of racist discrimination against Afro-Americans and their exclusion from the nation's civic life; the cultural information and social networks that Afro-Americans were denied as a result of their segregation from the mainstream of the industrial culture; and the oppositional coping strategies and other adaptations they were forced to make, which hardened into patterns of behavior that inhibit competence and full adjustment to an equal-opportunity environment.

It is impossible to measure the individual impact of such collectively accumulated Acts of History. Their effects are pervasive, collective, and diffuse. Afro-Americans experience these effects as Afro-Americans rather than as individuals. For this reason they can be dealt with only by representative agents whose task is to correct and remedy the lingering systemic impact of Acts of History on the "sensible" world of the Afro-American. This is precisely what affirmative action was meant to achieve. Whatever its flaws, this policy is one of the finest examples of a nation recognizing, and attempting to rectify, the collective impact of Acts of History on an especially disadvantaged group.

That conservatives object to such a policy on the grounds that collective agency and liability do not exist is sheer hypocrisy and self-contradiction. Collective reparation is a well-established principle in the laws of nations. And within the United States itself there are numerous counterparts to affirmative action in the treatment of corporate actors. What, after all, are antitrust laws but attempts to remedy Acts of History? When, for example, the extraordinary step was taken to break up AT&T, the legal and moral reasoning was identical to that underpinning affirmative action. While AT&T had committed no specific injury against any particular small communications firm, it was felt that it had, over time, committed Acts of History that were injurious to the growth of competitors, and that these accumulated Acts of History had created an environment in which it was nearly impossible for any other firm to fairly compete. The successful antitrust suit was a powerful form of affirmative action for small communications firms that wished for a fairer environment and a "piece of the pie."

This double standard in the matter of coercive constraints and the need for remedy is perhaps the most egregious aspect of contemporary conservative thought. As Robert E. Goodin observes, "If what the monopolist does when exercising his overwhelming bargaining power is described as infringing the freedom of others, as libertarians concede, then they must also concede that any contract predicated on unequal bargaining power (in capitalist employment markets, for example) infringes freedom to some greater or lesser extent."[8] Sauce for the goose of collective agents should surely be sauce for the gander of collective agents in their relations with less powerful individual agents.

All I am asking of the representative agents concerned with the plight of Afro-Americans is that they treat their collectively generated problems—problems accruing from their peculiar relation to the sensible American order—with the same compassion they bestow on corporate actors injured by similar collectively induced constraints on their freedom to act. The present conservative rhetoric that argues that the poor ought to be abandoned for their own autonomous good is hypocritical nonsense, not to mention a gross distortion of everything meant and implied by the ethics of autonomy.

Having argued the minimal case for collective representation on behalf of the Afro-American and other poor, I should clarify how my position differs from that of the Afro-American advocacy leadership criticized in the preceding essay. Could not this leadership argue that it is simply performing its representative-agent role, insisting on an autonomous policy for the sensible world that will empower Afro-American individuals and thus enhance their autonomy?

To the degree that Afro-American leadership sticks closely to the position I have outlined here, I obviously have no bones to pick with them. But they have done far more than this. Ironically, they have committed the conservative reductionist fallacy of thinking of their role in mainly face-to-face terms. But, unlike conservatives, they have compounded their representational reductionism by promoting a highly deterministic ideology of victimhood among their constituents.

A representative agent, a leader of any kind, has no business encouraging his individual supporters to think deterministically about themselves. To do so is the representative's task in his or her interactions with other representative agents. In a free, democratic, capitalist society that thrives mainly on the initiative and sense of—indeed, strong belief in and commitment to the dogma of—self-determination, a leader's role is to encourage individuals to think only in these terms, unless, of course, the individuals wish to become leaders themselves or professional social scientists. A society in which everyone thinks like a deterministic systems analyst or is only concerned with the collective impact on the individual is a society in dire trouble, for reasons explored in the last essay. Even if the dogma of self-determination were not true—and I am inclined to agree with Kant that, in terms of the pragmatic logic of human intelligibility, it is indeed true—we would have to make a holy lie of it.

Afro-American leadership, to the degree that they fight tooth and nail the conservative denial of the deleterious collective constraints on Afro-American individuals' capacity for self-determination, are on the right track. But to the degree that they encourage Afro-American individuals to adopt an ethic of determinism and victimhood, in which their very self-esteem requires a commitment to the belief that they have no control over their lives, they disastrously mislead those who need, above all else, to know and believe that only they can change their own lives.

FOR WHOM THE BELL CURVES

THE INTELLECTUAL AND CULTURAL
CONTRADICTIONS OF GENETIC DETERMINISM

The commercial success of *The Bell Curve* by Richard Herrnstein and Charles Murray a few years back reminds us of another form of "racial" discourse in America that has a long history dating from the nineteenth century: the genetic explanation of the problems of the poor generally, of Afro-American problems, and of the ordeal of integration that we all face.[1] Ironically, the insufficiency of social and economic explanations, combined with the political assault on all cultural explanations of the nation's "racial" dilemmas, has provided an intellectual opening that has been successfully exploited by the hereditarians.

It is not my aim to present another detailed critique of hereditarian ideology and scientism, since others have done so far more effectively than I could.[2] Instead, I will address here some of the more important intellectual, moral, and cultural issues raised by the hereditarian approach, ending with an exposure of one of the starkest contradictions in the ideology of liberal and Afro-American "racial" advocacy. I will lead into my analysis, however, with a brief review of some of the fundamental intellectual problems of hereditarian racialism.

THE INTELLECTUAL DILEMMAS OF THE HEREDITARIANS

Genetic determinism is, by its very nature, the most explicitly racialist of all attempts to explain differences between aggregates of human individuals. One basic problem that immediately confronts it is the fact that the social entities we call human groups differ in one fundamental respect from the other groups or aggregates of living creatures studied by biologists. Human groups are socially constructed, unlike other species that are classified solely by the scientific observer. These social constructions are sometimes arbitrarily imposed on aggregates. At other times they are developed by leaders of the collectivities themselves. More often, they emerge out of a complicated interactive process over long periods of time between the imposed and self-defined identities.

Being "black" in America means something quite different from being "black" in Brazil, Puerto Rico, Jamaica, Ethiopia, or India. If the hereditarian decides to stake everything simply on the basis of observed degrees of darkness of complexion, the problems multiply. In the first place, the range of colors covered by the social term "blackness" is almost as wide as the spectrum of colors in the human species, and certainly much wider than the spectrum of colors socially defined as "whiteness," with which it greatly overlaps. In Haiti and Brazil it means jet black as of unmixed West African ancestry; in the United States it embraces looking like the late Adam Clayton Powell, who was fairer than most Euro-Americans of Southern European ancestry. And second, it is now firmly established that there is no correlation between degree of darkness or amount of African ancestry and variation in whatever it is that IQ tests measure.

It is an odd biological science that begins with so amorphous an object of inquiry. It is, in fact, no science at all, but scientism, an ideology or form of advocacy that attempts to legitimize its claims with the tools and research strategies of science. As I have done with the other forms of advocacy examined in these essays, I will begin by taking seriously the claims made by its proponents, then proceed to examine their intellectual, sociological, and moral implications.

THE INTERPRETIVE PROBLEM

Beyond the amorphousness of their object of inquiry, a basic and insoluble problem emerges for the hereditarians. This is the fact that the best available data on variations in the attributes of socially defined aggregates of people are invariably open to more parsimonious and radically different interpretations than the one proposed by genetic determinists.[3] Herrnstein and Murray's measure of IQ, for example, was based on the Armed Forces Qualification Test. Using exactly the same data, which they analyzed with more rigorous statistical measurements and a far more sophisticated analytic framework, the economists Derek Neal and William Johnson were able to show that the test scores indeed explained nearly all of the wage gap between Afro-Americans and Euro-Americans. However, where Herrnstein and Murray attributed this relationship to inherent genetic differences, Neal and Johnson convincingly interpreted the test results as measuring a skill gap between Euro-Americans and Afro-Americans.[4]

There is no need to get overly technical here, because the basic point is clear: it is always possible and more parsimonious to interpret these measurements in socioeconomic terms using exactly the same statistical methods. The hereditarian response simply gets us into a fruitless chicken-and-egg quandary, with socioeconomic and background factors, hereditarians argue, themselves functions of a person's IQ. People have low status because their parents are genetically stupid and this stupidity is inherited by their children. Controlling for class, or parental background, then, disguises a good part of the effect of intelligence, which brings the whole procedure into question.

Quite apart from the fact that it is always better scholarship to explain a problem in terms of factors that are observable and measurable rather than something such as genetic intelligence that is inferred and amorphous, the hereditarian critique only holds if one is already persuaded by the genetic viewpoint. But the very same logic applies to someone persuaded by the environmental explanation, who can just as easily argue that, because a good part of IQ differences are class and culturally caused, controlling for IQ—whatever it may be—disguises a major part of the effects of class and culture.[5] There is no way out of this circle. The hereditarian debate is an endless chasing of tails. What's more, the very manner in which the relationship between environment and genes is treated has been devastatingly criticized, as I will discuss shortly. Before doing so I want to look at the fallacy behind one of the biggest scares in the hereditarian approach: the eugenic prediction of a general dumbing down of the population.

■

THE DEMOGRAPHIC FALLACY

One of the most alarming and seemingly most persuasive arguments of the genetic determinists goes all the way back to the beginnings of hereditarian advocacy around the turn of the last century, especially between 1890 and 1915.[6] *The Bell Curve* merely updated the old eugenic scare that the average intelligence of the nation is declining because less intelligent people breed more than do members of the cognitive elite. "Mounting evidence indicates that demographic trends are exerting downward pressures on the distribution of cognitive ability in the United States and that the pressures are strong enough to have social consequences," Herrnstein and Murray wrote. "If women with low scores are reproducing more rapidly than women with high scores, the distribution of scores will, other things being equal, decline, no matter whether the women with the low scores came by them through nature or nurture."[7] This dysgenic tendency, we are warned, is especially pronounced among Afro-Americans and Latinos as well as the post-1965 wave of predominantly non-European immigrants who differ from the earlier "classic American immigrant— brave, hard working, imaginative, self-starting, and often of high I.Q."

This intelligence-lowering fallacy is in many ways the most irresponsible and overtly dangerous part of hereditarian advocacy. It is irresponsible because it flies directly in the face of contrary empirical evidence, as well as against a powerful theoretical argument that I will briefly summarize below. And it is dangerous because eugenic hereditarians and "racial hygiene" advocates used exactly this argument during the twenties and thirties both in America—where they had a devastating effect on immigration laws—and in Germany, where they offered academic and ideological support to the eliminationist anti-Semitism of the Nazis.[8]

While it is true that the poor and people of lower IQ have higher fertility rates than the successful and those of higher IQ, it does not follow that we are facing a demographic apocalypse in which there is a general dumbing down of the nation due to the reckless breeding of underclass "welfare queens" and "white trash." This is precisely one of those seemingly commonsense conclusions that scholarship is able to correct, and the fact that hereditarians, including Herrnstein and Murray, choose to neglect the scholarly evidence in order to reinforce the misleading "commonsense" view, is yet another instance of their intellectual dishonesty.

The empirical evidence is overwhelming, and it comes from both the right and the left. In 1951 Psyche Cattell published findings in *Eugenics Review* that were quickly dubbed the "Cattell paradox," namely, that in spite of clear evidence of a negative relationship between fertility and IQ over several generations in Western countries, the average IQ in these countries had continued to increase.[9] Approaching the same issue from a somewhat different perspective, James Flynn has shown that there have been "massive gains" in mean national IQ over the four and a half decades between 1932 and 1978, and the so-called Flynn effect is now an accepted fact.[10]

In addition to the empirical evidence contradicting the eugenic scare, there is an elegant theoretical argument by the sociological demographers Samuel Preston and Cameron Campbell that completely demolishes all such eugenic predictions.[11] Preston and Campbell demonstrated that the so-called Cattell paradox is really not a paradox at all, once one understands that what is critical for national trends in IQ is how the differences in reproduction rates of smart and less-smart classes of persons relate to previously existing patterns. The basic error in the seemingly common-sense argument to which hereditarians irresponsibly appeal is the assumption that the subpopulations in question—the smart cognitive elite and the dumb masses—are closed off from each other. Only under this condition will the trait in the higher fertility population tend to become the norm for the entire population. As long as there is some intergenerational mobility between the classes the entire argument of a takeover of the trait from the higher reproduction group is vitiated. Negative fertility differentials are theoretically consistent with IQ distributions that are constant, falling, or rising.

Preston and Campbell's paper demonstrates that changes in the mean score of a trait such as IQ for a population from one generation to the next depends not on how the "current pattern of reproductive differentials" differs from "a uniform pattern of reproduction"—as most hereditarians think—but rather on how it differs from those in the past. The factors that permit the derivation of IQ distribution in one generation from its distribution in the previous one are complicated, but Preston and Campbell reduce them to three essentials: "assortative mating, differential fertility, and the process that relates the IQ of a child to that of his or her parents." Preston and Campbell proved mathematically that "there is no necessary association between fertility differentials by IQ and trends in the IQ distribution. Any persistent pattern of fertility differentials will eventually produce an equilibrium distribution of IQ in the population, that is, a distribution that is constant from generation to generation." The eugenic alarm that these fertility differentials will lead to a spreading of the low IQ trait of the population with higher fertility has no theoretical basis.

To be sure, if the low IQ group has a much higher fertility rate, the equilibrium distribution of the trait will settle at a point somewhat lower than would have been the case if the higher IQ group had the higher fertility. But Preston and Campbell's model shows that the difference resulting from these two demographic scenarios is surprisingly small, and it becomes even smaller when there is even a modest amount of intermarriage between the two groups, as there certainly is between subpopulations with different IQs in the United States. And most important, the intuitive position of the hereditarians is completely without foundation when it comes to making predictions about future trends.

The argument mathematically developed by Preston and Campbell is nicely illustrated in an accompanying "Comment" by the economist David Lam, who adds that the class of cases to which Preston and Campbell's model applies includes differential fertility between lower-income and upper-income groups: contrary to intuition, it does not follow that because the poor reproduce more than the prosperous that their trait—poverty— will gradually come to overwhelm the entire population.[12] The classist "welfare queen" scare is as empirically and theoretically groundless as the eugenic scare of the hereditarians.

THE INTERACTION PROBLEM

The most eminent population biologists have repeatedly cautioned that the entire hereditarian debate is couched in terms of an antithesis that may well be spurious: the nature versus nurture, or environment versus genes, dichotomy. Much energy is spent trying to decipher the relative causal determination of each. As Richard Levins and Richard Lewontin have argued, "There is no unique phenotype corresponding to a genotype; the phenotype depends on both genotype and environment."[13] Their often cited example is genetically identical seeds being planted in the desert and in a fertile environment and resulting in radically different plants.[14]

But the matter goes well beyond this. A further problem, Levins and Lewontin argue, is the failure of nearly all who approach this problem, including even those who take a liberal stand on the IQ issue, to distinguish between two kinds of causation: that in which separately working factors account for given effects, and that in which interacting sets, or streams, of causal factors account for a given outcome. "If an event results from the joint operation of a number of causative chains," they write, "and if these causes 'interact' in any generally accepted meaning of the word, it becomes conceptually impossible to assign quantitative values to the causes of that *individual* event."[15] IQ is a classic case in point. It is simply impossible to measure the relative determination of environmental and genetic factors in accounting for this phenotype.[16]

A related problem, although it is largely academic in nature, is disentangling the effects of natural and social selection. The two are not mutually exclusive and both kinds of selections may operate simultaneously. It is difficult sorting these influences out in the experimental study of lab animals and doubtful if we will ever be able to do so in the study of human populations. Significantly, the experimental studies on mice show that precisely with respect to traits involving a learning component, the genotype-environment interactions are most important.[17]

THE GENETIC IRONY OF HEREDITARIAN ADVOCACY

Finally, I want to draw attention to one fundamental issue in the genetics of heritability raised a few years ago by the Berkeley human biologist Jack R. Vale that has received almost no attention in the present debate.[18] All biologists agree that intelligence must have been strongly selected in the evolution of the human species. "Human evolution from its inception has been shaped by selection for behavioral characteristics, not the least of which is the capacity to comprehend, symbolize, and manipulate the psychological, social, and physical environment. We call this capacity intelligence."[19] The question then arises: does IQ have anything to do with this view of intelligence? I concur with Vale and a significant number of distinguished biologists, including Richard Lewontin, in the view that it has next to nothing to do with intelligence conceived of in this broader, more biologically meaningful way. There is no reason to believe that the capacity to do well at tests under test-taking situations has much to do with an individual's or group's ability to manipulate and succeed in its environment, or even to do well in practical applications of the skills that these tests measure.

Ironically, one of the best arguments against the entire hereditarian approach comes from the genetics of the selection process. Heritability is technically defined as the percentage of total phenotypic variance in a given trait that is explained by the genes in question *for a given population.*[20] Now, among all hereditarian psychologists, it is claimed that intelligence, as measured by IQ tests, is highly heritable: ranging between 40 and 80 percent. If we return to the concept of heritability in the light of one well-established principle of genetic selection, we are immediately faced with what Vale calls a "nice irony." The selection principle in question is that any trait which has been under strong selection for a long evolutionary period will demonstrate very little additive genetic variance, the only component of the three elements of total genetic variance that responds to evolutionary selection. It will have been "used up," so to speak. This being so, Vale says, the hereditarians are faced with an embarrassing dilemma:

> It is true of fitness characters that the proportion of additive genetic variance is small. It is therefore noteworthy that not only the total genetic component of variance (heritability in the broad sense or the degree of genetic determination) of IQ has been found to be so large, but that the proportion of additive variance within that component has been found to contribute the most to it.... The question is: If IQ is a fitness character, why should the additive variance be anywhere near .71.[21]

Or .60 or .40, or for that matter anywhere other than hovering close to a small fraction, which is where one expects to find the additive genetic variance of a trait that, as the hereditarian psychologists claim, and I fully agree, has been highly selected as an essential factor in the survival and fitness of the human species in its environment.

Hereditarians face the problem, then, that IQ scores are too heritable if they are to sustain the claim that these tests have any significance beyond the test-center and classroom. Whatever IQ tests are measuring, whatever g is, could have little to do with those vitally important behavioral qualities that meaningfully account for our survival in both broad evolutionary and narrower sociological terms.[22]

ONE FRIGHTENING IMPLICATION OF THE HEREDITARIAN DISCOURSE FOR AMERICA

I conclude this brief excursion into the demographic and genetic aspects of hereditarian advocacy with a conception of intelligence that is generally accepted among non-racist scholars. Intelligence is not an essence but a process, not some operationally inferred static entity indicated by IQ tests but that mode of thinking, symbolizing, acting and interacting which, in its totality, facilitates survival in, and/or mastery of, the environment by an individual or group. It is acknowledged that cognitive functioning is central to this behavioral configuration, along with other forms of intelligence,[23] and that genetic factors are important in its determination—that, indeed, intelligence was a major factor in our evolution as a

species. But there is absolutely no way in which we can meaningfully separate genetic and environmental effects, and given the impossibility of
conducting experiments on human populations, it is theoretically misguided, politically dangerous, and morally reprehensible to attempt to
separate the two as distinct processes.

Survival in and mastery of one's environment are not necessarily any
different in the degree of intelligence exhibited when conceived of in this
way, for survival or mastery must always be understood in terms of the chal-
lenges posed, or opportunities offered, by the environment. And the environment itself is not a static entity but partly chosen and made by the
population in question, or forced upon it by a dominant group, making
the concept of adaptation methodologically and epistemologically suspect, when it isn't a downright tautology, as Levins and Lewontin have
powerfully argued.[24]

The social intelligence demonstrated in the mastery of their environment by a George Washington, Charles Darwin, Jules-Henri Poincaré, or
Colin Powell—all of whom were average to poor students, with Poincaré
repeatedly scoring at the level of a moron in all the intelligence tests he
took—may be no higher, though more admired, than the social intelligence that is perhaps being exhibited, in gruesome evolutionary terms, by
the Afro-American underclass.

The point is frightening but has to be made since the discourse of the
hereditarians dictates it. If a population is under violent, relentless threat
from a dominant, predatory group with whom it shares its environment,
if the dominant group after centuries of enslavement, lynchings, and brutal oppression and public dishonoring continues to so manipulate the environment that the threatened group has been cornered like rats in blocked
sewers that we call ghettos, if the only option offered by the most powerful leaders of the dominant population is the scorched earth "contract"
of more and more incarceration in already overfilled jails aided by a
manifestly unfair drug-sentencing system, and more state-sanctioned exe-
cutions in already overcrowded death rows, then it is both brutally logical, in socioevolutionary terms, and fittingly intelligent, for the threatened group to arm itself to the teeth and behave as murderously, threat-
eningly, and aggressively as it can. The same principle accounts for the
survival of hyenas in habitats dominated by lions.

It is depressing to have to say it, but had the Jews of interwar Germany
possessed one-twentieth of the guns and exhibited one-tenth of the aggres-
siveness of the Afro-American underclass, millions of those six million

precious lives might have been saved, since the cost to the Germans of exterminating them simply would have been too high. So would be the cost in hereditarian American lives to get rid of the million Afro-Americans who constitute the despised Afro-American underclass.

In light of this horrifying logic, given the wholly negative and hostile attitude being expressed by the far right leaders of the dominant group, the resurgence of "white supremacist" and related militia organizations, and the more genteel academic advocacy of racism, one is led to wonder whether supporting gun control is a socially intelligent policy for underclass Afro-Americans, or for that matter, Afro-Americans in general. The Nazi Holocaust, a genocidal program supported by "scientific" hereditarian advocacy no different in principle from present arguments, is hardly a generation away. It is not only Jews who are under an obligation never to forget it. All hereditarian advocacy, whether the academic versions of writers such as Arthur Jensen, Richard Herrnstein, and Charles Murray, or the vulgar versions of the new "white supremacist" movements, points to one inevitable conclusion: that a eugenic policy is the best course of action for dealing with Afro-Americans and the growing "white trash" underclass.

When we talk or imply eugenics we are in the terrain of evolutionary competition and survival, for we are contemplating a cessation of the most basic evolutionary process—birth. However delicately expressed, however two-facedly denied, such talk amounts to a survival threat and, in turn, justifies a countercontemplation of what is most biologically logical and socially intelligent for a group that seeks to ensure its survival, especially one as historically used and abused as Afro-Americans.

I do not, let me hasten to add, condone this kind of talk. Indeed, as someone who is nearly always an incurable optimist, I find it depressing and dispiriting to have to follow the flow of this particular logic, and in what follows I will be pursuing an entirely different train of thought. But this, I feel obliged to make clear, is one path, the main path, down which the hereditarians lead us.

There are other discursive paths, and to these I now gladly turn.

BRINGING HISTORY AND CULTURE BACK IN

THE ANTI-ARISTOTELIAN LEGACY OF THE FOUNDERS

Let me begin this part with what strikes me, a historical sociologist, as one of the most puzzling aspects of the whole IQ controversy. Why is it that, in a land founded on the secular belief that "all are created equal," we are so obsessed with the need to find a scientific basis for human inequality? Now, the Founding Fathers, we have it on the authority of the hereditarians themselves, were very smart men, whatever backward extrapolations one may wish to draw about the revolutionary population as a whole from twentieth-century studies. When they inscribed for eternity in the Declaration of Independence that equality among persons was a self-evident truth, they clearly did not believe that there were no differences between persons. Most of them, certainly Jefferson, had at least a passing acquaintance with Aristotle and would have readily endorsed his view that both the equal treatment of unequals and the unequal treatment of equals are the height of injustice. The Founding Fathers, however, were aware of one cardinal ethical principle guiding social relations that we seem on the verge of abandoning, to our cost. I will return to it shortly.

Clearly, the members of our society differ in a vast number of ways— by gender, by age, by physical prowess, by beauty (more on this later), and most of all by intelligence, understood in the broad sense of capacity to compete and excel in one's society. Some of these differences, at any given time, we regard as very important, others less so, and still others we deliberately choose to disregard. On what basis do we make these decisions? My answer is that there is no known objective criterion for selecting which qualities are important or not. They are always based on value judgments—judgments that are subject to change over time, or even from one part of the country to another.

Now, when the Founding Fathers agreed to the dictum that all are created equal, they were not only encoding a major dictate for the new nation, but, with extraordinary perspicacity, they were implicitly drawing on, and condoning, a basic principle social life. Equality was being proposed as both an end and a means for determining how the new nation was to deal with the problems of difference and inequality. Their thinking may have gone something like the following: *We know that there are numerous differences and inequalities among people, and we live by them ourselves; for heaven's sake, we are nearly all major slaveholders! However, we are declaring as an end for the nation the idea that, whatever observable differences there may be between people, it will be accepted that in some profound respects they are to be treated as equal, especially in the legal and political areas of life. More generally, there is an essential core of humanity that, when all differences are shed, we all share, and in this essential core we are all to be considered equal. What*

*this core is, of course, has to be left vague. It is one of those things every-
one knows, but no one can define, for as Mr. Locke taught us, it is written on the hearts of men. An essential human core implies, in a fundamental way, that enslavement is wrong, even if there is not much we can
do about it for the nation as a whole at the moment.* (Actually, Washington,
the socially smarter, fitter, and morally stronger man, freed his slaves, at
great cost to his heirs; Jefferson, the morally weaker man with the greater
classroom intelligence and fluency—boy, and could he write a great line!
—did not.)

But equally important is the social principle of action implied by this
extraordinary decision to encode equality. This is the implicit recognition
that there are no objective grounds for selecting the ideals we consider
important and that therefore we must arbitrarily choose as best we can
based on our moral principles, and the way to do it is simply to declare
that in this, or that, respect people are to be treated as equal. This same
principle of action can be stated another—what may be called a deliberately anti-Aristotelian—way: namely, equal treatment for equals and
unequals in certain specified regards. Or to put it in still simpler terms:
whatever distinctions we may observe regarding the trait of interest, we
will treat as socially meaningless. So, for example, there is great observable inequality in body type and strength, but unequal will be treated
equally in this regard; there are great differences between Southerners
and Northerners, but the differences will be ignored; there are tremendous differences between Congregationalists, Baptists, and Catholics,
and we may be convinced that our faith is superior to theirs, but we will
behave as if all faiths are equal in our relations with each other. What
about the differences between men and women? In 1787 and for more
than two centuries thereafter it was agreed by nearly all men—unjustly,
we now agree— that the Aristotelian principle would prevail; they were
to be treated differently, and it was an injustice not to do so!

And that between Afro-Americans and Euro-Americans? Here, again,
there was little disagreement (apart from the distinction between slaves
and free, which confounded the issue with overlap but which nonetheless
was made to a surprising degree, many racists being ardent abolitionists):
it was an injustice to treat unequal "races" equally. Even so, the second
important aspect of the egalitarian injunction still held in 1787, as it
holds today: it was and is a matter of choice which observable distinctions we choose to make meaningful or choose to neglect. In spite of their
abominable "compact of death" with slavery, the Founding Fathers, to

their credit, left us with a method of dealing with "racial" and other differences when the time was ripe or forced upon us.

THE PRINCIPLE OF INFRANGIBILITY

I will briefly discuss three cases of differences that nicely demonstrate the workings of the anti-Aristotelian principle in American life: regional variation in intelligence; age variation in intellectual functioning; and somatic variation in the quality we call beauty.

It has long been established that significant differences exist in measured average IQ, as well as in performance assessed in terms of, say, contribution to the national income or to the nation's cultural life, among different regions of the country.[25] Euro-Americans in Tennessee and rural Georgia score significantly lower than Euro-Americans in the Northeast, and, on average, live in far worse conditions than their northern counterparts. No one, however, has ever chosen to call the nation's attention to these differences, except in a sympathetic and appropriately sensitive manner. We do not neglect them, but neither do we make a national issue of them, in the process wantonly insulting and dishonoring these people. No one dares to raise the issue of whether or not these two states in the South are an intellectual drag on the nation; no one bemoans the fact that were they not a part of the nation our ranking in the international IQ parade would be much higher. And if anyone—a Charles Murray in search of another hot topic for his next best-selling book—dared to do so, not only is it unlikely that he would find a commercial publisher, it is even less likely that he would find anyone willing to spend over thirty dollars on such a book. Why so? Because Euro-Americans in Tennessee and rural Georgia are seen as belonging to the social and moral community that constitutes the American people. Whatever we are incorporates them. If they are different from Northeasterners in one or more respects, the reasoning goes, that is just a fact of our national life, a part of the diverse fabric we take pride in.

This phenomenon explains why no one, certainly not any segment of the press, has taken seriously the discussion of genetic differences among Euro-Americans in *The Bell Curve*, or the seemingly inflammatory remarks by Murray on the "white trash" problem. I say "seemingly" because an undercurrent of disingenuousness runs through all of Murray's references to this "problem." It is precisely because the authors and their publishers knew that a book on the Euro-American IQ problem would interest no one but academic psychologists that the sections on Afro-Americans were given such prominence on the pretense of concern about the "controversy" the sections would generate—a controversy that authors and publishers were all praying for and positively salivating over as the race-conscious American press obliged. The implicit and unquestioning acceptance of low-IQ Euro-Americans, call them what you might, makes for little controversy and an uninterested press.

The same goes for the elderly. Until very recently, there was a consensus among psychologists that intellectual functioning declined with age, especially after middle age.[26] In this regard, three important changes over recent decades are worth noting. One is the growing size of the population over sixty-five years of age in America. According to recent estimates, by 2025 one in five of all Americans will be over sixty-five.[27] Second, with the growing demographic strength of senior citizens has come their increased political and economic power, the two closely related; it is now established that an extraordinary shift of resources has taken place from the population under twenty-five to that over sixty-five, a shift that continues relentlessly and is untouchable politically even though it threatens to bankrupt the country within the next quarter of a century.[28] The third major development has been the growing tendency of those over sixty-five to remain in the workplace, reflected most dramatically in the abolition of compulsory ages of retirement.[29] Hence we now face the prospect that one of the fastest growing and most powerful segments of the population—including the working population—is, according to the IQ specialists, an intellectually impaired group with rapidly declining cognitive competence.[30] This surely ought to provoke great alarm among those who make it their business to guard the intellectual integrity of the nation. After all, one in five is substantially larger than 13 percent, which is the menace posed by intellectually inferior Afro-Americans; and the elderly are growing a lot faster, from all demographic projections. And yet, we have heard almost nothing on this subject from any of those accustomed to warning the nation about impending psychological and related social disasters. Nor has anyone else chosen to make a crusade of the issue, certainly not in the United States.[31] No one has made a fortune frightening the nation with apocalyptic forecasts about the impending takeover by an intellectually spent gerontocracy.

Why not? For the same reason that we do not engage in public hand-wringing about the intellectual inferiority of rural Euro-American Georgians or Tennesseeans. The elderly are an integral part of our community; whatever we are as a people, the reasoning goes—and quite rightly, I might add—they help to define. If an important and essential part of what we are is in intellectual decline, then so are we, and so be it. The elderly are constitutive, and expressions of alarm in public debate about what to do with them are egregious and out of bounds, the occasional negative images of aging notwithstanding.[32]

A principle is at work here, one which takes to its sociological conclusion the anti-Aristotelian doctrine of the Founding Fathers. We may call it the principle of infrangibility. It refers to our commitment to a unity that cannot be broken or separated into parts, a commitment to the elements of a moral order and social fabric that is inviolable and cannot be infringed. I am proposing that Afro-Americans too are an infrangible part of the nation, and this morally vitiates all discussion about them that assumes or implies that they are a group apart, a drag on the national norm, however conceived.

We also find the infrangibility principle at play in our attitude toward beauty, that "outward gift which is seldom despised, except by those to whom it has been refused," as Gibbon once unkindly put it. We live in what some consider to be a culture obsessed with physical beauty among both men and women.[33] The observable differences are strikingly and, to many, painfully obvious. A few among us are beautiful or handsome; the majority range from attractive to homely to what is considered ugly. What is more, these differences strongly correlate with important indexes of psychological and socioeconomic well-being and success, and there is an unusual level of consistency in the assessment of attractiveness both over the life cycle and over the past half century. All available studies concur that more-attractive people have much greater self-esteem than others, a pattern reinforced from early childhood. They are perceived as smarter, kinder, healthier, saner, and morally better.[34] Less attractive people suffer just the opposite set of expectations; indeed, it is well documented that less attractive people are far more likely to be perceived as mentally unstable and neurologically impaired, even by health professionals.[35] The more attractive also achieve far more in socioeconomic terms, controlling for other factors, and are generally more upwardly mobile than others. Several carefully controlled studies have demonstrated that being perceived as more beautiful correlates highly with getting the jobs one seeks, and the job performance of the more attractive tends to be more positively evaluated than that of less attractive persons.[36] It also has been shown that taller, more handsome presidential candidates nearly always triumph over their shorter competitors.[37] As the short and less handsome Mike Dukakis learned to his cost, a high IQ, demonstrated managerial competence, and exceptional verbal fluency is no match against a candidate who is tall, handsome, and "classy" looking, however he may mangle the English language every time he speaks. Indeed, it may well be that the beauty quotient correlates more highly with success than IQ does, but let us not complicate the issue further. Gordon Patzer, in *The Physical Attractiveness Phenomenon,* correctly notes that aspects of physical attractiveness rank behind only gender and "race" as easily observable traits on which distinctions are made, and he only barely exaggerates when he claims that in many respects distinctions of physical attraction exceed "race" and gender differences as sources of discrimination.[38]

My point is that here we have a clearly observable pattern of genetically determined differences among people, correlating highly with social, economic, and psychological achievement, but that we deliberately choose to neglect as an issue for controversy. We nearly all admire and value the quality that beautiful people have; but at the same time, no one, to the best of my knowledge, has ever called for an aristocracy of the beautiful or for the denigration of the nonbeautiful. To the contrary, we have a well-developed countervalue that condemns any overt expression of favoritism to the beautiful.

Our tolerance for somatic differences is actually highly revealing of many of the more nuanced and complex aspects of our commitment to the anti-Aristotelian egalitarianism inscribed in the Declaration of Independence. And it is especially relevant to that other form of somatic differences among us on which so much heat is generated, the form we call "race," so bringing them into relief should be useful. The beauty bias of our society ought to be a matter of great concern to psychologists and others concerned with the issue of meritocracy. For, on the one hand, not only is there no known relation between beauty and intelligence—however conceived—but beauty is meritocratically dangerous precisely because it is a trait under strong selection in our society. It was undoubtedly for this reason that Darwin took a keen interest in the subject and called for detailed study of it by social scientists; but not even the great Darwin could get much of a research response, least of all from the hereditarian psychologists who otherwise make so many claims in his name.[39] For all the talk about assortative mating, little account is usually taken of the fact that a disproportionate number of beautiful lower-class women rise up the class ladder each generation by marrying smart, successful men. As Kin Hubbard once observed, "Beauty is only skin deep, but it's a valuable asset if you're poor or haven't any sense."[40]

If the lower class from which these women come is at the bottom of the ladder because its members are stupid—as the hereditarians claim—then untold millions of inferior genes are swarming their way up into the talented classes, dumbing them down. If I am correct, there is no danger in America of our class system hardening into a genetically determined hierarchy.

Sir Cyril Burt, the British hereditarian psychologist, once observed that genetic factors were a far better source of mobility in society than environmental ones. Environmental factors easily harden into class prejudice. However, because of the principle of regression to the mean, there will inevitably be a descent of the intellectually inferior members of the ruling class to the bottom and a rise of the smart lower-class members to the top. He may well have been right—but only for his native Britain, where class prejudices are rigid, people tend to marry assortatively within narrow circles, and upwardly mobile members of the lower classes desperately seek spouses, whatever their looks, from the higher classes.

The situation is very different in America. There is, to be sure, evidence of a fair level of assortative mating within classes here, but because of the higher volume of mobility, and wider range and fluidity of our classes, there will be tremendous genetic variance even within classes, and if the majority or even a substantial minority of successful men are choosing their mates on the basis mainly of their looks, the entire trend toward a genetically selected elite will be confounded, if not aborted. And a good thing too. The enormously successful movie *Pretty Woman* should send chills down the spine of every hereditarian. More seriously, as the sociologist Alan Wolfe makes clear, there is not a scrap of sociological evidence to suggest that America has experienced a cognitive revolution with a genetically hardening meritocracy.[41]

My point, however, is that Americans generally accept this somatic difference in their population, including all the patently unfair biases in favor of the beautiful, as well as its genetic randomization, with equanimity. No one finds these differences and their social consequences disturbing. And no one has ever chosen to make much of an issue of them. Interestingly, one of the most important findings of researchers in this area is the deep reluctance of Americans to acknowledge the role of physical attractiveness in their lives. So entrenched is this denial that social scientists attempting to study the phenomenon often encounter serious noncooperation, including a reluctance of fellow scholars, and funding organizations, to take the problem seriously. Gordon Patzer found that this deliberate "morphology neglect," as one researcher termed it, is invariably attributable "to one of America's most honorable... philosophies: *that philosophy being a hesitancy to suggest any form of genetic determinism in the relationship between physical appearance factors and personal characteristics. The sentiment for an egalitarian society has stifled research that may suggest an undemocratic situation in which those persons who possess higher physical attractiveness are, somehow, better than those persons lower in physical attractiveness* (emphasis added).[42]

"Beauty is not caused," Emily Dickinson once wrote, "it is." As are the differences among age groups and regions; whatever their consequences, they simply are.

Why, we may now ask, does not the same apply to the difference we observe in those somatic traits which together we call "race"?

WHOSE DILEMMA?

The simplest answer—perhaps too simple—is the persistence of racism, both personal and institutional. There can be no doubt that in many respects personal, or what has been called direct, "dominative" racism has declined substantially in this country. This has been one of the major achievements of the past three or four decades, and the nation can take much pride in this development, especially those Afro-Americans, and Euro-Americans, who struggled and gave their lives for it. Euro-Americans in general, too, can take credit for the changes in their "racial" attitudes, however reluctant they may be to actualize them, that are reflected in any number of surveys and in-depth studies. The main achievement of the civil rights movement was forcing the nation to apply the Founding Fathers' non-Aristotelian method of dealing with differences to the Afro-American population. Afro-Americans, in a real sense, are now generally accepted as a constitutive part of the moral order that embraces this great polity, even though they still remain too socially apart.

As we noted in the first essay, one of the tragic consequences of the unusual oppression of Afro-Americans—as is true of all other groups subjected to sustained exploitation—is that elements of the oppressed group develop illicit and harmful patterns of behavior as a way of coping, victimizing in-group members far more than those of the out-group; in other words, the group becomes its own agent of subjection.[43] As long as the group members were perceived as outsiders, such pathologies were of little concern to the dominant group: the best nigger, like the best Indian, was a dead nigger, however terminated.

Fellow Afro-Americans still are overwhelmingly the victims of law-less members of the population, but with the important difference that the dominant group now seems to care—whatever their politics, and however varied their proposed solutions—about this self-inflicted car-nage. It may be a case of spectacular naïveté on my part, but , in my view, this caring is an index of progress in the sense—and only in this sense—that it signals the moral incorporation of Afro-American people. The infrangibility principle has, at last, begun to be extended to the group. Tragically, one paradoxical consequence of this extension has been the increased incarceration of young Afro-American men, especially as a result of disparities in sentencing for drug-related crimes that, incidentally, Afro-American communities initially called for.

Mention of the pathologies of the Afro-American underclass brings me to my final reflection. When all is said and done, the dreadful statistics on the Afro-American lower class still need to be explained. Something is wrong, horribly wrong, in the condition of the bottom 3 percent of Afro-American people in the urban heart of this greatest of all experiments in pluralistic polities since the collapse of Rome. At the fragile core of its great cities, embracing the most advanced thought, the richest cultural life, the most sublime modern architectural structures on the face of the earth, a people rot in moral and social squalor, nod under the killing pal-liative of drugs, rape, rob and murder one another, and die the early, indiscriminate deaths of a late medieval city under plague. Beyond the underclass, we must explain the chronic failures of the bottom quarter of the Afro-American population.

All this takes me back to the first section of this essay, in which I briefly discussed the chicken-or-egg interpretive problem of the IQ debate. There can be no doubt that the answer lies somewhere in that inhuman record of oppression, the tragic net effect of which has been that a pat-tern of behavior emerged in which the problems of the underclass are now largely self-inflicted. Something is wrong with the value preferences, behav-ioral adaptations and socialization practices of the Afro-American lower class; we know what their historical causes were, but to spend more time arguing over who to blame is to play one's fiddle while the city burns.

This in essence is the meaning of the work of social scientists such as Derek Neal and William Johnson, Richard Nisbett, Howard Gardner, and many others who have taken a firm stand against the hereditarians, expressed here perhaps in less guarded language than they would prefer. Thus, Neal and Johnson, whose work was earlier touched on, convincingly demonstrate that "the black-white gap in mean scores is roughly equivalent to the skill building effect of just over four years of secondary schooling" and that this skill gap, in turn, explains the entire wage gap between Euro-American and Afro-American youth. While this knocks the wind from the sails of the hereditarians, it immediately poses a problem for Afro-American "racial" advocates and their liberal supporters. How are we to explain the failure of Afro-American youths to reduce this skill gap? Or, in Neal and Johnson's words, what are "the obstacles black children face in acquiring productive skill"?

Even after controlling for family socioeconomic characteristics and school environment, a substantial gap remains between the scores of Afro-Americans and Euro-Americans and, as such, the skills of the two groups. If the answer is not in the genes, then there is only one other place left to look: the subcultures and modes of socialization of children into their communities. As Gardner has written, "Cultural beliefs and practices affect the child at least from the moment of birth and perhaps sooner. Even the parents' expectations of their unborn child and their reactions to the discovery of the child's sex have an impact. The family, teachers, and other sources of influence in the culture signal what is important to the growing child, and these messages have both short- and long-term impact."[44]

Nisbett also points to fascinating evidence that suggests that the mother's role in the socialization of the child has a direct impact on his or her IQ score. Interestingly, it has been found that "children of black-white unions have IQs nine points higher if it is the mother who is white." This holds even after the mother's IQ is taken into account, strongly suggesting that "the higher IQs of the children born to white mothers would have to be attributed largely to socialization."[45]

Now there is a fascinating paradox in the two statements I have just quoted from Gardner and Nisbett. Both were made in the context of attacking the hereditarian position, and in that context are no doubt warmly approved by Afro-American intellectuals and other liberal "racial" advocates. However, had they been made in the context of a discussion of the educational problems of Afro-American youth, both men would almost certainly have been angrily corrected and dismissed as hopeless racists.

We come face to face with an awful contradiction. While Afro-American intellectual leaders, and all those who take a sympathetic interest in the plight of Afro-Americans, are quick to point to cultural factors in the defense of Afro-Americans against the onslaught of hereditarians, as well as nonracist conservatives, these very same leaders are equally quick to traduce, in other contexts, anyone who dares to point to the subcultural problems of the group in trying to explain their condition. It is now wholly incorrect politically even to utter the word *culture* as an explanation in any context other than counterattacks against hereditarians.[46] Indeed, so far has this politically correct position gone that it is not uncommon for people who even tentatively point to social and cultural problems to be labeled and condemned as racists. Consider the intellectual fate of Senator Moynihan.

We cannot have it both ways. If culture is the major intellectual weapon against the hereditarian racists, culture must contain the answers as we seek to explain the skill gap, the competence gap, and the wage gap, as well as the pathological social sink into which nearly a million Afro-Americans have fallen.

For all its imperfections, affirmative action has made a major difference in the lives of women and minorities, in the process helping to realize, as no other policy has done, the nation's constitutional commitment to the ideals of equality, fairness, and economic integration. In utilitarian terms it is hard to find a program that has brought so much gain to so many at so little cost. It has been the single most important factor accounting for the rise of a significant Afro-American middle class.

In the light of all this, it is hard to understand why affirmative action has become one of the most contentious political issues in the nation. One would think that a policy that was a major issue in at least two presidential elections, the focus of a bitterly fought California proposition, and the subject of repeated legal battles that ended up on several occasions in the Supreme Court must have adversely affected the lives of at least a substantial proportion of those opposing it. The facts show just the opposite.

In actuality, not one but two controversies surround affirmative action. One is a campaign largely contrived by politicians, pundits, and conservative intellectuals who have magnified the experiences and anger of a tiny but influential number of upper-middle-class professionals into a national economic threat. In the process they have divisively racialized a situation that, on closer inspection, reveals American people to be uncommonly fairminded and ethnically progressive when they are not being "racially" manipulated.

The other controversy, which parallels this campaign of distortion, refers to genuine issues of fairness, equality, and collective remediation in a heterogeneous society traditionally committed to a highly individualistic ethic. Hypocrites from the first camp often try to wrap themselves in the dignified mantle of the second, but it is usually easy to detect the camouflage.

THE CONCOCTED CONTROVERSY

There are, fortunately, excellent data on the actual effects of affirmative action on the lives of Americans as well as data on their views of the policy. These data, drawn from national samples surveyed by the National Opinion Research Center (NORC) of the University of Chicago in 1990 and 1994, and from a Harris poll conducted in 1995, tell us a very different story from the narratives of the media pundits and politicians.

In 1990 respondents were asked: "What do you think the chances are these days that a white person won't get a job or promotion while an equally or less qualified Afro-American person gets one instead? Is this very likely, somewhat likely, or not very likely to happen these days?" This question was followed with probes about the reasons the respondents held the views they did: "something that happened to you personally," "something that happened to a relative, family member or close friend," something the respondent "saw occurring at work," or "heard about on the media," and so on. I have analyzed the responses, and what I've found is remarkable.

First, it turns out that while over 70 percent of Euro-Americans asserted that other Euro-Americans were likely being hurt by affirmative action for Afro-Americans, only 7 percent claimed to have actually experienced any form of reverse discrimination and only 16 percent knew of someone close who had. Fewer than one in four could even claim that it was something they had witnessed or heard about at their workplace.[1]

So what was the source feeding all the outrage? This is what the NORC survey data indicated:

> ▢ The ethnic composition of the places where Euro-Americans work in no way accounts for their fears about affirmative action. Sixty-nine percent of Euro-Americans who work in exclusively Euro-American workplaces believed, *in the abstract,* that affirmative action harmed Euro-Americans, virtually the same as the 67 percent who work where the employees are predominantly Afro-American.

◻ The presence or absence of an affirmative action program where Euro-Americans work also, surprisingly, bears no relationship to how Euro-Americans think, in the abstract, about affirmative action's effects on Euro-Americans in general.

◻ The single most important source of information about affirmative action is the media, 42 percent of Euro-Americans mentioning it as their main source. Apart from the media, Euro-Americans said that they heard about it mainly from "another source." This would no doubt include political leaders exploiting the issue as well as casual discussions with friends and influential persons.

◻ There was no difference between Euro-American men and women on the issue of affirmative action, as a general policy, insofar as it relates to Afro-Americans. Almost exactly the same proportions of women and men think that it is harming Euro-Americans in general; and virtually the same small proportion of Euro-American women (6 percent) as Euro-American men (8 percent) claimed to have been affected by affirmative action in any way, in spite of their fears about it.

Before looking at more recent polls, two preliminary conclusions can be drawn from these unexpected findings: one is that Euro-American fears about affirmative action are a largely invented problem, based in almost all cases not on actual experience but on hearsay, on the by no means disinterested preoccupation of the media with the subject, on the exploitation of the issue by unscrupulous politicians, and on the unrelenting attack on it by conservative intellectuals and pundits. I suspect that the media has taken a more than normal interest in the issue because of fears felt by journalists themselves about the prospect of diversifying the newsroom.

The second tentative conclusion we may draw about Euro-American attitudes based on these 1990 responses is that as far as affirmative action is concerned, the much discussed "angry white male syndrome" is a complete myth. Euro-American women expressed the same level of fear as Euro-American men about affirmative action for Afro-Americans, in the abstract, and their fears were equally without any foundation in personal experience. What is extraordinary about this is the fact that Euro-American women constitute the largest group of Americans to have benefited from affirmative action programs.

The surprises are almost as great, however, when we turn to the responses of Afro-Americans to the 1994 NORC survey. Because of the overwhelming tendency to interpret all polls in polarized "racial" terms, and to see all 33 million Afro-Americans as a single group with a single set of interests, the differences within the Afro-American population regarding affirmative action have gone largely unnoticed.

The first point to note about the Afro-American response is that the support for affirmative action is nothing near as high as one would have expected. True, as figure 1 shows, a majority of Afro-Americans (57 percent) support such programs, in contrast with the very small fraction of Euro-Americans who do (11 percent). And this is the difference that our highly racialized media and policy analysts have fastened on: Afro-Americans, we hear endlessly, are five times more likely to support affirmative action in hiring than Euro-Americans.

However, a nonracialized approach to these figures allows us to be as impressed by the fact that only a slight majority of Afro-Americans support these programs. This may seem surprising, but on further reflection there is no real reason why these figures should not be as they are. The relentless attack on affirmative action by the media and politicians from center to right has clearly left its mark on Afro-Americans. It is interesting to note that, in spite of the fact that affirmative action has largely benefited middle-class Afro-Americans, the survey data do not indicate any statistically significant differences in support for affirmative action among the various classes of Afro-Americans. If anything, I found a slightly stronger level of support among the poorest Afro-Americans. Since this could not have been based on their own personal experience, I surmise that the poor continue to support affirmative action in substantially greater numbers simply because they are more insulated from the neoconservative and middle-class criticisms of the policy.

Another unexpected finding awaits us when we look at gender differences within the Afro-American population. As figure 1 shows, Afro-American men are actually split right down the middle on the question of preferential hiring: exactly one-half are opposed to it. On the other hand, of all Americans the strongest support for preferences in hiring comes from Afro-American women, over half saying they "strongly support" it, in contrast with a little under a third of Afro-American men and only 5 percent of Euro-American women. It should be added that the differences between Afro-American men and Afro-American women suggested by the graph are statistically significant.[2]

Earlier, I noted that there is no "angry white male syndrome" reflected in these results. Ironically, while it would be going much too far to speak about an Afro-American male syndrome, what we find here is a significant gender gap between Afro-American men and Afro-American women that has no counterpart in the Euro-American population (see figure 1) as far as this issue is concerned. The strong support for preferential

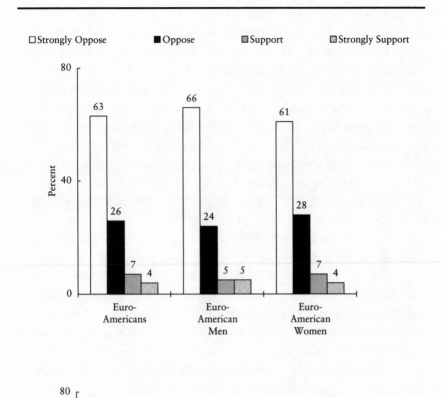

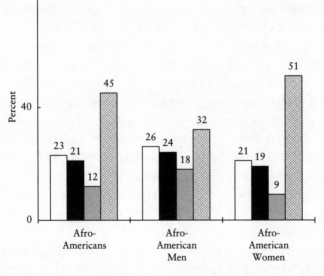

Figure 1. Percent of Different Groups that Support Affirmative Action in Hiring for Afro-Americans.
Source: Author's composition from the General Social Survey data base, 1994 (National Opinion Research Center, University of Chicago).

hiring by Afro-American women is, of course, consistent with the experience of middle-class Afro-American women that we noted in the first essay. Recall from the first essay that college-educated Afro-American women constitute the first group of Afro-Americans in the history of the United States to earn more than their Euro-American counterparts of comparable education. The intelligence, perseverance, character, and sacrifices of Afro-American women explain most of this success; let us be clear on that. But it simply cannot be denied that Afro-American middle-class women have seized the opportunities presented by affirmative action to a substantially greater degree than Afro-American men.

Does the general hostility to affirmative action *in the abstract* and the misbelief that it is harming Euro-Americans *in general* translate into Euro-Americans' negative attitudes toward affirmative action at their own workplaces? Here we come upon the biggest surprise of all, and a pleasant one at that. In light of all the hostile conservative and neoconservative rhetoric on the subject and its political saliency, it is astonishing to learn that the vast majority of Euro-Americans are actually quite content with the affirmative action programs *with which they are acquainted at their own workplaces.* This is the remarkable finding that came out of a Harris poll on the subject in June 1995, a year after the last of the NORC surveys. Figures 2 and 3 summarize the Harris findings.

First, the Harris poll offers impressive replication of the 1990 and 1994 NORC surveys: the same minuscule 7 percent of workers think that their employers have done too much, and one strongly suspects that this is the group that had earlier reported being personally hurt by affirmative action. As Humphrey Taylor, CEO of the Harris Poll, wrote: "There is a world of difference between people's *general attitudes* to such programs and their *actual* experiences with their own employers' policies" (emphasis added).[3] As figures 2 and 3 show, the vast majority of Euro-American workers say that their employers are doing just about the right amount or not enough for women (80 percent) and for minorities (79 percent).

Second, Taylor came independently to the same conclusion that I had from my analysis of the NORC data. "This Harris survey," he writes, "shows that the media has greatly overplayed the myth of the white male backlash, and failed to report that the overwhelming majority of workers feel they have been treated fairly in the workplace. *This is yet another case of a small, vocal minority being perceived as a majority*" (emphasis added).[4] Taylor was too restrained. It is much more than that. It is another case of how shamefully misinformed our commentators are about this important

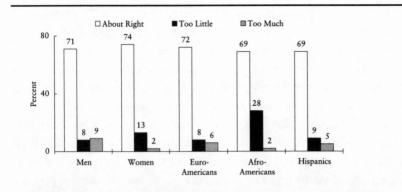

Figure 2. What American Employees Really Think About Affirmative Action for Women at Their Workplace. *Note:* Respondents were asked: "Do you feel that your employer has been doing too much, too little, or about the right amount to hire and promote women employees?" Percentages do not add up to 100 because respondents who were self-employed or who answered "not sure" were left out. *Source:* Author's composition from the Harris Poll on Affirmative Action, Poll No. 44, 1995, Table 1.

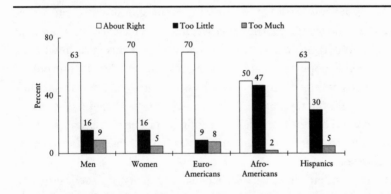

Figure 3. What American Employees Really Think About Affirmative Action for Minorities at Their Workplace. *Note:* Respondents were asked: "Do you feel that your employer has been doing too much, too little, or about the right amount to hire and promote Black, Hispanic, and Asian employees?" Percentages do not add up to 100 because respondents who were self-employed or who answered "not sure" were left out. *Source:* Author's composition from the Harris Poll on Affirmative Action, Poll No. 44, 1995, Table 2.

policy (including some who write long treatises on the subject), of how the basically decent and ethnically fairminded ordinary Euro-American workers have been misinterpreted and misled, and of how irresponsible and "racially" sensationalist and divisive all the nation's media have been on this issue—including the liberal media, which equally sensationalizes and racializes while pretending to be concerned.

Of course, these data would hardly matter were affirmative action something inherently evil. But this could scarcely be the case, since for more than twenty-five years American leaders of both parties and all ethnic groups, from Lyndon Johnson to Richard Nixon to 1996 presidential candidates Bob Dole and Governor Pete Wilson, supported this policy. Indeed, they lauded it as both morally defensible and one of the most effective means of remedying the intolerable exclusion of disadvantaged minorities and women from opportunities to train for, and be employed in, the better paying working- and middle-class jobs.[5]

What happened? How did so manifestly worthy and effective a policy so massively lose the political support of the nation, which has not been hurt by it, including even the backing of some of those who stood most to gain from it? As I suggested earlier, the media has played a significant role in all this, but it can account for only a part of the demonization of the policy. And the cynicism of our leaders, especially the transparent opportunism of former supporters such as Dole and Wilson, while a major contributing factor, does not sufficiently explain why so beneficial a policy could become an object of such political and intellectual condemnation. There are unquestionably several genuine moral and social issues fueling the controversy over affirmative action, which will be examined in the second part of this essay. In the remainder of this part, however, I look at several popular but baseless sources of hostility to the policy, which, when combined with the assaults of the press and politicians, sufficiently explain the mystery of why a policy that has benefited so many, hurt so few, and has the overwhelming support of Euro-American workers who actually experience it, could nonetheless emerge as a major national *political* issue.

The first is that the largely erroneous arguments of neoconservative and other right-wing critics somehow carried the day. Merit, we were repeatedly warned, was being undermined, resulting in both individual inequities and, worse, severe threats to the efficiency of our national economy and its preparedness for the demands of a high-tech society. Nonsense, both. Only a minuscule number of Euro-Americans, we now know, are affected unfavorably by affirmative action, and of this small fraction, a still smaller percentage is able to claim genuine grievances. The claim that the nation's efficiency is being threatened is simply laughable. The American economy is currently experiencing one of its most robust and productive periods since the great postwar boom, generating jobs paying above median-level income at a phenomenal rate; indeed, its performance now exceeds that of all the other G-7 countries.[6]

At the same time, there is no evidence of any shortage of the scientists, engineers, other highly educated persons, and trained technicians to meet the demands of the growing postindustrial service and high-tech sectors. We may well be on the verge of an oversupply of scientists and mathematicians—with one major institution of higher learning, the University of Rochester, recently closing its graduate math program. And the gatekeepers of the medical profession have already raised the alarm that the nation faces a crisis of oversupply of highly specialized doctors. Euro-American men still control over 99.9 percent of all the important top positions in private and public institutions in the nation, as well as the vast majority of middle-level and high-paying jobs, and will continue to do so until well into the next millennium.

The argument that affirmative action has done almost nothing for the underclass and poor but favors middle-class workers, while correct, deliberately misleads. Rhetorically it is extremely effective. This argument figured prominently in the recent propaganda of Governor Wilson and University of California regent Ward Connerly against the university's affirmative action policies and later in the successful campaign on behalf of Proposition 209, which outlawed the policy in California. However, affirmative action was never intended to help the poorest and least able members of the minority classes and women. It is, by its very nature, a top-down strategy, meant to level the field for those middle- and working-class persons who are capable of taking advantage of opportunities denied them because of their gender or ethnic status. For the underclass and working but chronically poor, an entirely different set of bottom-up strategies are called for, some of which I will mention in the concluding essay.

The common neoconservative refrain that affirmative action brings into question the competence and dignity of truly qualified women and members of minorities is such a blatant prevarication that it often leaves many minority persons speechless. Where were these conservatives when the most basic dignities of Afro-Americans were, for centuries, being ground in the dust by legalized segregation, racist persecution, and exclusion from all but the lowliest levels of the nation's economy? Why are these neoconservatives wasting their anguish on the problems of upper-middle-class Afro-Americans, who if they know one thing in life it is how to protect their dignity, when all around them millions of fellow Americans daily suffer the chronic indignities of homelessness and impoverishment in a land of affluence? If the occasional sneer of racists and sexists, not to mention the not infrequent tut-tuts of anguished neoconservative colleagues, is the price to be paid by the truly qualified for the extension of the opportunities and access they have enjoyed to others waiting on the bench, it is a burden most of them are only too happy to bear. Besides, uninvited anguish over another's honor is itself an insidious dishonor.

The University of California's experience of affirmative action demonstrates beyond a doubt the shallowness of the conservative criticisms. While achieving its goal of incorporating students from disadvantaged minorities over the period 1984 to 1996, the university, far from experiencing a decline in standards, not only fulfilled its mandate of selecting students from the top eighth of the state's graduating class but increased its eligibility requirements five times during this period. It is now a far more selective institution than before the introduction of affirmative action, with improved graduation rates for both Afro-American and other students.[7]

Nothing could be more hypocritical and self-contradictory than the spectacle of a Republican governor and his board of regents mandating their state's university system to rely solely on the crude instrument of test scores to select incoming students. Republicans never tire of reminding the nation that what counts most in leadership in all domains of life, what makes America great, are the virtues of hard work, honesty, courage, initiative and imagination, integrity, loyalty, and sportsmanship and fair play, all best demonstrated by a person's track record and especially his or her perseverance in the face of adversity. If there is one thing to which American conservatives have shown a chronic propensity throughout the nation's history, it is what Richard Hofstadter has called "the suspicion of intellect," a decided preference for practical intelligence and character over mere raw intelligence.[8] Why, then, are conservatives traducing the great universities of this nation for taking their values seriously in selecting the next generation of leaders?

Afro-American ancestry, we are told, should have nothing to do with the assessment of these virtues. Ethnic ancestry, however, refers to several aspects of a person. It sometimes refers to a person's physical appearance, and this, all but extremist Afro-Americans would agree, should be a matter of no importance. But for Afro-Americans, their ancestry also means surviving an environment in which racism is still an important obstacle. It has to be taken into account in assessing the content of any Afro-American person's character, and to assert that this amounts to a divisive glorification of "race" or ethnicity is as disingenuous and as absurd as claiming that we are divisively glorifying poverty and broken families when we account for these background factors in assessing the content of a Euro-American student's character, as the University of California and other institutions currently do.

But there is a third, important meaning of ancestry and ethnic identity in America, and here we enter tricky ground. Being Afro-American also connotes something positive: the subcultural heritage of a minority that, in spite of centuries of racial discrimination, has vastly enriched American civilization out of all proportion to the numbers, and treatment, of the group creating it. The University of California, like the other great institutions of learning in the nation, rightly sees as part of its educational mission the exposure of all its students to this great minority culture as well as the recognition of its influence on the mainstream.

This is a noble goal, but it is fraught with dangers. My vision of affirmative action, what brought me around to it after some severe initial reservations, was not simply its effectiveness as a strategy for reducing inequality, but the possibility of greatly increasing cross-pollination of our multiethnic communities, in the process promoting that precious, overarching national culture—the envy of the world—which I have come to call ecumenical America.[9]

Unfortunately, affirmative action has accomplished nothing of the sort, as Connerly and Wilson were able to argue truthfully and with devastating impact. On the contrary, both on and off our campuses, affirmative action seems to have been distorted by its beneficiaries into the goal of balkanizing America both intellectually and culturally. One has only to walk for a few minutes on any of the nation's great campuses to witness the extent of ethnic separatism, alternating with periodic outbursts of ethnic, gender, and other chauvinistic hostilities. The thought that repeatedly haunts me as I travel the nation's campuses is that the South did indeed finally win the moral battle over integration, for no group of people now seems more committed to segregation than Afro-American students and young professionals. The motto now seems to be an in-your-face "separate yes, but make damn sure it's equal, by affirmative action or any other means." To a lesser extent, the tendency of the new Afro-American middle class to segregate itself residentially and to scoff at the norms and values of the ecumenical mainstream are simply the off-campus versions of this lamentable betrayal and abandonment of the once cherished goal of integration. It comes as no surprise to learn that the NAACP is now rethinking its fundamental commitment to school integration.

Ethnic separatism has also had deleterious academic consequences. In a controlled experiment conducted at the University of Michigan by psychologists Claude Steele and Richard Nisbett, disadvantaged minority students who were encouraged to participate in mainstream university activities and made to understand that the highest standards were expected of them consistently performed above the average for Euro-American students and the university as a whole, whereas those who went the familiar route of ethnic solidarity and consciousness-raising performed well below the average.[10]

Affirmative action has also been hurt by a certain amount of cheating, although this has been exaggerated. The cynical promotion of clearly unqualified people, even if it happens only occasionally, greatly damages the legitimacy of the entire policy since it takes only one such mistake to sour an entire organization. So, too, do clearly illegal practices such as using Afro-Americans and women as entrepreneurial fronts in order to gain access to affirmative action contracts.

In spite of these problems, we have seen that the vast majority of Euro-American workers continue to support affirmative action in their own workplace, however misinformed they may be about its impact on other workers throughout the nation. This support, in addition to what is known of the actual effects of affirmative action, suggests that progressive leadership can continue to support the policy without fear of any serious negative political consequences.

But should they do so? Earlier I noted that there is a sincere debate about the moral and intellectual issues posed by affirmative action. The fact that the policy has now been shown to be politically feasible and of little practical harm does not mean that it is the right action to pursue. Let's turn now to these issues.

THE GENUINE DEBATE

Whatever its practical merits, affirmative action does conflict with some of the moral presuppositions of American society, and any defense of the policy must account for these tensions. There is a deep reluctance in the Anglo-American moral and legal tradition to accept the principle of group rights and claims. This stems from the strong commitment to individualism and its supporting ethic of self-determination.[11]

As I argued in the essay on conservative advocacy, it is simply not possible for a modern—or indeed any—society to work without some recognition and acceptance of the ideal of group obligations and claims. We accept the reality of states as actors in the international community, and within states we accept the existence of corporate groups such as firms and trade unions. Noncorporate groups are, in principle, not recognized as holders of claims or government preferences. Nonetheless, there is a strong precedent for such recognition in recent American history. Veterans, for example, have for decades been granted special privileges and rights. As John David Skrentny points out, "Unlike racial preferences, which have been called 'underhanded' by Harvey Mansfield, Jr., and 'covert' by Thomas Sowell, veterans' preferences are naked, particularistic affronts on the meritocratic rules of the American job market—they are simply called veterans' preferences, rather than hidden with an ambiguous term like affirmative action. At the same time, they are relatively uncontroversial and are protected by the courts." These privileges certainly cannot be viewed solely as payment for their recipients' war effort, since what they did was a moral duty required by all, and in any event would have been paid for long ago when measured in terms of lost wages during wartime.

Equally problematic is the implicit challenge to the nation's undergirding ethic of self-determination implicit in many arguments in favor of affirmative action. As I argued in the essay on liberal advocacy, the dominant American tradition insists on self-determination and autonomy. But here again, the degree of commitment to this principle is very much a function of the experience of Americans. I think that one may safely make the generalization that all excluded or disadvantaged groups pressing for inclusion are going to challenge the doctrine of autonomy on the grounds that it blames the victim and discourages the government intervention that they favor; whereas all groups already securely "in" are going to defend the doctrine's sanctity and favor a hands-off position by government.

This was nicely demonstrated in a poll conducted by the *New York Times* in December 1995. When a sample of Americans was asked, "Do you think government should step in to do something about layoffs and loss of jobs, or is this something the government should stay out of?" only 42 percent of those Americans who had not been affected by layoffs felt the government should step in, while 63 percent of those who had been affected by such layoffs favored government action. Other responses made it clear, also, that those who had experienced layoffs, including former corporate executives who said they were Republicans, tended to blame the system rather than themselves for their situation, while those still unaffected held firmly to the autonomy dogma.[12]

Now, while the doctrine of autonomy is a moral and sociological imperative of modern life, it is evident that a person's capacity to act autonomously can be stunted by being disadvantaged and excluded.

Behaving autonomously is itself something we learn mainly by doing. This is a classic case of the divine paradox: to him that hath it shall be given; to him that hath not it shall be taken away. Success breeds success; failure, failure. How do the "hath-nots" break out of the trap? They do so by struggling for access. The most important way in which affirmative action helps those who are on the outside is to provide them with access to circles and networks that they would otherwise almost never penetrate. For Afro-Americans, one of the most egregious effects of past ethnic exclusion has been their isolation from cultural capital and personal networks that are essential for success in America. This important sociological fact is usually simply neglected by those who imagine capitalist America to be a perfectly competitive, meritocratic system in which people rise to their positions based solely on their training and motivation. There is some truth in this, but it is at best a half-truth.

An important argument against affirmative action has been advanced by the distinguished economist Glenn Loury.[13] In his speeches and writings Loury presents the following scenario. Imagine that there are ten equally qualified persons in a firm, nine of whom are Euro-American and one Afro-American, and that they are all candidates for promotion to a single slot. The firm has an affirmative action program and the Afro-American person gets the job. Now, eight of the Euro-American candidates would not have gotten the job, whether there was an affirmative action program or not. Yet in the presence of such a program all nine Euro-Americans who did not get the job blame racial preference for their nonpromotion, harbor deep grievances over the apparent unfairness, and may even become hardened racists as a result. A program that generates such enormous social conflict and resentment, Loury argues, is simply not worth it. One Afro-American person benefits, but to the detriment of all Afro-Americans, who bear the major cost of increased ethnic conflict.

This is a theoretically powerful argument. In light of the unusual level of social and political tension surrounding affirmative action, it seems highly plausible. However, it crumbles under closer empirical and theoretical scrutiny. The empirical argument against it has already been given. Contrary to all the heat, only 7 percent of Euro-Americans can actually claim that they have been affected unfavorably by affirmative action, and the vast majority of Euro-American workers support affirmative action in their own workplace.

But there is a theoretical response to Loury's argument, and in pursuing it we come to one of the best defenses of affirmative action. My argument, in a nutshell, is that two features of American society make it impossible for Afro-Americans ever to achieve parity without some sustained, although not permanent, policy of affirmative action. These are, first, the ratio of Afro-Americans to Euro-Americans, which, second, operates in conjunction with certain well-known characteristics of internal labor markets.

Let us assume that there is a firm with one hundred entry-level employees, exactly 13 percent of whom are Afro-American, and that all these employees have been shown by objective measures to be perfectly equal in ability, educational attainment, and motivation. Let us assume further an ethnically unbiased organization: the owner of the firm and the personnel officers are all good Americans with not a trace of ethnic prejudice. Even under these circumstances, I am saying, it is almost certain that the Afro-American entry-level employees will never make it to the top echelons of the organization if there is no account taken of ethnicity in promotion; indeed, they will hardly move beyond their entry-level jobs.

This claim seems counterintuitive because we assume that, in the normal course of events, each equally qualified entry-level Afro-American will have a 13 percent chance of being promoted, resulting eventually in a similar ratio of Afro-Americans moving up the firm's opportunity ladder. This is what misguided liberals and neoconservative critics have in mind when they speak naively about a "color-blind" system. The problem with this logic is that it disregards the fact that when firms promote workers they consider not simply the characteristics of employees, but organizational criteria, among the most important of which is the degree to which a candidate for promotion will fit into the upper echelon for which he or she is being considered. And it is precisely here that Afro-Americans lose out because of their small numbers, their ethnic differences, and the tendency of personnel officers to follow one well-established law of microsociology, first formally propounded by the sociologist George Caspar Homans.[14]

This very simple principle of human behavior—call it the principle of homophyly—is that people who share common attributes tend to marry each other, tend to play more together, and in general tend to get along better and to form more effective work teams. Thus, a nonracist personnel officer, under no pressure to consider ethnic attributes—indeed, under strong misguided pressure to follow a "color-blind" policy—would always find it more organizationally rational to choose a Euro-American person for promotion. There are more than six candidates for every one Afro-American candidate, which means that unless the Afro-American person is a genius of sociability, outperforming Euro-Americans at their own social game, the organizationally rational act will be to select one of the Euro-American candidates. In spite of the technical equality of the Afro-American candidates, the Euro-American person's organizational fit—which comes simply with being Euro-American—will so significantly reduce the cost to the organization of incorporation and training that it would be irresponsible of our ethnically unbiased personnel officer, under orders to select in a color-blind manner, ever to promote an Afro-American person.

Of course, when one introduces one well-known real-world feature of American society to this model of "color-blind" organizational behavior, the cards are even more heavily stacked against our thirteen Afro-American entry-level employees: this is the fact that Euro-American workers have a hard time taking orders from Afro-American supervisors. There is no need to belabor this fact. This being so, the cost to our non-racist, "color-blind" personnel officer becomes even greater; and it gets worse the more real-world attitudes and behaviors we introduce.

Incidentally, many Asian-American recruits to American organizations face exactly this problem, although often at a higher level of the organizational hierarchy than Afro-Americans. With their well known "model-minority" technical qualifications and "work-ethic" reputation they are often more qualified than their Euro-American counterparts in the organizations where they work, but somewhere in the middle of these organizations Asians come crashing headlong upon Homans's first law of group behavior. They find themselves filling up the technical departments and being passed over for those higher level jobs requiring less emphasis on technical knowledge and individual attributes and more on organizational knowledge and social or interactional attributes.[15]

Clearly, unless ethnic diversity is made an organizational goal, promoting minorities will never be in the interest of firms, except in very special cases where, for instance, an organization wishes to penetrate the Afro-American market. In such a case the Afro-American person's ethnic distinctiveness gives him an organizational edge—for example, a cosmetic firm introducing a new line of texturizers for the Afro-American hair type, an insurance firm wanting to tap into the ghetto market, or a record company seeking vice-presidents who can relate to its Afro-American entertainers and music shop owners.

A policy of deliberate ethnic (and gender) diversity, then, is essential if Afro-Americans (and women) are ever to achieve parity with Euro-

Americans in anything approaching their proportion in the population at all levels of the organizational hierarchy. There is no foundation to the charge of critics that such affirmative action policies will become permanent. The reason for this is Homans's second principle of human group behavior: the more people who are unlike each other live and work with each other, the more they will come to share the same sentiments and social attributes, and consequently the better they will come to work together as a team. There has been overwhelming empirical support for this law. Perhaps the best-known real-world case is that of the army, a once segregated institution with a disproportionate number of ethnically biased Euro-American officers from the Deep South. Integrated by executive order, the army, as I noted in the first essay, eventually became a model of integrated ethnic teamwork. It is no accident that from its ranks America produced the first Afro-American man with a realistic chance of becoming president of the country. How did the army do it? As the work of Charles Moskos and John Sibley Butler demonstrates, the army practiced affirmative action on a massive scale, combined with an extremely effective program of training Afro-American recruits to ensure that they achieved skill parity with Euro-Americans.[16]

To argue that we should begin to solve the problem of "racial" exclusion by assuming a color-blind world is to assume away the very problem we are trying to solve: only voodoo priests and rational choice theorists can get away with this kind of mumbo-jumbo. The simple truth, the simple reality, is that "racial" categorization is a fact of American life, one that we can do away with only by first acknowledging it. We must also acknowledge that Afro-Americans did not originally create or construct the social reality of their "blackness." In the West Africa of the sixteenth to eighteenth centuries from which they came there was no meaningful notion of "blackness," since everyone there looked African. Afro-Americans are the only group of persons whose ancestors were dragged here, kicking and screaming. For nearly three centuries they were held in chains here, during which time the social category of "blackness" was constructed and imposed upon them. Eventually, the logic of their situation dictated that they accept and invert the "racial" status forced upon them in their heroic struggles to overcome the centuries of enslavement and victimization. In their struggles, they made something positive of the ethnic markers imposed upon them, even in the face of the continuing negative conception of, and response to, them on the part of still too many Euro-Americans.

The eventual goal of all but the small minority of extremist chauvinist

Afro-Americans is a world in which the social fact of their ethnic difference will not have to be considered in the organizations where they work as far as evaluations of their work performance and promotion go. But to achieve such an objective, ethnic factors must be considered for some time to come, both for the reasons I have mentioned earlier and for the more obvious reasons that overt racism persists, even if it is declining.

I think it will be very difficult ever to find consensus on affirmative action. Beyond the immediate question of improving access for minorities and women looms a deeper issue. Assuming a moderate level of success in the recruitment and promotion of formerly excluded persons, the newcomers may soon begin to find that they just don't like the organizational game or the way it is played. After enormous effort to enter the executive suite, for example, many women have discovered that they do not particularly enjoy "kicking a little ass" for the hell of it, as former President Bush once so joyfully expressed it.

It is at this point that a new phase in the egalitarian struggle emerges. The struggle at this point is not about getting on the playing field or playing the game, but about the very rules of the game, about who sets the rules, and about the style and purpose of the game. And at this point we have moved well beyond the boundaries of a policy such as affirmative action, which in essence is designed to remove bias and promote access within the existing system. In defending affirmative action, or any other policy, it is important to be clear about its limits. Using it to achieve objectives for which it was not designed will result in the baby being thrown out with the bathwater. Let me therefore turn to a few of these broader egalitarian goals for which affirmative action is not appropriate.

A great deal of the heat in the debate over affirmative action, I suspect, is generated by the usually unstated assumption that changing the rules, style, and purpose of the game is really what the struggle is ultimately about. Those who control our society like to think there is something immutable and sacred about the rules of the game. Simply to bring them into question excites anxiety and outrage. If comparative and historical sociology teaches us one thing about societies, however, it is the fact that the rules by which we play in our social organizations are not like genetic codes. They can and do change.

Furthermore, we also know that the same objective can often be obtained by different means. A good case in point is provided by the differences between the American and Japanese patterns of management. For decades, many people thought that the rules of management were those encoded in the case studies of the Harvard Business School. Real culture shock reverberated when corporate America learned that there are radically different ways of maximizing profits. My point is not to idealize the Japanese alternative, which is currently showing many signs of its own peculiar failings, but rather to illustrate the fact that the rules of the game more often reflect the interests, values, and class of those who are at the center of power than they do any hard-to-grasp essences that only the select, meritocratic few can fathom.

To put the matter another way, if we insist on running our car factories the way Detroit does, then it follows, as night follows day, that only people who look, think, feel, and behave like Lee Iacocca will ever end up at the top of the executive ladder. No Afro-American and no woman could exhibit the kind of Euro-American male executive macho with which Mr. Iacocca so obligingly regaled TV viewers in his commercial spots for Chrysler during the early eighties. The example of top executive positions in the auto industry represents the most extreme heights of power. But my argument applies to nearly all areas and levels of exclusion, from firefighting and police work to law and medicine.

We can now understand the true nature of the crisis that affirmative action creates when it is mistakenly associated with these more radical goals. It is not just the presence of the formerly excluded that presents problems for the establishment, but the fear that they might change the way we run things. These fears are indeed justified, since it is true that if women and minorities are to be included in significant numbers at the top layers of the system, the rules will have to change.

Before I am wholly misunderstood by those who wave the banner of high standards (rarely, I might add, are they those who most often achieve these standards), let me make it clear that the redefinition of rules in no way entails a lessening of standards or the abandonment of the merit principle. I am not proposing that we do away with rules and structures, but that we redefine them in a manner that makes it possible for those now excluded to play by them. I am, in short, urging a commitment to the very values that critics of affirmative action insist on, a genuine universalization of the rules of conduct. Such a universalization cannot stop short of the rules by which we change the rules.

To put the matter in somewhat more formal terms, the intensity of the debate over affirmative action may be attributed to deep-seated disagreements over three kinds of rules—what may be called the rules of allocation, of application, and of determination.

It is a struggle, first, over the age-old problem of equality and the difficulty of arriving at some acceptable conception of distributive justice. People disagree over what constitutes fair distribution of wealth and power, and even where they agree that some effort ought to be made to reduce the gap between the haves and have-nots, they disagree over the rules of allocation, the means by which we achieve less inequality. In a nutshell, those who support affirmative action believe that inegalitarian rules of allocation are fair where the objective is a more egalitarian distribution of rewards. Many of those opposed to affirmative action take the opposite view, questioning even the long-established principle of a graduated income tax—the classic example of an inegalitarian rule of allocation aimed at a more egalitarian distribution—as the unexpected surge of support for Steve Forbes's 1996 primary campaign indicated.

Second, the conflict is over the rules of application, that is, the problem of whether groups, especially noncorporate disadvantaged groups, are entitled to special claims as a result of the special damages and exclusions they have suffered historically and continue to suffer in institutional and personal terms. Supporters of affirmative action accept the legitimacy of such claims; those opposed insist that only individuals, as individuals, rather than as members of disadvantaged groups, can claim damages and are entitled to compensatory treatment, in stark contrast with the realities of the capitalist system, as I argued in the earlier essay on conservative advocacy.

Finally, the covert agenda of the struggle for affirmative action is that it seeks to change the underlying rules of determination in our society, what, to use the terminology of Daniel Bell, might be called the axial rules.[17] Affirmative action does restrain the freedom and power of some people to maintain an order that results in the chronic disadvantage of others. This is clearly a power struggle, and as with all such struggles in a democracy, it can and should be waged politically.

There are striking precedents for such political struggles. American history is a remarkable and inspiring record of the successful struggle of the disadvantaged and excluded to overcome their constraints and to be included. They accomplished their goals by personal merit, by the use of political and other means to achieve access to meaningful positions in their society and, just as importantly, by insisting on having a say in the way the rules by which they lived were defined, maintained, and changed.

The history of the Irish in America is only one, although the classic, case in point. The post-famine Irish who came to America in the nineteenth century were called every name that has been used to abuse Afro-American folks. Indeed, it was common lore among Euro-Americans that the Irish were "niggers turned inside out" and that Afro-Americans were "smoked Irish."[18] More to the point, the Irish were culturally different, "as different as could be imagined in mood and tempo from those natives of Anglo-Saxon Puritan stock," wrote William Shannon in his standard history of the group, and "they did not seem to practice thrift, self-denial and other virtues desirable in the 'worthy laboring poor.'"[19] In their struggle for inclusion, the Irish used their control of city governments to institute massive programs of "affirmative action" biased in favor of the working and middle classes of their group. There can be no gainsaying the fact that political patronage and preferential hiring in the nation's city bureaucracies were decisive factors in the rise of the Irish out of poverty into respectability.

But it is equally important to note two other elements of their success: an amazing capacity for hard work, and a deep and abiding commitment to the sanctity of their families. Even in the face of oppressively low wages and nativist hostility, including the burning of their churches and convents, the Irish worked long, backbreaking hours for their families, the men often dying young as a result. And, contrary to present sociological dogma that it is poverty that creates familial dislocation, destitution and anti-Irish bigotry resulted in a tightening of familial bonds among the Irish who were seemingly trapped in the ghettos of nineteenth-century America.[20]

Another important lesson of Irish-American history confirms a point made earlier. When the Irish got on the playing fields of American politics and economics, they did not turn themselves into good little Celtic models of the Protestant ethic, meekly playing by the rules they found. Instead, once on the field they moved to the next stage of their struggle: they changed the rules of the game. "The newer Irish," wrote Shannon, "challenged the code of the community at almost every point.... Their politicians pressed to the fore; their priests raised new issues of religious discrimination in public schools. The activities of both disturbed the smug, clublike atmosphere in which the large towns had formerly been governed. Their 'grating brogue' was heard everywhere."[21] Even in the highly traditional arena of Catholic church government, the Irish insisted on changing the rules as soon as they took over. What another historian of the Irish-Americans, George Potter, wrote of the powerful John Hughes, the first Irish-American to take over the diocese of New York in 1840, holds true of Irish rule-changing generally: "He trampled on the prudence and rejected the diplomatic suavity [of his more conformist predecessors], once saying that he did not hold with the 'generally good, cautious souls who believed in stealing through the world more submissively than suits a freeman.'"[22] Afro-American Baptists of the late twentieth century can relate to that.

The end result of this struggle, which combined politically based "affirmative action" on a grand scale for over three quarters of a century, hard work, strong family ties, and an insistence on not simply playing hard by the rules, but also changing them, is one of the great success stories of America. Contrary to common knowledge, Irish Catholics are today the second most prosperous group of people of European ancestry in America, trailing only Jews, with their household income 118 percent of the U.S. average, way above Americans of Protestant British ancestry, who ranked a distant fifth in 1989.[23]

Today, of course, the Irish no longer need affirmative action, in much the same way that, not long from now, women and Afro-Americans will no longer need it. And there is something else about the Irish-American story that informs the present debate. The men who controlled Tammany Hall and the other city governments in the earlier part of this century would have considered it laughable, if also a pretty lousy Protestant joke, had they been told that preferential treatment of the Irish poor and lower middle classes was un-American and brought into question the qualifications of worthy Irish-Americans who had succeeded solely by their merits and work ethic. These men all knew that to transcend the limitations and constraints of being Irish, they had to emphasize their Irishness. Today, there is less need for them to do so, except in a symbolic, "cut-flower" kind of way or on St. Patrick's Day.

In their struggle for inclusion and prosperity, the Irish redefined themselves. By changing the rules of the game, they profoundly redefined what it is to be American. This, above all, is perhaps the greatest lesson of their prototypical American story for Afro-Americans and women. What Joseph O'Grady wrote in his book *How the Irish Became Americans* holds for all those who are still struggling for full equality and integration into the great, ever-changing cultural process that is America:

> In effect, the people of America did not bring their democracy with them, nor did they find it here. They made it from the interaction of many ideas and interests as defined by many groups. The clash of these ideas generated pressures upon both individuals and groups to make decisions that, in turn, simply created new demands for new groups. In that momentum one finds the origin, meaning and purpose of America.[24]

Today, Afro-Americans and women are simply extending the struggle and renewing the momentum that is the source of America's greatness in ways that will ensure their own integration and meet their peculiar needs and interests. The affirmative action program is a start in this struggle for Afro-Americans and women, but as I indicated earlier, we are approaching its limits, and broadening its scope may simply overstrain it. The broader struggle for inclusion will have to be waged within the corporate system itself by those who gain entry through affirmative action.

The struggle is endless even at the entry level and will continue even after Afro-Americans have won their battle for full economic inclusion, because in our competitive capitalist democracy with its great tradition of immigration there will always be inequality, not to mention new outsiders to be integrated. The world will not leave America alone, because America remains its only global power, generating the world's first truly global culture, thanks in good part to the creativity of its Afro-American and Irish-American populations. Not only will some justly do better than others, but many will unjustly do so. As Rousseau saw more than two centuries ago, an inevitable tendency toward inequality in modern societies is no reason to accept inequality: "It is precisely because the force of things always tends to destroy equality that the force of legislation should always tend to maintain it."[25]

CONCLUSION
WHAT IS TO BE DONE

The failure to grasp both the paradoxes of the "racial" situation and the contradictions and paradoxes in the prevailing perceptions, experiences, and interpretations of it not only badly obscures a major national problem but undermines all attempts at change, playing right into the hands of the most extremist forces in society. I have no certain answers, but I propose we bear the following thoughts in mind as we struggle out of the quagmire in which we are now trapped.

RECOGNIZE THAT THE REAL AFRO-AMERICANS ARE DIVERSE, SURPRISINGLY HAPPY, AND VERY AMERICAN

The great majority of Afro-Americans—some 23 million persons making up more than 70 percent of the aggregate—have benefited from the enormous progress made by both Afro- and Euro-Americans over the past forty-five years in resolving the nation's "racial" crisis. They are a hard-working, disproportionately God-fearing, law-abiding group of people who share the same dreams as their fellow citizens, love and cherish the land of their birth with equal fervor, contribute to its cultural, military, and political glory and global triumph out of all proportion to their numbers, and, to every dispassionate observer, are, in their values, habits, ideals, and ways of living, among the most "American" of Americans. It is striking that, as of October 1995, some 67 percent of Afro-Americans said that they still believed in the American Dream, and Afro-Americans were only 2 percent less likely than Euro-Americans to say that they were farther away from attaining the American Dream than they had been ten years ago.[1]

For this two-thirds of the Afro-American population, Martin Luther King Jr.'s dream has *not* been deferred, as so many Euro-American liberals and Afro-American advocates insultingly insist, misleading the world. They have, indeed, inherited the fruits of what Anita Patterson refers to as King's "abiding faith in the political efficacy of civil disobedience and love."[2]

A sound grasp of this remarkable achievement must be the starting point of any assessment of America's "racial" problem. There is still a serious problem: let that be clear. Failures, especially in the persistence of urban slums and the ethnic bias in incarceration, rightly outrage most Afro-Americans as well as caring Euro-Americans. But it is irresponsible, patronizing, and downright racist of analysts and reporters in academia, public life, and the media to persist in viewing all Afro-Americans as a single, homogeneous group of downtrodden outsiders, racked with chronic problems and constantly sour about their lot and their country. For those who find it hard to believe that there are any happy, contented Afro-American persons out there in America, let the facts speak for themselves. When the National Opinion Research Center of the University of Chicago asked a random sample of Afro-Americans the following question in 1994— "Taken all together, how would you say things are these days, would you say you are very happy, pretty happy, or not too happy?"—fully 78 percent of them said that they were either very happy or pretty happy.[3]

This response was no fluke. A Gallup poll in June 1997 found equally high levels of satisfaction in most areas of life by Afro-Americans.[4] Thus, 74 percent were satisfied with the way things were going in their personal lives, up from 55 percent in 1979; three-fourths were satisfied with their housing condition, up from 49 percent in 1973; 74 percent were satisfied with their present standard of living, up from 45 percent in 1973; and 73 percent were satisfied with their jobs, compared with 66 percent in 1973. While only 53 percent of Afro-Americans were satisfied with their household income, this was entirely explained in class terms. Their dissatisfaction is an accurate reflection of their relatively lower income and not any chronic ethnic unhappiness with their lot; once class is taken into account, the difference in levels of satisfaction with standard of living between Euro-Americans and Afro-Americans vanishes.

WE MUST CHANGE THE WAY WE TALK ABOUT AND INTERPRET
OUR SO-CALLED "RACE" PROBLEM

▫ One of the first things to be done is to change the language of inter-group relations. The term *race* itself must be abandoned, or, as Ashley Montagu suggested years ago, where absolutely necessary it should be used only in quotation marks. We should, instead, talk about ethnic groups and relations—if we must—rather than racial groups and rela-tions; and the distinction between "race" and ethnicity should be aban-doned as meaningless and potentially dangerous. It is incredible that the United States Census Bureau still continues to ask Americans to classi-fy themselves according to "race" in addition to ethnic ancestry. Quite apart from the absurdities into which this distinction has gotten the agency with respect to so-called Hispanics, it is pernicious that the nation's Census Bureau is perpetuating this relic of the Nazi era. The term *race* should be banished from the Census questionnaire immediately.

▫ We should drop the terms *black* and *white* when talking about Afro-Americans and Euro-Americans. I find it hard to believe that the nation's writers do not shudder at the sheer infelicity of referring to someone as a "black" or a "white." Not only are the terms *black* and *white* denotatively loaded in favor or Euro-Americans—as a check in *The Oxford English Dictionary* will attest in lurid detail—but by their emphasis on the somatic, they reinforce and legitimize precisely that biological notion of "race" that we claim we want to be rid of.

The term *racist* is still a meaningful one, but should be used only to designate persons who believe in the existence of ranked, genetically separate "races" and who explain human behavioral differences pri-marily in genetic or somatic terms. These include academic racists such as Arthur Jensen, Charles Murray and Leonard Jeffries, politicians such as David Duke and Louis Farrakhan, and the declining minority of the U.S. population—presently about a fifth of the nation—who still hold to this execrable dogma.

▫ In most cases where supposed racism is at issue, the more appropriate charge is either ethnocentrism or class prejudice. All human beings are prejudiced, Afro-Americans no less than others. It is natural to discrim-inate and categorize. These qualities are fundamental to all thought and sensibility. Indeed, we actively cultivate many kinds of prejudices, such as our prejudices toward freedom, democracy, and altruism, and much of what we call education, especially in the arts and humanities, is sim-ply the cultivation of our capacity to discriminate between good and evil, the beautiful and the coarse, and refinement and vulgarity.

Ethnocentrism is the hurtful misapplication of our capacity to categorize and discriminate to particular aggregates of persons, especially those
that are self-identified as ethnic groups. It consists of two egregious errors,
and it is very important that we recognize its twofold nature. One error is
the stereotyping of ethnic *aggregates* with negative attributes: "Jews are
clannish and deceptive"; "Italian-Americans are prone to organized crime";
"The Irish are drunkards who beat their wives"; "Poles are stupid"; "Afro-
Americans are socially and intellectually inferior"; and so on. The second
is the tendency to judge *individuals* entirely or primarily in terms of the
stereotyped attributes of the groups with which they are identified: John
Brown over there is stupid because he is an Afro-American; Sidney
Weinstein next door cannot be trusted because he is Jewish.

I distinguish between these two related aspects of ethnocentrism
because, contrary to what many analysts think, they do not necessarily
go together, especially in America. It is possible to be prejudiced against
a collectivity of persons, especially one that is self-identified as an ethnic
group, without being prejudiced against individual members of that
group. In other words, it is possible to be anti-Semitic, or to dislike Afro-
Americans as a group, and yet treat individual Jews and Afro-Americans
one encounters quite fairly. The sardonic expression "Some of my best
friends are Jews, Afro-Americans, etc." is aimed precisely at this apparent contradiction. The nation's newspapers often present tragic cases of
it: Afro-American and Euro-American youth who maim and kill persons
from the other ethnic group in what are clearly "racially motivated" acts
often turn out to have close personal friends from the group they have so
viciously stereotyped. And every middle-class minority person knows of
at least one or two supervisors in organizations who are scrupulously fair
with minority persons even though they are known to be racists. As
Sniderman and Piazza found, many Euro-Americans, faced with an *individual* who is Afro-American, are likely to be supportive of that individual in, for example, his claim to government assistance, but "confronted
with blacks *as a group,* a significant number of whites practice a racial
double standard."[5]

On the other hand, it is possible to be individually prejudiced in
"racial" or ethnic terms without holding such prejudices about the ethnic group with which the person is identified. This may be so because the
prejudiced individual, on principle, does not believe in attributing qualities to groups. Many conservatives, for example, simply reject the reality
of groups over and beyond individuals and families, as Margaret Thatcher

famously made clear. However, this kind of individualized nongroup ethnic prejudice can exist even in the absence of Thatcherite reductionism.
Recent studies of the attitude of employers toward Afro-American inner-
city youths reveal marked individualized ethnic prejudice toward them
even in cases where we know that these employers are not prejudiced
toward Afro-Americans in general. How do we know? Not simply
because the employers all insist they are not group prejudiced, but, more
tellingly, because a large proportion of Afro-American employers exhibit exactly similar prejudice toward these youths.[6] These employers are
often themselves prominent members of the local Afro-American community, and it is obviously absurd to claim that they are racists against
their own self-identified ethnic group. What we have, instead, is the kind
of prejudice that has come to be known by the awkward term *statistical
discrimination*. Whatever we call it, it is a clear example of individualized
ethnic prejudice in the absence of generalized group prejudice.

Both versions of ethnocentric prejudice are wrong and dangerous,
and we have to work hard toward their elimination, but we must recognize that formidable barriers stand in the way. In a large, heterogeneous
society like America it can sometimes be costly to always do the right
thing and judge every person one meets solely on the basis of reliable,
individualized information on them. If I find myself walking alone on a
street near South Boston and I see a large, rednecked Euro-American with
a bulbous nose and long dirty blond hair dressed in studded black leather
lumbering toward me, I am going to take evasive action, however statistically prejudiced against working-class Irish-Americans I know such an
act to be. I would react the same way if I saw a group of hooded Afro-
American homeboys bopping down the street with stony-eyed stares. How
we sanction this kind of prejudice will depend on the relative probabilities
of injury to both individuals and the potential damage of such injuries. In
what may be called the menacing youth situation, the probability of being
injured, while small, is nonetheless nonnegligible.

We cannot assume that there is no probability of injury to the party
avoided in this situation. Minority youth, especially Afro-Americans, often
suffer hurt feelings as a result of such evasive action. Indeed, when the frequency of psychological injury in casual ethnic encounters and the actual
statistics of victimization by strange youth are considered, it may well be
true that the probability of injury is greater for the avoided person than it
is for the avoider. The problem, however, is not simply a matter of the odds
of injury, but of the nature of the costs incurred in the event that one

guesses wrong. In the menacing youth situation, the costs run the gamut from verbal abuse to catastrophic physical injury for the person making the judgment call whether to trust or to take evasive action. For the avoided person there is no such range of injury, since it does not extend beyond a temporary sense of being slighted.

With an employer, however, the probabilities of injury and the range of such injuries are different. Employers have the resources to gain more information on people seeking employment, and while the cost of being rejected for work can be catastrophic for the job seeker, not to mention the inner-city communities from which he and the majority of similarly rejected youth come, they do not go beyond the costs of firing and rehiring for the employer. These should be viewed as the necessary costs of doing business in a heterogeneous society that for generations willfully and maliciously shut out the vast majority of a subpopulation from the discipline and culture of the industrial process solely on the basis of their appearance. What is more, in the long run the society of the employer who statistically discriminates ends up paying far more in taxes to maintain the unemployed and to correct the social problems they create. Such costs may not be acknowledged by the prejudiced employer for classic free-rider reasons. It is to solve this free-rider problem, and to make sure that employers do the right thing, that strictly enforced laws against discrimination in hiring are essential. The fact that Afro-American employers engage in this kind of prejudice is neither an excuse for it nor a reason for not strictly enforcing antidiscrimination laws. It does suggest, however, that this kind of discrimination is really a form of class prejudice rather than ethnic prejudice. Unfortunately, there are no laws against class prejudice, and it is unlikely that such laws will ever be passed or implemented.

Against the group version of ethnocentrism we should continue to educate young and old alike about the dangers of attributing negative stereotypes to particular groups or aggregates of people. Multicultural education's main claim for support is that, at its best, it attempts to do this. The main obstacle in the elimination of ethnic group prejudice, however, is the ironic fact of the very salience of ethnicity in American life and our commitment to the slippery ideal of ethnic pride. Some have seriously questioned whether it is possible to promote ethnic diversity without inciting ethnic hostility and division. It can be done, as the case of Switzerland, with its French-, German-, and Italian-speaking subpopulations, attests, but it is difficult, and I am not sure whether the conditions that made the

Swiss model possible hold in America. I will have far more to say on this subject in the third volume of this trilogy.[7]

For the time being, I propose that we talk about ethnic rather than "racial" differences as the lesser of two evils, and that in our ethnic discourse we do everything to avoid negatively stereotyping other groups. Since the promotion of ethnic diversity encourages the celebration of positive stereotypes about other ethnic groups, and since most people find it hard to accept positive stereotypes without slipping into negative ones, we have our work cut out for us.

◗ Our entire approach to the study and interpretation of the Afro-American condition and of relations with Euro-Americans is fundamentally flawed and must be changed. The assumptions and conventions of academic scholarship as well as popular writings on this subject now do more harm than good. What should illuminate dispassionately, now distorts and reinforces the very dilemma it attempts to clarify.

Most important of all, we should stop overracializing our discussion of the Afro-American condition. One way we could begin to do this is to reduce the almost reflexive tendency to measure the progress of Afro-Americans solely using that of Euro-Americans as a yardstick. Euro-Americans had a head start of three and a half centuries on Afro-Americans, during which Afro-Americans were not simply left alone but were actively parasitized for the economic, cultural, and psychological benefit of Euro-Americans. This horrendous past morally dictates some redress, but it also necessitates restraint in our expectation of the speed with which Afro-Americans can be expected to catch up with Euro-Americans. Unrealistic or false expectations can have, and have had, unfortunate consequences.

First, such comparisons will backfire after a time and might begin to buttress racist views, when they are not themselves incipiently racist. The endless stream of negative comparison with Euro-Americans must sooner or later raise the suspicion that "these poor people" just do not have what it takes. After a while, the one liberal excuse—racism—begins to wear thin, especially for Americans who do not consider themselves racist and may even have tried hard to rid themselves of any conscious racist attitudes. It is just these Euro-Americans whom one wants to persuade and encourage. One cannot tyrannize people intellectually into accepting "racism" as a universal, monocausal, utterly overdetermining explanation of every observed difference between Euro-Americans and Afro-Americans. It is natural, and perfectly reasonable, to begin to wonder what is really going on other than the same old liberal ding-dong:

> It's racism dat dunnit,
> racism dat dunnit.
> If you dare to deny it
> you're a racist, I know it.

I cannot believe that social scientists, especially sociologists, who are trained to be sensitive to the social construction and uses of knowledge, and who know perfectly well that there is no such thing as an objective, decontextualized factual observation, are unaware of the two-edged nature of the verbal swords they thrust incessantly in their analysis of the Afro-American condition. We know why professional racists such as Charles Murray magnify these "racial" comparisons and distort the nation's record in solving the problems of the Afro-American lower class, but why on earth do liberals compulsively play this "two-nations" game? Do left-leaning social scientists get some deep-seated pleasure in exposing the "racial" failures of their society? With the triumph of capitalism and the cooptation of the Euro-American working class by the right, have the Afro-American poor become the last remaining stick with which the left can morally and politically beat the gloating corporate elite? Has "racial" analysis become not just a surrogate for class analysis, but the means whereby the left abandons issues of class while rhetorically seeming to remain radical? Why is the American left spending far more time on ever more intricate statistical exposures of inequalities between Afro-Americans and Euro-Americans than on the far greater and more fundamental problem of the nearly obscene growth in income disparity in the nation?

Which is the more important problem: the fact that the income gap between Afro-American and Euro-American workers has been *reduced* by only a few percentage points since 1974 or the fact that the income gap between the average worker and the average CEO has *increased* by 340 percent over the same period, from 35 times the earnings of the average worker in 1974 to over 120 times during the 1990s? The view that a focus on general inequality will lead to a neglect of the specific problem of the Afro-American poor is simply inane. Neglecting the broader problem of inequality in favor of an obsessive and unwittingly disparaging emphasis on the Afro-American poor not only obscures the real national problem but precludes an understanding of the Afro-American problem itself. As we saw in the first essay, the main problem of the Afro-

American poor, especially adults, is not lack of work. The problem, rather, is one they share increasingly with their Euro-American counterparts: when they work they simply do not earn enough to get out of poverty. The problem of the great majority of the Afro-American poor is the problem of income inequality. In a land of extraordinary abundance, the top fifth greedily takes so much that the bottom fifth, even working two jobs, sinks deeper and deeper into poverty.

There is another way in which the repeated and careless allegation of racism diverts attention from the real issues, recently pointed out by Paul Sniderman and Thomas Piazza. "The over-readiness to make blanket charges of racism—against people, points of view, institutions—has had an effect very nearly the opposite of the one intended," they lament. "How seriously can one take the idea of racism if everyone is said to be a racist?"[8] They then show that the idea of a pervasive covert racism in America in which prejudice against Afro-Americans is disguised as traditional American values is simply incorrect. Conservatives do not discriminate against Afro-Americans in their opposition to government activism; if anything, they discriminate in favor of Afro-Americans over Euro-Americans when discussing who should get support. There is, they found, a marked double standard in Euro-American attitudes toward Afro-Americans, but it has nothing to do with ideology. Instead, its source is precisely what believers in covert racism tend to neglect: low educational attainment. The advocates of the view that there is a new, subtle or covert racism, however, tend to disparage the positive role of education in eliminating prejudice, arguing that education merely teaches Euro-Americans how to conceal their true attitudes toward Afro-Americans. The result is another tragic paradox: "Seeing racism where it is not and failing to see it where it is," write Sniderman and Piazza, "some contemporary commentators on race have tended to ignore what they should criticize, and to criticize what they should defend."[9]

In addition to these pitfalls of ethnocomparison, there is the irony that the incessant comparison with the status of Euro-Americans as a measure of Afro-American progress is itself a highly patronizing view of Afro-Americans, since nearly all these indexes of progress are preferences dear to Euro-Americans, not Afro-Americans. Suppose it were the case, for example, that working-class Afro-Americans preferred socializing with friends and engaging in participative cultural activities such as dancing or attending blues concerts more than Euro-Americans, whereas their Euro-American counterparts preferred to invest more of their time and resources in ever more elaborate refinements of their homes, thereby enhancing the value of their major material asset? Were this the case, as some research suggests,[10] then assessing the progress of Afro-Americans in terms of their accumulation of material assets relative to Euro-Americans—as many "racism forever" analysts do—amounts to a rather vulgar form of ethnocentrism. One could just as reasonably gauge progress by looking at the frequency of friendships and the support of cultural activities.

Assessments of Afro-American development should pay far more attention to the growth and vitality of Afro-American cultural and social life, as well as Afro-Americans' involvement with and contributions to the mainstream culture. Social scientists who can only count, who cannot get through a Toni Morrison novel, who cannot tell a Langston Hughes or Rita Dove poem from a doggerel, who do not like the blues and are mystified by jazz, who think that cultural analysis should be left to people in departments of English, and whose strait-jacketed linearity of vision blinds them to the tragic dialectics of history and to the interplay of good and evil, should all get out of the business of assessing the progress of Afro-Americans, for they are the equivalent of a house painter with a computer-generated color chart trying to evaluate the progress of a Picasso.

I am not suggesting that we do not make comparisons with other groups when assessing the progress of Afro-Americans. However, I propose the following guidelines. As far as possible, comparisons should be made with the nation as a whole, rather than with Euro-Americans. National averages will, of course, include the influence of Afro-Americans. This should not be viewed as a liability, but an asset. It means that Afro-Americans are being compared to national norms or averages that embrace their contributions, whatever they may be. Such a comparative strategy is in keeping with the principle of infrangibility for which I argued in the fourth essay.

Finally, when comparisons with Euro-Americans and other ethnic groups are made, we should be sure that we are making meaningful comparisons. For instance, we should compare specific family types across ethnic groups, and not all families indiscriminately. To take a more invidious case, we should stop making comparisons between immigrant groups and Afro-Americans. There is a virtual academic and journalistic industry around this theme. Here are some generic examples: "The Cubans came here as refugees and look how successful they are; compare them to those Afro-Americans in Liberty City." Or, "Look at the wonderful Asian immigrants; Asians do it, why can't *they*?" Or, to take the most vicious of all such comparisons, "Look at the Jamaicans and other West Indians who are black like *them;* the West Indians do it. Why can't *they?*" The answer in every case is the same, and it is very simple: immigrants almost always do better than natives, and this holds equally for Euro-American natives in comparison with European and Asian immigrants. The Cuban Americans are not a success story, by any meaningful standard. Take any elite group from any society, resettle them in the most affluent society in the world, pamper them with the most extraordinarily generous resettlement grants in the history of refugees, and the interesting research question thereafter is not why Cubans have been so successful, but why have they not been more successful? While not resettled at taxpayers' expense, much the same holds for the Jamaican and Asian success stories. East Indians do well in Silicon Valley not because they are Indians—if this were the case, India would not have remained one of the poorest countries on earth after decades of development effort—but because they are highly motivated bourgeois immigrants as atypical of their homeland as they are of America.

IN INTERPERSONAL RELATIONS, FOLLOW A MODIFIED VERSION OF THE GOLDEN RULE

America's long history of segregation and ethnic prejudice toward Afro-Americans has created serious problems of interaction in face-to-face relations between Afro-Americans and Euro-Americans. We have seen that, in spite of this history, Afro-American and Euro-American individuals have been able to establish friendships across spatial ethnic boundaries to a surprising degree. Nonetheless, interpersonal relations are still plagued by distrust and confusion. If there is to be greater integration we must establish clear-cut rules to facilitate the crossing of ethnic barriers erected over the centuries. Simply ridding oneself of ethnic prejudice and enforcing laws against discrimination are not enough. Antidiscrimination laws tell us what not to do and how to behave under specified formal circumstances. They do not, and cannot, dictate how we are to interact in everyday encounters.

The most common current strategy employed by well-meaning liberals is some version of relativism. I think this creates more problems than it solves. The philosophical contradictions of relativism are well known and need no repetition here.[11] Doing unto others as one imagines they do unto themselves is an interactional strategy best left to professional anthropologists doing fieldwork among exotic tribes. Applying it in relations with fellow Americans can easily lead to patronizing behavior and misunderstanding. Afro-Americans, as I have emphasized throughout these essays, are not a different tribe or people with exotic cultural practices. They are, to repeat, among the most American of Americans, with as much variation as exists among Euro-Americans. These variations, however, are well within the cultural compass of all ordinary Americans.

Even where Afro-Americans appear to be very different, closer examination reveals that they are merely emphasizing, sometimes to extremes, certain values and traditions that are very American. Take the most limiting case of Afro-American youths from the inner city who live by the cool-pose street culture. Afro-American chauvinists, relativistic liberals, and racist pundits would all like to believe that their way of life is fundamentally different, although motives for believing this differ. For liberals, the motivation is the laudable but mistaken idea that this is the path to tolerance in a diverse society. In the recent pseudo-controversy about Ebonics we find the Afro-American bourgeois chauvinists' claim to exotic difference descending to outright buffoonery. And for racists, the motive is the intellectual and psychological need to confirm that "these people" are fundamentally and irreconcilably different.

But what is the real truth about underclass youth culture, the source of so much convoluted commentary? In one of the best recent studies of Afro-American ghetto youth, Carl Nightingale shows that, far from being different, the problem of Philadelphia inner-city youths is that they have too completely embraced and taken to their pathological extreme some of America's most cherished values: its materialism and conspicuous expenditure, its cutthroat competitiveness, its celebration of masculine bravado, its love of aggression, its Wall Street dictum that "greed is good."[12] In the pathologies of the urban underclass youth, Americans see the values of their own materialist culture in broad billboard colors, staring back at them. What is the difference between the gaudy display of jewelry by underclass young men and the vulgar extravagance of a Donald Trump? And where did underclass youth acquire their murderous code of responding to being dissed with the violent defense of their honor? They learned it, Nightingale shows, from spending countless hours in front of their television sets where Euro-American stars such as Marlon Brando, John Wayne, and Clint Eastwood—beloved by all Americans, especially conservatives, as models of manhood—portray the murderous honorific code of an earlier, even more violent underclass, the one we now celebrate as cowboys of the Wild West, or the more recent Euro-American "gangsta" heroes portrayed in movies glorifying everyone from the real Al Capone to the fictional Godfather. Violence is not an Afro-American pathology; it is an American pathology. One of the tragic contradictions of this culture is its obsession with violence and the instruments of destruction—its perverse tendency to decry and celebrate violence at one and the same time. Underclass youth, like the cowboys and Godfathers and more recent heroes played by actors such as Sylvester Stallone and Arnold Schwarzenegger, whom they slavishly emulate, expose this contradiction by their unrestrained destructiveness. An American suburbanite attempting to understand "these people" does not need an expert in urban anthropology or diversity training to advise him; all he has to do is recall his old John Wayne and Clint Eastwood movies.

What is true of the pathological side of Afro-American culture holds equally for all that is cherished within it. A Euro-American does not need an expert to get to the heart, the pivotal source, of stable working- and middle-class Afro-American life because that vital source is none other than Protestant Christianity itself. The secular Euro-American suburbanite who wants to understand "these people" need do no more than recall what she learned in Sunday school.

Insofar as Afro-Americans are different, then, they differ not in any exotic, inexplicable way, but merely in those quintessentially American values and traditions they have chosen to emphasize. It is for this reason that the best strategy in face-to-face relations between individuals from different ethnic groups is the good old Golden Rule—do unto others as you would wish them to do unto you. There are, to be sure, some limits to the working of this rule in a society as heterogeneous as America. The Golden Rule symmetrically implies that others should be allowed to do unto you as they would wish you to do unto them. In some circumstances, this might be a socially hazardous assumption. A masochistically inclined person is not one with whom I would wish to share the Golden Rule. Even more dangerous are cases where individuals live by a violent code of honor. If a man accidentally insults me, I am prepared to accept his explanation and apology and forget the matter. If a man lives by a violent honorific code, as do most members of many organized crime families as well as the thousands of members of street gangs around the nation, an accidental insult on my part will result in my head being blown off, since this is how such a person expects to be done unto in the event that he accidentally insults or "disses" another. We are back to the menacing stranger situation discussed earlier, where it was concluded that avoidance is the best strategy.

The heterogeneity problem in employing the Golden Rule strategy is not peculiar to relations with Afro-Americans. Indeed, it crops up more often in relations among different Euro-American ethnic groups. The Brahmin elite of Boston, or what is left of it, still do not comprehend the working-class Irish of South Boston and have long given up trying. If an upper-middle-class, Euro-American New Yorker ever needs an experience in interethnic relations, he should meet working-class Euro-Americans from the Deep South. They barely speak the same language, if I may exaggerate a bit. Like democracy, the Golden Rule may not be perfect, but in a multiethnic society such as America, it is by far the best and safest strategy when dealing with fellow citizens, especially ones as traditionally American as Afro-Americans. All that it requires is a modicum of good faith and a willingness to negotiate one's way around the tricky social situations inevitably encountered in heterogeneous societies.

THE PROBLEMS OF THE BOTTOM QUARTER OF
THE AFRO-AMERICAN POPULATION MUST BE MORE EFFECTIVELY
ADDRESSED AND NOT JUST TALKED ABOUT

◻◼ We have seen that a major problem of the poor, most of whom work, is that they simply do not earn enough on which to survive. I entirely agree with the sensible recommendation of Mary Jo Bane and David Ellwood that "people who play by the rules shouldn't lose the game." They add: "If we want to reinforce our values of family, work, independence, and responsibility, we cannot allow working families to be the poorest of the poor. We cannot abide a system that traps women who want to work on welfare. We cannot let absent parents shirk their responsibilities. We must ensure that if people work, they can achieve a measure of financial security. This means making work pay."[13]

◻◼ One major reason why the Afro-American poor who want to work cannot find adequate jobs is that the better-paying manufacturing jobs are located in suburban areas far from where they live. This geographical mismatch can be solved in two ways. One, recently emphasized by William Julius Wilson, is to create incentives for the relocation of better jobs to the inner cities, in addition to the institution of Depression-style government job creation schemes. I hold out little hope for this proposal, given the present mood of the country's economic and political leaders and the present trends in the American economy. The United States is now experiencing one of the highest growth rates since the postwar boom and outperforms all other industrial countries in the creation of jobs at all levels of income. Calls for more jobs under these circumstances are likely to fall on deaf ears.

The second alternative is to move the residents of the inner cities who want to work to where the remaining good industrial jobs are. This entails a well-organized housing voucher program with administrative support committed to steering low-income families into suburban areas and helping them adjust to the suburban environment. We know from the federal experimental housing programs of the seventies that without such administrative support and commitment to integration, vouchers will have no effect on the mobility of poor Afro-Americans out of the ghettos. In a definitive evaluation of the Federal Experimental Housing Alliance Program, in which housing voucher policies were systematically compared with other strategies for meeting the housing needs of the poor between 1970 and 1981, Raymond Struyk and Marc Bendick Jr. found that while housing vouchers provided housing equivalent to other programs at significantly lower costs, they have "little if any impact on locational choice, economic or racial concentration, or neighborhood quality" when administered in a "passive way."[14] Their study also demonstrated how segregation operates as a self-perpetuating process in urban America. Because low-income Afro-Americans live in segregated neighborhoods, they were simply unaware of the much better housing opportunities in nearby suburbs and were cut off from the information necessary in the search for adequate housing. What Struyk and Bendick wrote of segregated housing holds true of many other aspects of segregation in America: "The bifurcation of most urban areas into segregated housing markets constrains the perceived and actual housing opportunities of minorities. Segregation does this in part by limiting the development of informal, interpersonal-information networks, possibly the most effective source of search/move information due to its low cost and low-risk nature."[15]

While passive voucher programs have no effect on desegregation, the Gautreaux program in metropolitan Chicago, which actively promotes the goal of integration, shows without a doubt that this approach can work. What it requires is not just the provision of housing vouchers but a well-organized support system that helps families in their transition to the suburban areas with tight labor markets. Such a policy also has the laudable added effect of enhancing educational integration. If America's leaders are really serious about the goal of integration, then a major path in that direction will be the implementation of a national version of the Gautreaux program.

▪ For those remaining in the ghettos, out of either choice or necessity, one way to bring immediate, short-term relief will be to effectively apply the laws against the employment of illegal immigrant labor, and to reduce the inflow of low-skilled immigrants for at least a decade or so. As we saw in the first essay, immigration does not adversely affect the economy as a whole, but there is powerful evidence that it creates extreme hardship for the urban poor. Immigrants, especially illegal ones, migrate in disproportionate numbers to the urban centers where Afro-Americans are located. There they not only depress the wage level below what is required for survival, but by placing inordinate pressure on the low-income housing market, they greatly increase the cost of housing. I am not by any means suggesting a retreat from the nation's great tradition of immigration, only a temporary halt to the entry of unskilled labor, and the prosecution of employers who break existing laws against hiring illegal immigrants.

◼ In the final analysis, of course, the economic plight of unemployed youth in the inner cities will be solved only when they acquire the education and skills necessary for good jobs in a postindustrial economy. Job training programs may compensate to some degree for earlier educational failures, but the record of these programs is disappointing, with some studies even suggesting that they might be counterproductive.

But there can be no doubt that the major part of the solution must come from the lower quarter of the Afro-American population itself. As the recent work of economist Susan E. Mayer makes abundantly clear, even if the income of the poor were to double, the effects on their children and related social problems would be "relatively small." It would "reduce the high school dropout rate from 17.3 to 16.1 percent, and increase the mean years of education from 12.80 years to 12.83 years. Male idleness would increase, and the percentage of women who become single mothers would hardly change."[16] Mayer's research comes to another, rather ironic conclusion: the main reason that increasing income will have little effect on existing social problems is the very success of liberal welfare policies over the past thirty years. Food stamps, housing subsidies, AFDC, and Medicaid have met the basic "material needs" of all Americans. Children's opportunities remain unequal, but we have very nearly exhausted the potential of income transfers as a remedy for them. The irony is that liberals who see income transfers as the *only* effective means of solving the remaining social problems hate to be told that they have actually succeeded in what they have tried so hard to achieve, namely, the elimination of income inequality as the *primary* reason for social problems. Mayer's research seems to confirm the divine injunction that people "cannot live by bread alone," with her bracing conclusion that it is to "parents' noneconomic characteristics" that we must turn to find the solutions to the social problems that remain.[17]

At the heart of these problems among Afro-Americans, I argued in the first essay, is the *further* breakdown of the institutions of marriage and the family, an important dimension of which is the growing rate of out-of-wedlock teenage births. I emphasize "further" because this breakdown has been long in the making, originating in the deliberate, ethnocidal destruction of marriage, fatherhood, and the sanctity of the family as an inviolable social unit during the two and a half centuries of slavery. This is where this horrible tragedy began, disregarding the absurdities of revisionist historians of slavery on the subject, and the entire nation—but especially the Afro-American poor whose postslavery ancestors simply never recovered from the familial ethnocide—are paying the price of the rapacity and wickedness of Southern slaveholders, *and let no one forget it.* There is no known case in the history of human societies in which a people have, in such huge numbers, found themselves unable to practice and commit themselves to well-instituted social structures for the stable interaction of couples and the rearing of children. By whatever means, and through whatever new or existing social patterns, lower-class Afro-Americans have got to recommit themselves to the institutions of stable cohabiting unions and the joint custody and socialization of children by men and women.

The knee-jerk liberal view that there is no deep institutional problem here, that the familial and gender problems are all due to poverty and lack of jobs, is sociohistorical nonsense. The world is full of horribly poor people who have not abandoned the institutions of marriage and the family. Indeed, the comparative sociology of the family indicates that just the opposite is generally the case: poverty and other severe environmental shocks tend to reinforce the close and intimate bonds of marriage and family, people retreating to them as a haven from the hostile world around them. Instituting stable structures for the union of adults and the socialization of children—call them what one wishes—will not be sufficient to solve the problems of the underclass, or any other group of poor people, but it is an absolutely necessary precondition for any meaningful change.

With regard to the related problems of teenage births and high rates of dropping out from high school, where many of the problems of the inner cities originate, I have a specific proposal based partly on a study of a large urban high school that I conducted with my graduate students a few years ago. This proposal focuses on young men in contrast with the prevailing tendency of policymakers to emphasize female students in attempting to reduce teenage childbearing. The cool-pose culture of Afro-American youth focuses on two behavioral patterns that have become normative. One is a pattern of early sexuality in which older male youths sexually exploit younger girls. As repeated studies have by now demonstrated, early sexuality is not sanctioned in Afro-American lower-class adult culture—any more than it is among lower-class Euro-Americans — but it has become an ideal in the oppositional cool-pose culture of lower-class male youth. At its worst, this oppositional norm becomes a misogynistic compulsion to impregnate and destroy the life-chances of innocent young girls before they have time to realize just how disastrous are the sexual encounters they are being pressured into.

The second, related pattern is the obsessive involvement with sports on the part of Afro-American youth. This, too, must be seen not as a peculiar cultural pattern—since Euro-American youth are also sports involved—but the selective overemphasis of a dominant cultural norm. The patterns of precocious sexuality and overemphasis on sports are closely related. Many of the sports heroes at school tend to be the very same young men who sexually exploit and impregnate teenage girls. Getting a young girl pregnant and being good at sports, or just being sports-obsessed, are together the coolest things one can do and be.

A way must be found to break this devastating conjoint pattern. The solution is simple: make getting a high school girl pregnant socially costly and very uncool. The way to do this is for all schools to bar any male student who gets a female student pregnant—at any school—from playing any kind of varsity sport. Furthermore, a boy who gets a girl pregnant should be required to pay for part of the costs to the city or state of caring for the mother and child. Finally, any student who gets a female student pregnant for a second time—whether the same girl or another—should be immediately expelled.

These simple measures, all well within the law, will almost certainly have the immediate effect of reducing teenage pregnancy. Getting a girl pregnant will become a most uncool thing to do if the cost is giving up the dream of becoming a professional athlete. The fact that the most athletically talented students—the ones looked up to and emulated—will be the ones most committed to avoiding becoming fathers will immediately change the normative structure of the cool-pose culture. In time, avoiding pregnancy will become the cool thing to do.

SCHOOL INTEGRATION SHOULD REMAIN A PRIMARY GOAL BUT SHOULD BE PURSUED WITH FLEXIBILITY AND IMAGINATION

The Supreme Court's landmark decision in 1954, *Brown v. Board of Education,* initiated the social revolution that resulted in the integration of America's schools and other areas of social and economic life. For the next twenty years both Congress and the Court, in other rulings, extended this initiative. In spite of tremendous resistance and conflict over busing during the seventies, the long-term trend has been toward greater integration of the nation's schools.

However, a recent report by the Harvard Project on School Desegregation warns that this historic trend toward educational integration has been halted and is even being reversed in certain areas of the Deep South and in the nation's major cities.[18] The Reagan administration "turned actively against school desegregation in 1981" and the Supreme Court has reversed its former pro-desegregation stand, ruling in 1995 in *Missouri v. Jenkins* that court-ordered plans were temporary and could be discontinued before fully achieving their goals.[19]

As an ardent supporter of integration, I naturally share the concerns of the authors of this report, and I am in complete agreement with them that "there is no evidence that separate but equal today works any more than it did a century ago."[20] School integration is important, not only because it improves the educational opportunities for Afro-Americans, but also because it increases ethnic tolerance and gives Afro-Americans access to broader social networks. However, I think the authors of the Harvard Project grossly exaggerate in their claim that "in American race relations, the bridge from the twentieth century may be leading back into the nineteenth century."

Their own data fail to support such pessimism. One of their three measures of desegregation, "calculated as the number of students experiencing intense isolation in schools with less than one-tenth whites (i.e., 90–100 percent minority enrollment)" has fallen considerably—from 64 percent in 1968–69 to 34 percent in 1994–95)—and was still declining at the time of their study.[21] And on their two other indexes, the time-series changes are not statistically significant for Afro-American students. It is certainly the case that Latino students are being increasingly segregated, but this is the result of recent rapid changes in the size of the Latino population due mainly to immigration, and it makes little sense comparing this group either with the Afro-American case or with the nation's historic pattern of segregation.

Other data also fail to support this pessimistic picture of school integration. Thus, the Gallup poll on relations between Euro-Americans and Afro-Americans, which was conducted two months after the Harvard study, found that the oldest child of the family of 61 percent of Afro-Americans went to a school that was either mostly or nearly all Euro-American or was half Afro-American and half Euro-American. Equally remarkable is the fact that one in four of the oldest children of the Euro-American respondents went to a school that was either half Afro-American or nearly all Afro-American.[22] This does not look like a bridge to the nineteenth century, but rather a preparation for the twenty-first, when Euro-Americans will themselves decline as a proportion of the population.

The real problem, as the researchers of the Harvard Project acknowledge, is that current trends in segregation are largely a function of economic or class factors rather than of racist prejudices against Afro-American and Euro-American children going to school together.[23] Only 12 percent of Euro-Americans claim that they would object to sending their children to a school that was half Afro-American in enrollment.[24] The question, then, is how sensible it is to attempt to solve a class problem with the blunt and contentious instrument of school busing, which, in effect, is what the authors of the Harvard Project are insisting on.

Busing was an essential tool during the fifties, sixties, and seventies, when outright racism and unequal expenditures on schools were the central issues, and there are many areas of the country where this strategy is still essential. Today, however, it makes more sense in many cases to concentrate on those measures that will first integrate neighborhoods and occupations and let the integration of schools follow from them. The continued growth of the Afro-American middle class will naturally lead to greater educational integration as parents seek out and pay for better schools for their children, including private ones. Instead of moving children out of their neighborhoods to schools elsewhere, with all the friction that creates, we should concentrate our resources and energies on moving whole families out of the ghettos into integrated neighborhoods using a housing voucher plan along the Gautreaux model discussed earlier. There will, of course, be objections to such a policy from the remaining racist fifth of Euro-Americans as well as chauvinistic Afro-Americans and their leaders who have a vested interest in continued segregation, but this is where antidiscrimination laws and the forceful support of the majority of Americans who favor integration will be critical.

Finally, for Afro-Americans who remain in segregated neighborhoods either by choice or by necessity, the emphasis should be on the improvement of their schools, although this is likely to have only limited impact. It is now well established in the sociology of education that improved school resources have only negligible effects on the educational performance of schools. There is, however, one possible exception to this. For children from severely deprived Afro-American homes with multiple social problems, same-sex schools focusing on their special social, psychological, and educational needs might be a productive approach. It is too early to say whether experimental schools along these lines are effective, but the experience of other countries suggests that they are worth trying. Apart from such experiments, however, we should remain firmly committed to educational integration, although we must rely on a broader set of approaches to achieve it.

Now a backlash is growing among a minority of Afro-American leaders against desegregation measures such as court-ordered busing, reflected in increased pressure on the NAACP from both within and outside its ranks to alter its firm historic stance in favor of school integration. A strange bedfellowship has emerged between ethnic chauvinists such as Louis Farrakhan, the leader of the Nation of Islam, and Clarence Thomas, the conservative Supreme Court justice, in support for segregated Afro-American schools. Both argue that integration demeaningly suggests "that black students can achieve a quality education only in largely white schools."[25] This is arrant and hypocritical nonsense, as both men, who benefited greatly from the integration of the nation's schools, should know.

In the first place, school integration works not because the schools are better endowed but because the majority of children in such schools come from homes that better prepare their children to learn. It is no insult to lower-class Afro-Americans to acknowledge this axiom of educational sociology. Second, integration is to be pursued not only because it improves the education of the less privileged students, but because it brings Afro-Americans and Euro-Americans together at a time when their life-long attitudes are being formed. The sociological evidence is now overwhelming that Euro-Americans who went to school with Afro-Americans tend to be more tolerant and more in favor of greater educational and economic opportunities for Afro-Americans. At the same time, Afro-Americans who went to school with Euro-Americans not only make more friends among them, but establish important networks in the broader Euro-American group and learn to relate more easily to Euro-Americans. These networks and learned modes of interaction account for the fact that Afro-Americans who went to integrated schools perform better as adults even when they have performed poorly in educational terms.

It is truly extraordinary how few people—including avid supporters of school integration such as the scholars of the Harvard Project on School Desegregation—make the most important case for school integration, namely, that it is not only about improving the formal education of Afro-Americans, but also about providing an informal education in the ways and networks of the majority population. Integration is about the acquisition of social and cultural capital. The acquisition and application of this social and cultural capital will eventually obviate the need for affirmative action.

AFFIRMATIVE ACTION IS STILL NEEDED BUT SHOULD BE PHASED OUT OVER THE NEXT FIFTEEN YEARS, EVENTUALLY TO BE REPLACED BY A CLASS-BASED PROGRAM

The continued institutional and direct discriminatory biases against Afro-Americans and women in the workplace require that affirmative action continue for at least another fifteen years. This policy is a major factor in the rise of the Afro-American middle class, the single greatest success story of the past forty years.

The moral and political problems notwithstanding, the benefits of affirmative action far outweigh its costs. It must be viewed, however, as a medium-term solution. After a quarter of a century, the time has come to think about not only how to extend it for a while longer, but how to phase it out with as much grace and as little harm as possible. In doing so, we should consider both the areas to which the policy applies and the categories of persons who should benefit.

This is not the place to specify the areas of public and private life from which affirmative action is to be excluded or when this should be done. Such a complex matter requires detailed study on a case-by-case, level-by-level, industry-by-industry basis. One general guiding rule should be that access to the opportunities to acquire skills vital for competence in society remain as readily available as possible, whatever the costs, while rigorously universalistic criteria are used in assessing performance once entry has been granted.

Such a policy is "wasteful" only if we evaluate it in narrow recruitment terms. In broader, systemic terms over the long run, this approach is generally better in that the system will be seen as fair and legitimate. And it will lead to positive gains in the number of capable persons it screens in, more than compensating for the incompetents it fails to screen out of the initial recruitment process. The danger of this approach is the possibility of lowering the standards of the recruiting organization so as to maintain as large a proportion as possible of those who are recruited. But this is a failure of administration, and not an inherent flaw in the approach.

Regarding the categories of persons eligible for affirmative action, I think we can begin immediately to make changes that will reduce its costs.

It is ridiculous that all persons of so-called Hispanic ancestry are considered disadvantaged minorities. The only Hispanics who should qualify for affirmative action are Puerto Ricans, of any generation, and Mexican-Americans of second or later generations. First-generation persons of African ancestry from Africa, the Caribbean, and elsewhere should also be excluded from affirmative action recruitment, although they may be considered where diversity—a secondary goal—is the objective, as should underrepresented Euro-Americans. Like Mexican-Americans, their children and later generations should be eligible in light of the persistence of racist discrimination in America. In addition, all Asians except Chinese-Americans descended from pre-1923 immigrants should be immediately excluded from all affirmative action considerations.

The next phase of change should begin about five years from now, when all women and minority persons currently eligible for affirmative action who are from upper-middle-class backgrounds or higher—that is, those from families with household incomes above $75,000 in 1997 dollars—should be excluded from affirmative action considerations. Ten years from now we could move to a third phase of change, when only disadvantaged minorities and women from working- and lower-class backgrounds should be considered for affirmative action. At that time we could begin to phase into the program all other American-born persons of lower-class background. Finally, fifteen years from now all ethnic criteria should be dropped from affirmative action consideration and the program should be converted to a wholly class-based program. From that point onward the nation should institute an affirmative action program for all American-born persons from poor families. This program should be indefinite, lasting as long as there is poverty in the midst of affluence.

ULTIMATELY, INTEGRATION MUST MEAN INTERMARRIAGE

People who discuss "race" tend to skirt one central issue. Of all groups of persons in America, Afro-Americans are unusual in the low rate of intermarriage with other ethnic groups. Miscegenation was, of course, the ultimate taboo in the South and in the nation generally. The taboo's purposes were acidly clear: on the one hand, it gave meaning to the racist idea of "racial purity" and pollution. "Whites" of presumably "pure" European stock were to avoid at all costs pollution with Afro-Americans. One drop of the latter's blood immediately made the offspring "non-white," touched by the tar brush, forever "black."

On the other hand, it also served a sociopolitical function: Afro-Americans were quintessentially the people who did not belong, the domestic outsiders who by their very exclusion defined who truly belonged. Afro-Americans were the unfree, the degraded, the people whom "we" do not marry. We the people, the citizenry, were a "white" nation.

There is no gainsaying the fact that in every known human society, a group of people are never considered truly a part of those who constitute the people until they are considered people whom "we" marry. The evidence from historical linguistics suggests that these associations go back as far as extant human history. Thus, in the Indo-European family of languages the very earliest meanings of the word *free* were "belonging to the people," which was synonymous with those whom we "hold dear," who are also those "not in bondage," those who are "beloved"—no, Toni Morrison did not originate this idea—and, above all, those whom we marry.

In the first essay I pointed out the ironic developments in this area of ethnic relations: Afro-American leaders are now among the most vociferous defenders of the one-drop rule and of endogamous marriages. But, as in so many other areas, Afro-American leadership is out of touch with the attitudes and behavior of ordinary Afro-Americans as well as Euro-Americans. Sociologists have emphasized the low rate of "interracial" marriages even after taking into account compositional factors such as population size.[26] However, within recent decades there has been a major shift not only in the attitudes of Euro-Americans and Afro-Americans toward interethnic dating and marriage, but in their actual practices. It is these recent developments that should be emphasized and encouraged by anyone seriously committed to integration.

There have been striking changes in attitudes toward mixed marriages in the past two decades: the June 1997 Gallup poll previously cited found that 77 percent of Afro-Americans and 61 percent of Euro-Americans now express approval of such marriages, up from 61 percent among Afro-Americans and 25 percent among Euro-Americans in 1972.[27] Even more telling are the differences between age groups: Euro-Americans over age 50 are still largely opposed to such marriages, only 36 percent agreeing with them; but the figure increases to 68.4 percent in the 35–49 age group, and increases further to 82.7 percent among Euro-Americans between 18 and 34. We find the same age-related differences among Afro-Americans: a little under two-thirds of the over-50 age group, slightly over three-quarters of those between 35 and 49 and 86 percent of those between 18 and 34 approve of mixed marriages.[28] What these figures suggest is that the potential for a truly integrated, intermarried America already exists. What is more, practice is also changing, although in complicated ways: according to Douglas Besharov and Timothy Sullivan, 12 percent of all new marriages by Afro-Americans in 1993, as distinct from all existing marriages, were with Euro-Americans, which was four and a half times the rate in 1970.[29] They also emphasize "another enormously portentous change," the fact that current mixed marriages have "an equal likelihood of producing children" as intraethnic Euro-American marriages, unlike mixed marriages of the past, which were often second marriages, "obviating the issue of having children." The dating patterns of younger Americans suggest not only that this rate is likely to escalate in coming years, but that it belies an even greater degree of cohabitation taking place between Euro- and Afro-Americans.[30]

The neglect or outright hostility of most Afro-American leadership to marital integration marks another sad retreat toward separatism and away from what the mass of Afro-Americans whom they claim to lead really believe and want—as does the pernicious opposition of the national association of Afro-American social workers to "cross-racial" adoption. It is a wholly self-interested position, since the only people likely to be adversely affected by an increase in intermarriage are those Afro-American leaders who capitalize on their broker role between the "two hostile nations," the more separate the better.

All other American ethnic groups, including the more recently arrived Asians, are intermarrying at record rates, partly for the age-old reasons of inclusion mentioned above, but also for another, more immediately beneficial reason discussed in the essay on affirmative action. When one marries into another ethnic group, one greatly expands one's social networks. Every spouse brings a cultural dowry of social networks and cultural capital in the form of childrearing patterns, and it is to reap this rich harvest of social and cultural capital that Americans of all other ethnic groups are busily intermarrying with each other, fully exploring what the sociologist Mary Waters calls their "ethnic options."[31]

Afro-Americans, more than any other group of Americans, should be aware of the deleterious consequences of exclusion from these broader networks and pools of cultural information: antimiscegenation and segregation laws were explicitly aimed at keeping them isolated from these sociocultural resources. As the network sociologist Edward Laumann and his team observed in their recent study of American sexuality, "The small number of interracial partnerships is part of a larger social process that functions to maintain social 'distance' between racial groups since sexual partnerships (and to an even greater extent marriages) often create social bridges between families and groups of acquaintances."[32]

Affirmative action, I have argued, partly compensates for the absence of these acquired affinity networks. However, it is a poor substitute for intermarriage, for while it may partly compensate for attenuated social networks it does nothing to make up for the cultural isolation of Afro-Americans from the nation's rich resources of childrearing patterns. A false and dangerous kind of cultural pride leads Afro-Americans to believe that they have within their traditions sufficient resources to enable them to neglect the abundance around them. This is not a cultural deprivation argument but rather a resource-utilization view of our rich multicultural society.

Afrocentrists and other chauvinists have got to learn that the whole point of diversity is not to separate and endogamously purify, but to share and cross-pollinate. Even if Afro-Americans assumed they were the most successful group socially and culturally, they would still be in serious error to exclude themselves from the intimate networks and cultural resources of other groups, especially the dominant one. It is no accident that Jewish- and Japanese-Americans are among the two most successful ethnic groups in America, as well as being the two most exogamous in spite of the fact that their source cultures strongly prohibit exogamy.

The Jewish- and Japanese-American marital behavior fully exemplifies the American tendency toward what Herbert Gans calls "symbolic ethnicity."[33] This is the tendency to completely reorient one's ethnic allegiance in a manner that facilitates rather than interferes with one's integration into, and full competence in, the dominant society. What this means is that outmoded traditions are sentimentalized but kept at bay, and ritual patterns are selectively retained or ruthlessly abandoned depending on how well they serve the material and social interests of members. Indeed, the most vital traditional foundation of the group may be abandoned altogether and replaced by new sociopolitical markers of ethnic identification, the most dramatic case in point being secular Jews' replacement of synagogue worship with support for Israel as their primary identity marker, a replacement that served the double purpose of modernizing their ethnic base and moving them into the interstices of American politics. And of course, accompanying all this was an escalation of their intermarriage rate, the threat of bereaved fathers saying kaddish notwithstanding.

At the same time, Jews, like Japanese-Americans, demonstrate that high out-marriage rates do not mean the death of the ethnic group, as chauvinistic leaders simplistically believe and intone. Jewish ethnicity is alive and well, so much so that in spite of being one sixth of the population size of Afro-Americans, Jews exercise far greater power on their national government: far more aid goes to the small state of Israel than to the entire plague-ridden and desperately needy continent of Africa.

The lesson of these successful ethnic groups is unambiguously clear: if you want in, you marry in. And if you come from a group with impoverished social networks, you have even more reason to do so. It is not as if Afro-American leaders are unaware of the great value of cultural dowries. The problem is that they have too often attempted to acquire them illicitly. It is a matter of some notoriety among elite Afro-Americans that the men of this group have disproportionately relied on Euro-American lovers to provide them with a link to networks and cultural information that are critical for their success. This pattern goes all the way back to Booker T. Washington and Frederick Douglass, the latter having the decency to do the right thing and marry the Euro-American who brought him the cultural dowry he so brilliantly exploited. The recent exposé of the late Ron Brown's complicated love affair with Texas businesswoman Nolanda Hill, a well-connected and culturally as well as economically savvy Euro-American on whom he heavily depended for counsel, funds, and contacts, is merely the tip of a long historical iceberg.[34] The role of Euro-American women in the history of Afro-American advancement is a major episode in American cultural history waiting to be written. It is time, however, for such underhanded practices to stop. After nearly four centuries of imposed social—although not sexual and reproductive—endogamy, Afro-Americans could do with a good deal of exogamy.

Incidentally, marrying out will not only socially and culturally enrich the aggregate of Afro-Americans, but will also solve a major social problem that increasingly besets Afro-American women, especially those of the middle and upper classes. This is the chronic shortage of marriageable men, a problem that is getting daily worse as Afro-American women outcompete their male counterparts in the educational system and increasingly in the corporate world. The high endogamy rate of Afro-American women—perhaps the highest of any Western industrial subpopulation—is not due to any marked nonpreference for them among the men of other ethnic groups. It is time for Afro-American women to expand their options by widening the network of men whom they are prepared to marry. They may have no choice in the matter. The increasing tendency for Afro-American middle-class men to marry out, or to ruin their marriages by illicit relations with attractive unmarried Afro-American women (exclusively available to them in large numbers) as well as with Euro-American women, is turning a bad marriage market into a virtual slump.

Afro-American men and women, then, have every reason to out-marry: it will enrich the repertoire of childrearing practices among them; it will vastly expand their weak social ties and other social capital; it will help to solve the internal crisis of gender and marital relations among them; and it will complete the process of total integration as they become to other Americans not only full members of the political and moral community, but also people whom "we" marry. When that happens, the goal of integration will have been fully achieved.

AMERICAN CHRISTIANITY SHOULD BEGIN TO RID ITSELF OF THE SCANDAL OF SEGREGATION

There have been many ironies and contradictions in the long history of Christianity, but foremost among them must be its role in America's tortured ethnic history. The Puritans' persecution of Quakers and other dissenters soon after achieving their own religious independence in America and the nativist antagonism to Catholics and Jews suggest that these contradictions are by no means restricted to relations between Euro-Americans and Afro-Americans. Nonetheless, it is in these relations that we find Christianity both at its best and at its worst. At its best, Christianity offered comfort, solace, and dignity to Afro-Americans during their long time on the cross of slavery, rural semiserfdom, and racist persecution; it also eventually provided the organizational framework and leadership for the triumphant civil rights movement.

But we find Christianity being practiced at its worst in the way the creed was used by racists to justify racism, lynchings, and social obscenities such as the KKK, a disproportionate number of whose leaders were Southern clergymen. Sadly, this pattern persists in the continued segregation of the Christian churches of America. The Christian churches, as the Gallup Poll reported in June 1997, together remain the one "highly segregated" major institution of American public life. In contrast with the dramatic changes in all other areas in recent decades, 73 percent of Euro-Americans and 71 percent of Afro-Americans still go to churches that are, respectively, almost or nearly all Euro-American and Afro-American.[35] Surely, one of the greatest ironies of modern America, the most devotedly

Christian nation in the West, is that its army, the most powerful instrument of war and destruction in the history of mankind, is the nation's model of integration while its churches remain the last bastion of "racial" segregation.

Both Afro-Americans and Euro-Americans now promote this pattern of segregation. It is time to remind the clergymen and worshipers of America that this practice is in complete opposition to the most basic tenets of their creed. Christianity is nothing if not a profoundly universalist religion. Its definitive break with Judaism, under the leadership of Paul—"the apostle to the Gentiles"—was on precisely this issue. In Christ, said Paul, "there is neither Jew nor Greek, there is neither slave nor free, there is neither male nor female." What is more, the fellowship that the faith demands is one not only in spirit and belief but in the corporate body of Christ. Segregation is outright un-Christian, and both Afro-Americans and Euro-Americans are guilty of it.

This is, of course, all very naive sociologically. What about the hardnosed social science accounts of sects and cults, and of religion as a conservative force around which a community's values converge? I know all that, but it is just the problem: we have all come to talk about religion as if we are professional sociologists. It is perhaps appropriate, then, that a professional sociologist remind Americans how to talk about religion and the behavior of the church: idealistically and moralistically. What ought to be and what is are separate epistemological realms. Religion is about what ought to be. I am not here attempting to explain with my sociological tool kit of "value-free," hardheaded, scientific survey and historical data why the Christian church has failed miserably in the promotion of ethnic fellowship and is now the mainstay of segregation. I am, instead, talking to readers of the most Christian nation on earth the way they talk religiously. Segregation is a sinful denial of everything Christianity stands for, and it is time the churches of America return to the spirit and partial start of the sixties in helping to desegregate the country, beginning with the desegregation of churches themselves.

I strongly suspect that this change might be easier than people imagine. The more moderate sections of both the Afro-American and Euro-American churches offer distinct spiritual and ritual practices and versions of the faith that may appeal to significant numbers of people in the other ethnic group. Many Euro-Americans, especially younger people, are likely to find the more intense spirituality and aesthetic emphasis of the Afro-American church far more appealing than the churches in which they grew up. On the other hand, a growing number of Afro-Americans, especially those from the middle classes, might find the liberal Protestant and Catholic churches more ritually and theologically uplifting, not to mention the possibility of greater intimate fellowship with their middle-class Euro-American church members.

WHILE FULLY RECOGNIZING PERSISTING ETHNIC PROBLEMS, WE SHOULD STOP EXAGGERATING THEIR INTRACTABILITY AND START EMPHASIZING THEIR SOLUTIONS BY FOCUSING ON WHAT WORKS

Failure to understand and sympathize with the contradictory nature, and often paradoxical outcomes, of ethnic change penalizes precisely those organizations and members of American society that are most willing to take its egalitarian creed seriously and have tried hardest to make it work. To embrace change is to embrace conflict, and it is natural to resent the pain that goes with it. But when internal resentment overwhelms any recognition of what has been achieved, and outsiders mock the missteps and turmoil besetting those who attempt to change, there is little motivation to try harder. A conservative firm or college or newspaper may well find, as many have already done, that the best way to keep out of the "racial" limelight is to adopt a strategy of minimal contact with Afro-Americans. No Afro-American editors or executives, no accusation of racism, no pain, and no embarrassing books by aggrieved bourgeois Afro-Americans about "volunteer slavery." Affirmative action increased the costs of such a strategy, but with the current assault on this policy, the minimal-contact/minimal pain approach may well become the most appealing for many organizations and people.

The insistence that things are getting worse when in fact they are getting better, though more complicated and conflictual, also has a debilitating effect on Afro-Americans and Euro-Americans who do wish to get on with the task of Afro-American integration and improvement of the condition of Afro-Americans in poverty. If, after forty years of trying, the only news is an endless litany of inter-ethnic failure, many otherwise well-meaning Euro-Americans, and an increasing number of Afro-Americans, will understandably conclude that ethnic harmony is a hopeless dream and that only some form of ethnic separation, with the lines fairly drawn, will work. Separate but truly equal becomes the new order of the day. Indeed, this is the position taken by the growing school of Afro-American critical race theorists.

As Sniderman and Piazza have correctly observed, while the "commitment of many Americans to racial equality is qualified and conflicted," the real problem today is the fact that "the politics of race is emotionally charged, and differences in opinion and inclination over highly publicized issues are therefore read, by commentators on all sides, as evidence of deep and lasting cleavages."[36] It may well be that the politics of "race," not the complex realities of ongoing interethnic relations, is driving America's "racial crisis."

Euro-Americans should appreciate the fact that Afro-Americans are not necessarily exaggerating their plight or denying the obvious when they complain that the situation remains painful or seemingly unchanged. For many poor, working Afro-Americans trapped in inner-city neighborhoods, the situation has indeed gotten worse, their lives a daily struggle with economic insecurity burdened by the nightmarish shuffle between the lawless terror of the underclass and the legalized terror of unrelentingly racist police.

However, Afro-Americans tempted down the separatist path have got to understand that no society has ever succeeded in treating its minority groups separately and equally. Egalitarian ethnic separatism, as we cautioned earlier, is a dangerous myth. The comparative sociology of ethnic relations strongly suggests that separate always means unequal for the mass of minority group members. The only members of minority groups to benefit from such a system are leaders who enjoy the collective spoils permitted by the dominant group as a payoff for keeping the groups separate, ensuring the continuation of the deprived condition of the majority, a deprivation which, in turn, becomes the rhetorical fodder for the coopted separatist leadership. In the first essay, we found a classic instance of this in the gerrymandering of the Georgia legislative seats by Afro-American political leaders in collusion with conservative Republicans.

Above all, what both Euro-American and Afro-American leaders must learn is to tone down the overheated rhetoric of "race," especially in the political arena, and to acknowledge a major aspect of Euro-American attitudes recently reinforced by the research of Sniderman and Piazza: "the extent to which whites can be induced to change their minds about racial attitudes." Group prejudice remains an important factor in Euro-Americans' attitudes toward Afro-Americans, especially on issues relating to social welfare, but the pliability of even the most prejudiced of attitudes is remarkable. Most Euro-Americans can be easily talked out of nearly all their negative positions. This encouraging feature of ethnic prejudice strongly suggests the need for cool-headed dialogue. As Sniderman and Piazza rightly conclude, "Since preferences are pliable on both sides of racial issues, majorities can be assembled either in favor of or in opposition to many public policies aimed to assist blacks. Our future is not fixed by our past."[37]

To acknowledge the destructive impact of the past and present conditions and the ways in which dysfunctional adaptations lead to self-victimization by some members of a collectivity is not to blame the victim. This is as absurd as saying that we are blaming when we recommend to a self-destructive victim of rape or child-abuse—an all too frequent tragedy—that they seek therapy to change their behavior.

To identify the source of one's problems is not necessarily to identify the agent for change. To return to the child abuse analogy, it is, tragically, true that only the victim can change him- or herself. This is not to deny that the abusive parent is also responsible for facilitating the process of healing. The analogy holds directly for relations between Afro-Americans, who were violently abused for most of their history in this country, and Euro-Americans, who collectively and individually abused and exploited Afro-Americans and gained collectively from it. Hence, a strong commitment to socioeconomic change that equalizes the opportunities of Afro-Americans is as much the responsibility of Euro-Americans as is the full assumption for healing themselves and changing their situation—especially their dysfunctional gender and familial relations—the only meaningful path for Afro-Americans.

Nonetheless, one painful truth from the comparative sociology of intergroup relations must be acknowledged by Afro-Americans: except for those now rare cases where a minority constitutes the elite, the burden of ethnic change always rests on a minority group. Although both Euro-Americans and Afro-Americans have strong mutual interests in solving their most serious ethnic problem, and the solution must eventually come from both, Afro-Americans will have to play the major role in achieving this objective, not only because they have more to gain from it, but because Euro-Americans have far less to lose from doing nothing. It is Afro-Americans who must take the initiative, suffer the greater pain, define and offer the more creative solutions, persevere in the face of obstacles and paradoxical outcomes, insist that improvements are possible, and maintain a climate of optimism concerning the eventual outcome.

And it is they, more than any other group of Americans, who must draw on their deep spiritual faith and heritage of creative dissent in leading the way toward Martin Luther King Jr.'s glorious ideal of America as the "beloved community": free, egalitarian, and as integrated in its social life as it already is in the triumphant global culture that Afro-Americans have done so much to fashion.

Introduction

1. Paul M. Sniderman and Thomas Piazza, *The Scar of Race* (Cambridge: Harvard University Press, 1993), p. 178.

2. Ritchie Witzig, "The Medicalization of Race: Scientific Legitimazation of a Flawed Social Contact," *Annals of Internal Medicine* 125:8 (1996): 675-679.

3. National Opinion Research Center, *General Social Survey, 1994*, University of Chicago.

1. The Paradoxes of Integration

1. I called attention to the paradoxical nature of the Afro-American condition and of attitudes toward them in my article "The Paradox of Integration," published in the *New Republic*, November 6, 1995, pp. 24-27. Others have been equally struck by the paradoxical nature of "racial" attitudes and behavior. Lawrence Bobo, for example, comments on the paradox of growing commitment to the principles of racial equality and integration along with opposition to specific policies aimed at improving the economic situation of Afro-Americans. See his "Group Conflict, Prejudice and the Paradox of Contemporary Racial Attitudes," in Phyllis Katz and Dalmas Taylor, eds., *Eliminating Racism: Profiles in Controversy* (New York: Plenum Press, 1988), p. 88. Paul Sniderman and Thomas Piazza have attempted to explain this paradox, but in the process unearthed several more, such as the contradictory positions of conservatives and liberals on the issue of government help for Afro-Americans, on which see their *The Scar of Race* (Cambridge: Harvard University Press, 1993), especially chapter 3.

Paradox has characterized the Afro-American experience and American racism from the earliest period of American history. American democracy, for example, first emerged on a large scale in the slave-holding state of Virginia precisely because of the existence of Afro-American slaves who made possible a bond of solidarity among equally free "white" citizens, the "we" in "we the people," who belonged, versus "them," the domestic enemy, the black slaves who were the quintessential outsiders defining by their otherness and slaveness the meaning of freedom and citizenship. For the classic study on this ultimate paradox of "race" in America, see Edmund Morgan, *American Slavery, American Freedom: The Ordeal of Colonial America* (New York: Norton, 1975).

2. See Michael B. Preston, Lenneal J. Henderson Jr., Paul Puryear, et al., eds., *The New Black Politics* (New York: Longman, 1987); Thomas E. Cavanagh, *The Impact of the Black Electorate* (Washington, D.C.: Joint Center for Political Studies, 1984); Patricia Gurin, Shirley Hatchett, and James S. Jackson, *Hope and Independence: Blacks' Struggle in Two Party Politics* (New York: Russell Sage Foundation, 1988); Michael Dawson, *Behind the Mule: Race and Class in African-American Politics* (Princeton: Princeton University Press, 1994); and National Research Council, "Black Political Participation," in Gerald D. Jaynes and Robin Williams, eds., *A Common Destiny: Blacks and American Society* (Washington, D.C.: National Academy Press, 1989), chapter 6.

3. The Afro-American population as of June 1997 was 33,856,000 persons, or 12.7 percent of the total U.S. population of 267,177,000 persons. It is now well established, however, that the Afro-American population is undercounted, so it is reasonable to round their percentage of the population up to 13. Source: U.S. Bureau of the Census, Population Division, *U.S. Population Estimates by Age, Sex, Race and Hispanic Origin,* June 1997.

4. For an excellent collection of studies on the influence of Afro-American popular culture and the struggle for acknowledgment of this influence in the media, see Jannette L. Dates and William Barlow, eds., *Split Image: African Americans in the Mass Media* (Washington, D.C.: Howard University Press, 1993).

5. Albert Murray, *The Omni-Americans* (New York: Outerbridge & Dienstfrey, 1970), p. 22; see also Mabel M. Smythe, ed., *The Black American Reference Book* (Englewood Cliffs, N.J.: Prentice Hall, 1976); Henry Louis Gates Jr., *The Signifying Monkey: A Theory of African-American Literary Criticism* (New York: Oxford University Press, 1988).

6. Survey results cited in *U.S. News and World Report,* March 31, 1997, p.18.

7. David Samuels, "The Real Face on Rap," *New Republic,* November 11, 1991.

8. Times Mirror Center for the People and the Press, *The Pulse of Europe: A Survey of Political and Social Values and Attitudes* (Washington, D.C.: Times Mirror Center, 1991).

9. Charles C. Moskos and John Sibley Butler, *All That We Can Be: Black Leadership and Racial Integration the Army Way* (New York: Basic Books, 1996), p. 2.

10. See also Bureau of the Census, *Current Population Reports: The Black Population of the United States, 1994 & 1993,* Table E; and James P. Smith and Finis R. Welch, *Closing the Gap: Forty Years of Economic Progress for Blacks* (Santa Monica: Rand, 1986), chapter 3.

11. Jonathan Kozol, *Death at an Early Age: The Destruction of the Hearts and Minds of Negro Children in Boston Public Schools* (Boston: Houghton Mifflin, 1967); idem, *Savage Inequalities: Children in America's Schools* (New York: Harper Perennial, 1992).

12. David Armor, "Why Is Black Educational Achievement Rising?" *Public Interest,* Summer 1992: 65-80.

13. Armor, ibid. More recently, The Education Trust, an education advocacy organization, has raised the alarm that the gap in reading and math scores increased

slightly between 1988 and 1992. However, it is much too early to figure out what the long-term trend is. Since 1992 the gap has begun to narrow once again, as the Education Trust's own data clearly show. See *Education Watch: The 1996 Education Trust State and National Data Book* (Washington, D.C.: The Education Trust, 1996), pp. 4-5.

14. Gary Orfield, Mark D. Bachmeier, David R. James, and Tamela Eitle, *Deepening Segregation in American Public Schools* (Cambridge: Harvard Project on School Desegregation, 1997), p.1.

15. I will discuss these gender differences at greater length in the second volume of this trilogy. For now, see Orlando Patterson, "The Crisis of Gender Relations Among African Americans," in Anita Hill and Emma Coleman Jordan, eds., *Race, Gender and Power in America: The Legacy of the Hill-Thomas Hearings* (New York: Oxford University Press, 1995), pp. 56-104.

16. See Bart Landry, *The New Black Middle Class* (Berkeley: University of California Press, 1987).

17. Smith and Welch, *Closing the Gap*, p. 19.

18. See Landry, *The New Black Middle Class;* Melvin Oliver and Thomas Shapiro, *Black Wealth/ White Wealth: A New Perspective on Racial Inequality* (New York: Routledge, 1997), especially chapter 5. These authors emphasize lower estimates and draw attention to the fragile economic base of the Afro-American middle class. In contrast, see Stephan and Abigail Thernstrom, who view these developments in more optimistic terms: *America in Black and White: One Nation Indivisible* (New York: Simon & Schuster, 1997), chapter 7.

19. Bureau of the Census, Current Population Reports, Series P-20, *The Black Population in the U.S.: March 1995,* unpublished on-line data: Table 2, "Selected Economic Characteristics of Persons and Families, by Sex and Race: March 1995."

20. Bureau of the Census, Income Statistics Branch/HHES, Current Population Reports, Series P-60, Historical Income Tables—Households, Table H-3.

21. Ibid., Tables 13 & 14. As of March 1995, 36 percent of year-round, full-time male workers belonged among the top four white-collar occupations of the Census Bureau. The median incomes of these middle occupational categories ranged from $24,336 for men who were administrative support workers, including clerical workers, to $34,858 for men in executive, administrative and managerial positions. If we exclude men in these occupations without a high-school diploma, the percent falls to 35. Using the more limiting criterion of persons with some college education, the percent is reduced to 26, but this is clearly too restrictive.

22. Ibid., Tables 12 & 13.

23. Sharon M. Collins, *Black Corporate Executives: The Making and Breaking of a Black Middle Class* (Philadelphia: Temple University Press, 1997).

24. Oliver and Shapiro, *Black Wealth/White Wealth*, p. 103.

25. On which see, Claude S. Fischer, Michael Hout, Martin Sanchez, et al., *Inequality by Design: Cracking the Bell Curve Myth* (Princeton: Princeton University Press, 1996), especially pp. 107-28.

26. The Gini coefficient, one of the most commonly used measures of inequality, was always higher among Afro-Americans than Euro-Americans, and the internal inequality has been growing. Thus in 1967 the rate for Euro-Americans was .391 and it increased to .442 in 1995; for Afro-Americans the respective ratios were .432 and .468. Source: Bureau of the Census, Income Statistics Branch/ HHES, Current Population Reports, Series P-60, Historical Income Tables—Households, Table H-4. (Unpublished on-line census data, December 1996.)

27. Bureau of the Census, Income Statistics Branch/HHES, Historical Income Tables (Unpublished on-line data, December 1996), Table F-7.

28. Bureau of the Census, Income Statistics Branch/ HHES, Current Population Reports, Series P-60, Historical Income Tables (Washington, D.C.: U.S. Bureau of the Census, 1996), Household Table 5.

29. Bureau of the Census, Income Statistics Branch/ HHES, Current Population Reports, Series P-60, Historical Income Tables—Persons (Washington, D.C.: U.S. Bureau of the Census, 1996), Table P-13.

30. Ibid.

31. Bureau of the Census, *The Black Population in the United States, 1994 and 1993,* Table 28, pp. 121-25.

32. Bureau of the Census, *Poverty in the United States: 1988 and 1989,* p. 2.

33. Daniel H. Weinberg, "Press Briefing on 1995 Income, Poverty and Health Insurance Estimates" (Bureau of the Census, HHES Division, September 26, 1996). I have estimated the impact on the Afro-American poverty rate by taking account of the greater reliance on these noncash payments by the Afro-American population. For the entire U.S. population, the rates in 1995 declined from the official rate of 13.8 percent to a low of 9 percent depending on how much noncash transfers are considered. See the chart accompanying Weinberg's press release: "Poverty Rates Using Experimental Definitions of Income: 1959-1995."

34. William Julius Wilson, *When Work Disappears: The World of the New Urban Poor* (New York: Knopf, 1996), p. xix.

35. William Julius Wilson, *The Truly Disadvantaged: The Inner City, the Underclass, and Public Policy* (Chicago: University of Chicago Press, 1987); idem, *The Declining Significance of Race: Blacks and Changing American Institutions* (Chicago: University of Chicago Press, 1980).

36. For the very best study of the impact of immigration on unskilled Afro-American labor market prospects, see Roger Waldinger, *Still the Promised City? Afro-Americans and New Immigrants in Postindustrial New York* (Cambridge: Harvard University Press, 1996). In general, economists seem lost in a sea of technicalities on this subject, unable to distinguish local, especially metropolitan, from national impacts or the causal links, if any, between immigrant and native worker mobility. See George Borjas, "The Economics of Immigration," *Journal of Economic Literature* 32 (December 1994): 1667–1717, and more recently, his "New Economics of Immigration," *Atlantic Monthly,* November 1996.

37. Harry J. Holzer, "Black Employment Problems: New Evidence, Old Questions," *Journal of Policy Analysis and Management* 13:4 (fall 1994): 699-722. See also J. Kirschenman and K. Neckerman, "We'd Love to Hire Them But...The Meaning of Race for Employers," in Christopher Jencks and Paul E. Peterson, eds., *The Urban Underclass* (Washington, D.C.: The Brookings Institution, 1991), 203-32, and Richard B. Freeman, "Employment and Earnings of Disadvantaged Young Men in a Labor Shortage Economy," in idem, pp.103-21.

38. Bureau of the Census, March Current Population Survey, Table 18 (Unpublished on-line data, April 1997). The figure is lower for Afro-Americans.

39. Rebecca M. Blank, *It Takes a Nation: A New Agenda for Fighting Poverty* (New York: Russell Sage & Princeton University Press, 1997), pp. 18-20.

40. Ibid., p. 39.

41. National Research Council, *Risking the Future: Adolescent Sexuality, Pregnancy, and Childbearing* (Washington, D.C.: National Academy Press, 1987), pp. 83-90.

42. S. J. Ventura, J. A. Martin, S. C. Curtin et al. "Report of Final Natality Statistics, 1995," *Monthly Vital Statistics Report* 45:11(S) (June 1997), p.8 and tables 10, 11, and 14; see also Blank, *It Takes a Nation,* Table 1.1, p. 35.

43. See Waldinger, *Still the Promised City?,* especially chapters 5 & 6.

44. See, in particular, Wilson, *When Work Disappears,* chapter 3.

45. Blank, *It Takes a Nation,* pp. 79-80.

46. I draw here on several major recent joint studies on this subject: National Research Council, *Risking the Future;* Rebecca A. Maynard, ed., *Kids Having Kids: Economic Costs and Consequences of Teen Pregnancy* (Washington, D.C.: The Urban Institute, 1997); S. J. Ventura, S. C. Clarke, T. J. Mathews, "Recent Declines in Teenage Birth Rates in the United States: Variations by State, 1990–1994," *Monthly Vital Statistics Report* 45:5 (S) (December 1996); and the "Report of Final Natality Statistics, 1995."

47. Maynard, *Kids Having Kids,* chapters 1 & 3.

48. Arline T. Geronimus and Sanders Korenman, "The Socioeconomic Consequences of Teen Childbearing Reconsidered," *Quarterly Journal of Economics* 107 (1992):1187-1214. See also K. Luker, "Dubious Conceptions: The Controversy over Teen Pregnancy," *American Prospect* 7 (1991):73-83.

49. Saul Hoffman, E. Michael Foster, and Frank F. Furstenberg Jr., "Reevaluating the Costs of Teenage Childbearing," *Demography* 30:1 (February 1993):1-13.

50. Maynard, *Kids Having Kids,* pp.18-19 and chapter 10.

51. Ibid., chapters 3-9.

52. See Ronald B. Mincey's excellent review of the complex and often contradictory literature on this subject. The standard works are William Julius Wilson, *The Truly Disadvantaged,* and the collection of papers in response to this work edited by Christopher Jencks and Paul E. Peterson, *The Urban Underclass,* in which see especially, Christopher Jencks, "Is the American Underclass Growing?" pp. 28-100.

53. Jencks, ibid.

54. Blank, *It Takes a Nation,* pp. 47-56.

55. W. E. B. Du Bois, *The Philadelphia Negro: A Social Study* (New York: Schocken, 1967 [1899]), p. 241.

56. Ibid., p. 236.

57. Ibid., p. 238.

58. Ibid., p. 241.

59. For one of the best studies of this process, see Stanley Lieberson, *A Piece of the Pie: Black and White Immigrants Since 1880* (Berkeley: University of California Press, 1980), pp. 319-25; 339-54.

60. Roger Lane, *Roots of Violence in Black Philadelphia: 1860-1900* (Cambridge: Harvard University Press, 1986), p. 95.

61. Children's Defense Fund, *The State of America's Children, 1992* (Washington, D.C.: Children's Defense Fund, 1992), p. xii.

62. Marc Mauer and Tracy Huling, *Young Black Americans and the Criminal Justice System: Five Years Later* (Washington, D.C.: The Sentencing Project, 1995), p. 1.

63. Ibid., p. 3.

64. Ibid., p. 2.

65. Michael Tonry, *Malign Neglect: Race, Crime and Punishment in America* (New York: Oxford University Press, 1995), p. 79.

66. U. S. Department of Justice, Office of Justice Programs, Bureau of Statistics, National Crime Victimization Survey, 1994-95. (Office of Justice Programs: Bureau of Justice Statistics, April 1997.)

67. One of the central arguments of William Julius Wilson in *The Truly Disadvantaged.*

68. Douglas S. Massey and Nancy A. Denton, *American Apartheid: Segregation and the Making of the Underclass* (Cambridge: Harvard University Press, 1993).

69. Paul A. Jargowsky, "Ghetto Poverty Among Blacks in the 1980s," *Journal of Policy Analysis and Management* 13:2 (April 1994):288-310.

70. Reynolds Farley and William H. Frey, "Changes in the Segregation of Whites from Blacks During the 1980s: Small Steps Toward a More Integrated Society," *American Sociological Review* 59 (1994): 23-45.

71. Reynolds Farley, Charlotte Steeh, Maria Krysan, Tara Jackson, and Keith Reeves, "Stereotypes and Segregation: Neighborhoods in the Detroit Area," *American Journal of Sociology* 100:3 (1994):750-780.

72. John R. Conlon and Mwangi S. Kimenyi, "Attitudes Towards Race and Poverty in the Demand for Private Education: The Case of Mississippi," *The Review of Black Political Economy* 20:2 (Fall 1991):5-22.

73. The Gallup Poll Social Audit, *Black/White Relations in the United States* (Princeton, N.J.: The Gallup Organization, June 1997), p. 18.

74. Lee Sigelman and Susan Welch, *Black Americans' Views of Racial Inequality: The Dream Deferred* (New York: Cambridge University Press, 1991).

75. The Gallup Poll Social Audit, *Black/White Relations in the United States*, p. 16.

76. Christopher Ellison and Daniel Powers, "The Contact Hypothesis and Racial Attitudes Among Black Americans," *Social Science Quarterly* 75 (1994):385-400.

77. Lee Sigelman, Timothy Bledsoe, Susan Welch, and Michael Combs, "Making Contact? Black-White Social Interaction in an Urban Setting," *American Journal of Sociology* 101:5 (1996):1306-32.

78. Ibid., 1325.

79. See the excellent report and evaluation of this program in James Rosenbaum, Nancy Fishman, Alison Brett, and Patricia Meaden, "Can the Kerner Commission's Housing Strategy Improve Employment, Education and Social Integration for Low-Income Blacks?" *North Carolina Law Review* 71 (June 1993):1519-56.

80. See, in particular, William Clarke, "Residential Segregation in American Cities: Common Ground and Differences in Interpretation," *Population Research and Policy Review* 8 (1989):193-97; and idem, "Residential Preference and Neighborhood Racial Segregation: A Test of the Schelling Segregation Model," *Demography* 28:1 (1991):1-19. An alternate position is taken in Lawrence Bobo and Camille Zubrinsky, "Prismatic Metropolis: Race and Residential Segregation in the City of Angels," Russell Sage Foundation, Working Paper No. 78, October 1995. The authors consider and dismiss economic factors, or assumptions about housing costs, and attribute minor significance to what they call "ethnocentrism," i.e., people wanting to live with their own kind, claiming Euro-American racism as the main factor. Nonetheless, they found that all groups, including Afro-Americans, appear to want both integration and a "significant number of same-race neighbors."

81. The Gallup Poll Social Audit, *Black/White Relations in the United States*, p. 24.

82. Margery A. Turner, Raymond J. Struyk, and John Yinger, *Housing Discrimination Study: Prepared for U.S. Department of Housing and Urban Development* (Washington, D.C.: The Urban Institute and Syracuse University, 1991).

83. Farley, et al., "Stereotypes and Segregation: Neighborhoods in the Detroit Area," 755-57.

84. On which see Howard Schuman, Charlotte Steeh, and Lawrence Bobo, *Racial Attitudes in America: Trends and Interpretations* (Cambridge: Harvard University Press, 1985).

85. The Gallup Social Audit, *Black/White Relations in the United States*, p. 15.

86. National Research Council, *Risking the Future*, p. 52. See also Maynard, *Kids Having Kids*, pp. 36-38.

87. U.S. Department of Health and Human Services, Administration for Children and Families, "Change in Welfare Caseloads" (Data sent to author in personal communication from Michael Kharfen, director, Office of Public Affairs); see also *The New York Times*, February 2, 1997. On the recent welfare law— "The

Personal Responsibility and Work Opportunity Reconciliation Act of 1996"—see Mark Greenberg and Steve Savner, *A Detailed Summary of Key Provisions of the Temporary Assistance for Needy Families Block Grant of H.R.3734* (Washington, D.C.: Center for Law and Social Policy, 1996); David A. Super, Sharon Parrot, Susan Steinmetz, and Cindy Mann, *The New Welfare Law* (Washington, D.C.: Center on Budget and Policy Priorities, 1996), which is generally critical of the new Act. For the most balanced, preliminary assessment of the new Act's possible impact, see Rebecca M. Blank, *The Effect of the 1996 Welfare Reforms* (Evanston: Center for Urban Affairs and Policy Research, Northwestern University, 1996). None of these early assessments anticipated the remarkable decline in welfare caseloads recently reported by the U.S. Department of Health and Human Services. Between January 1993 and January 1997, there was a 20 percent decline in the number of individual AFDC/TANF recipients, down from 14,115,000 in 1993 to 11,360,000 in 1997. Source: U.S. Department of Health and Human Services, Administration for Children and Families, "Change in Welfare Caseloads," on-line data, revised April 1997.

88. Anthony J. Lemelle Jr., *Black Male Deviance* (New York: Praeger, 1995), p. 139.

89. Already showing strain when the movement originated in the early eighties, the coalition has fallen apart with the strong stand taken by the critical race theorists on behalf of hate-speech codes. For a brilliant analysis and critique of the movement, see Henry Louis Gates Jr., "War of Words: Critical Race Theory and the First Amendment," in Henry Louis Gates Jr., Anthony P. Griffin, Donald E. Lively, et al., eds., *Speaking of Race, Speaking of Sex: Hate Speech, Civil Rights and Civil Liberties* (New York: New York University Press, 1994), pp. 17-58.

90. *New York Times*, May 5, 1997.

91. Derrick Z. Jackson, "Other Barriers to Break," *Boston Globe*, April 16, 1997.

92. Amos Quick as quoted in Steven A. Holmes, "At N.A.A.C.P., Talk of a Shift on Integration," *New York Times*, June 23, 1997, A15.

93. Ellis Cose, *The Rage of a Privileged Class* (New York: Harper Perennial, 1995), p. 35.

94. Ruth Shalit, "Race in the Newsroom," *New Republic*, October 2, 1995, pp. 20-37.

95. Joe R. Feagin, Hernan Vera, and Nikitah Imani, *The Agony of Education: Black Students at White Colleges and Universities* (New York: Routledge, 1996); Feagin and Melvin P. Sikes, *Living with Racism: The Black Middle-Class Experience* (Boston: Beacon Press, 1994); Cose, *The Rage of a Privileged Class*.

96. Rosenbaum et al., "Can the Kerner Commission's Housing Strategy Improve Employment, Education, and Social Integration for Low-Income Blacks?" *North Carolina Law Review* 71:5 (1993): 1519–56.

97. Ibid, pp.1539-40.

98. Ibid, p. 1540. It should be noted that these correlations were not statistically significant, possibly due to the small sample size. I agree with the authors that they are nonetheless "substantively very important." The program cries out for further studies, hopefully focusing on precisely these counterintuitive interactional patterns.

99. The Gallup Poll Social Audit, *Black/White Relations in the United States*, p. 11.

100. Ibid., p. 22.

101. The Washington Post/Kaiser Family Foundation/Harvard University Survey Project, *The Four Americas: Government and Social Policy Through the Eyes of America's Multi-Racial and Multi-Ethnic Society* (Menlo Park, CA.: Kaiser Family Foundation, 1995).

102. See Sigelman and Welch, *Black Americans' Views of Racial Inequality*.

103. Schuman, Steeh, and Bobo, *Racial Attitudes in America*; Jaynes and

Williams, eds., *A Common Destiny,* chapter 3.

104. These figures are derived from the data base of the General Social Survey, 1972-1994. See *Cumulative Codebook, Nov. 1994* (Chicago: NORC, 1994).

105. Feagin and Sikes, *Living with Racism;* Bob Blauner, *Black Lives, White Lives: Three Decades of Race Relations in America* (Berkeley: University of California Press, 1989).

106. On the greater prejudice of the less educated, working- and lower-class Euro-Americans, see Sigelman and Welch, *Black Americans' Views of Racial Inequality.*

107. "Crime and the Administration of Criminal Justice," in Jaynes and Williams, eds., *A Common Destiny,* pp. 473-74.

108. Dennis Rodman and Tim Keown, *Bad As I Wanna Be* (New York: Delacorte Press, 1996).

109. These figures were calculated from The General Social Survey data base.

110. These data are discussed at greater length, and their sources given, in chapter 5. There it will be pointed out that the "angry white male" syndrome is a misnomer, since Euro-American females respond in similar terms.

111. Henry Louis Gates Jr., *Colored People: A Memoir* (New York: Knopf, 1994); Sterling A. Brown, "When de Saints go Ma'ching Home," in Michael S. Harper, ed., *The Collected Poems of Sterling A. Brown* (Chicago: TriQuarterly Books, 1989), p. 28.

112. Jean Paul Sartre, *Black Orpheus,* trans. S. W. Allen (Paris: Presence africaine, 1963).

113. David Lublin, *The Paradox of Representation: Racial Gerrymandering and Minority Interests in Congress* (Princeton: Princeton University Press, 1997).

114. Signithia Fordham and John U. Ogbu, "Black Students' School Success: Coping with the 'Burden of Acting White,'" *Urban Review* 18:3 (1986):176-206.

115. See F. James Davis, *Who Is Black: One Nation's Definition* (University Park, Penn.: The Pennsylvania State University Press, 1993); Joel Williamson, *New People: Miscegenation and Mulattoes in the United States* (New York: Free Press, 1980); Paul S. Spickard, "The Illogic of American Racial Categories," in Maria P. P. Root, ed., *Racially Mixed People in America* (Newbury Park: Sage, 1992), pp. 12-23.

116. See Alexander Saxton, *The Rise and Fall of the White Republic: Class Politics and Mass Culture in Nineteenth-Century America* (New York: Verso, 1991); David R. Roediger, *The Wages of Whiteness: Race and the Making of the American Working Class* (New York: Verso, 1991); Noel Ignatiev, *How the Irish Became White* (New York: Routledge, 1995).

117. Stanley Lieberson and Mary Waters, *From Many Strands: Ethnic and Racial Groups in Contemporary America* (New York: Russell Sage, 1988); Maria P. P. Root, ed., *Racially Mixed People in America.*

118. MIT Center for International Studies, "The Politics of Counting: Race, Ethnicity and Censuses," *Precis* 8:1 (winter 1997).

119. Bureau of Labor Statistics, "A CPS Supplement for Testing Methods of Collecting Racial and Ethnic Information: May 1995" (Washington, D.C.: U.S. Department of Labor, 1996).

120. Michael Vannoy Adams, *The Multicultural Imagination: "Race," Color, and the Unconscious* (New York: Routledge, 1996), p. 11.

121. Lawrence Wright, "One Drop of Blood," *New Yorker,* July 25, 1994, p. 53.

122. For references, see Orlando Patterson, *Slavery and Social Death: A Comparative Study* (Cambridge: Harvard University Press, 1982).

123. Cited in L. Perry Curtis Jr., *Apes and Angels: The Irishman in Victorian Caricature* (Washington, D.C.: Smithsonian Institution Press, 1971).

124. Ibid., p.104.

125. Gareth S. Jones, *Outcast London: A Study in the Relationship Between Classes in Victorian Society* (New York: Pantheon, 1984), pp. 12-13, 127-29, and chapter 16.

126. Cited in ibid., p. 330.

127. Karen Brodkin Sacks, "How Did Jews Become White Folks?" in Steven Gregory and Roger Sanjek, eds., *Race* (New Brunswick, N.J.: Rutgers University Press, 1994), pp. 78-102.

128. Roediger, *The Wages of Whiteness;* see also, Ignatiev, *How the Irish Became White.*

129. Virginia Dominguez, *White by Definition: Social Classification in Creole Louisiana* (New Brunswick: Rutgers University Press, 1986).

130. W. E. B. Du Bois, *The Philadelphia Negro;* idem, *The Negro American Family* (Cambridge: MIT Press, 1970); John Hope Franklin, *From Slavery to Freedom* (New York: Knopf, 1963), pp. 177, 201-204; E. Franklin Frazier, *The Negro Family in the United States* (Chicago: University of Chicago Press, 1939); idem, *The Negro in the United States* (New York: Macmillan Co., 1949), esp. chapter 13; Malcolm X, *The Speeches of Malcolm X at Harvard,* ed. Archie Epps (New York: Morrow, 1968).

131. See my essay "Rethinking Black History," *Harvard Educational Review* 41:3 (August 1971):297-315. And for more recent excellent critiques of the revisionists of the sixties and seventies, see Peter Parish, *Slavery: History and the Historianas* (New York: Harper & Row, 1989); Peter Kolchin, "Reevaluating the Antebellum Slave Community," *Journal of American History* 70:3 (1983). Among the best of the counter-revisionist works are: Deborah Gray White, *Ar'n't I a Woman: Female Slaves in the Plantation South* (New York: Norton, 1985); Brenda Stevenson, "Distress and Discord in Virginia Slave Families," in Carol Bleser, ed., *In Joy and in Sorrow: Women, Family and Marriage in the Victorian South, 1830-1900* (New York: Oxford University Press, 1991); and Elizabeth Fox Genovese, *Within the Plantation Household: Black and White Women of the Old South* (Chapel Hill: University of North Carolina Press, 1989).

132. For the best account of this whole sorry episode and its disastrous consequences for the study of Afro-American social conditions and problems, see Wilson, *The Truly Disadvantaged,* pp. 99, 125-39.

133. See Robert H. Haveman, *Poverty Policy and Poverty Research: The Great Society and the Social Sciences* (Madison: University of Wisconsin Press, 1987).

134. Andrew Billingsley, *Climbing Jacob's Ladder: The Enduring Legacy of Black Families* (New York: Simon & Schuster, 1992).

135. The media's greatest failure in this regard has been in its growing obsession with violence, especially ethnic and sexual violence. It is a reasonable guess that persisting Euro-American fears of neighborhood integration can be attributed to the irresponsible, profit-driven reporting of crime in the media, especially the local television news medium. On violence in the press generally, see the special issue on media violence in *Nieman Reports* 50:3 (fall 1996). On the theme of ethnicity and violence see, in this issue, the article by Lester Sloan, "Race and Violence," pages 28-29. For a persuasive experimental study of the negative impact on "racial" attitudes produced by TV news reporting on crime, see Franklin D. Gilliam Jr. and Adam F. Simon, "Can Media Cues Change Thinking about Race? An Experimental Study of Television News Crime Coverage" (paper presented at the 1996 annual meeting of the American Political Science Association, San Francisco, August 28–September 1). On the "tabloidization" of America's television networks in the search for ratings and profits, see John Dancy, "Lights in a Box: Gotcha Journalism and Public Policy" (unpublished paper). And on the resistance of ordinary

Americans to these trends in the mass media and their strong support for measures to "watch the watchdogs" so as to ensure responsible reporting, see Robert Lichter, "The People versus the Press" (lecture delivered on March 17, 1997, at the Research Roundtable Series, The Joan Shorenstein Center on the Press, Politics and Public Policy, Kennedy School of Government, Harvard University).

2. The Moral and Intellectual Crisis of Liberal Afro-American Advocacy

1. *New York Times,* December 9, 1995.

2. Quoted in David Remnick, "Kid Dynamite Blows Up," *New Yorker,* July 14, 1997, p. 50.

3. Quoted in Ian Fisher, "Tainted Hero: Neighbors Split on Tyson," *New York Times,* July 2, 1997, p. 1.

4. Andrew Hacker, *Two Nations: Black and White, Separate, Hostile, Unequal* (New York: Charles Scribner's Sons, 1992), p. 34.

5. Mitchell Duneier, *Slim's Table: Race, Respectability, and Masculinity* (Chicago: University of Chicago Press, 1992), pp. 45-46.

6. John Rawls, *A Theory of Justice* (Cambridge: Harvard University Press, 1971), p. 440.

7. Morris Rosenberg, Carmi Schooler, Carrie Schoenback, and Florence Rosenberg, "Global Self-Esteem and Specific Self-Esteem: Different Concepts, Different Outcomes," *American Sociological Review* 60 (1995):141-56, especially 144-56.

8. For the two best reviews of this subject, see Judith R. Porter and Robert E. Washington, "Black Identity and Self-Esteem: A Review of Studies of Black Self-Concept, 1968-1978," *Annual Review of Sociology* 5 (1979):53-74; and William E. Cross, "Black Identity: Rediscovering the Distinction Between Personal Identity and Reference Group Orientation," in M. B. Spencer, Geraldine K. Brookins, and Walter R. Allen, eds., *Beginnings: The Social and Affective Development of Black Children* (Hillsdale, N.J.: Lawrence Erlbaum, 1985).

9. Another explanation is that these earlier works from the late forties, fifties, and sixties were simply methodologically flawed. The most famous of these earlier works were K. B. Clark and M. P. Clark, "Racial Identification and Preference in Negro Children," in T. M. Newcomb and E. L. Hartley, eds., *Readings in Social Psychology* (New York: Holt, 1947), pp. 169-78; and A. Kardiner and L. Ovesey, *The Mark of Oppression* (New York: Norton, 1951). For criticisms of these works, see R. G. Simmons, "Blacks and High Self-Esteem: A Puzzle," *Social Psychology* 41 (1978): 54-57.

10. David H. Demo and Keith Parker, "Academic Achievement and Self-Esteem Among Black and White College Students," *Journal of Social Psychology* 127 (1987):345-55.

11. Porter and Washington, "Black Identity and Self-Esteem."

12. Ibid. See also V. Gecas, "The Self-Concept," *Annual Review of Sociology* 8 (1982):1-33; and more generally, Bonnie Bhatti, David Dezerotes, Seung-Ock Kim, and Harry Specht, "The Association between Child Maltreatment and Self-Esteem," in Andrew M. Mecca, Neil J. Smelser, and John Vasconcellos, eds., *The Social Importance of Self-Esteem* (Berkeley: University of California Press, 1989), especially pp. 33-39.

13. Porter and Washington, "Black Identity and Self-Esteem," p. 65. The psychologists who most advocate this position are Patricia Gurin and Edgar Epps in their *Black Consciousness, Identity and Achievement: A Study of Students in Historically Black Colleges* (New York: Wiley, 1975).

14. Rosenberg et al., "Global Self-Esteem and Specific Self-Esteem," p. 143.

15. H. W. Marsh, "Global Self-Esteem: Its Relation to Specific Facets of Self-Concept and Their Importance," *Journal of Personality and Social Psychology* 51 (1986):1224-36.

16. Rosenberg, et al., "Global Self-Esteem and Specific Self-Esteem," p. 144.

17. Claude Steele, "Race and the Schooling of Black Americans," *Atlantic Monthly*, April, 1992, pp. 68-78. Steele's theory of disidentification has recently been strongly supported by Jason W. Osborne in his "Academics, Self-Esteem, and Race: A Look at the Underlying Assumptions of the Disidentification Hypothesis," *Personality and Social Psychology Bulletin* 21:5 (1995): 449-55. However, in a footnote Osborne notes that there might be a much simpler explanation for the discrepancy between Afro-American global self-esteem and academic performance: the fact "that individuals' self-esteem is based on the social groups they belong to" (p. 454). More recent experimental work has confirmed this, on which see Brenda Major, Anne M. Sciacchitano, and Jennifer Crocker, "In-Group vs. Out-Group Comparisons and Self-Esteem," *Personality and Social Psychology Bulletin* 19 (1993):711-21. The problem for Steele's theory here is that Afro-American students may not be disidentifying with academic studies at all, but simply evaluate their performance in comparison to other Afro-Americans, leaving Euro-Americans completely out of their evaluative framework. There might also be a simpler, alternate explanation for Steele's finding that Afro-American students disidentify with academic performance—or at any rate do not let it influence their self-esteem—as they grow older. This is the fact that all students, including Euro-Americans, are doing the same thing. This is the conclusion reached by David H. Demo and Keith D. Parker in their paper, "Academic Achievement and Self-Esteem Among Black and White College Students," *Journal of Social Psychology* 127:4 (1987): 345-55, especially pp. 352-53. Afro-American students may not be that unusual in the discrepancy between their academic performance and their self-esteem. Indeed, Morris Rosenberg and his associates flatly conclude that, among young Americans, "the value placed on academic performance is not a function of either academic or global self-esteem" (quoted in Rosenberg et al., "Global Self-Esteem and Specific Self-Esteem," p. 153).

18. Porter and Washington, "Black Identity and Self-Esteem," pp. 65-66, 68.

19. Most notably, B. F. Skinner in his book *Beyond Freedom and Dignity* (New York: Knopf, 1971).

20. The question of moral freedom is very closely linked to that of autonomy, and some writers even identify the two as synonymous. Moral freedom, however, is not strictly the same thing as autonomy. Rather, it is the philosophical problem posed by the reality and necessity of autonomy. Autonomy itself is the moral and psychological commitment to the belief in self-determination. It is the insistence on, and strong valorization of, the notion that, regardless of the dictates of causation—whether divine or natural or both—one nonetheless always has the choice to behave other than the way one in fact behaved at any given time. Moral freedom is the philosophical argument for such a position. Obviously, one may be strongly committed to the ideal of autonomy without even being aware of the philosophical problem. What is more, one may even reject the philosophical case for moral freedom while remaining strongly committed to the secular ideal of autonomy. This, in fact, is the position of all strict Calvinists, who are as fiercely committed to the valorization and realization of personal autonomy as they are to the doctrine of divine predestination.

How all this relates to the broader issue of outer freedom or liberty as ordinarily understood is an extremely complex matter that cannot be entered into here. On the one hand, it is clearly erroneous to conflate the two. But, on the other hand, it is as great an error to argue that the two are to be treated as distinct problems. In the history of freedom, as I have shown elsewhere, the Christian notion of inner freedom was one of the major factors in the rise and institutionalization of the West's commitment to, and understanding of, outer, secular freedom. See my *Freedom: Volume 1: Freedom in the Making of Western Culture* (New York: Basic Books, 1991), especially parts 4 & 5.

21. See my discussion of Epictetus in *Freedom, Vol.1*, pp. 275-84. And for one of the best discussions of the Stoic problem of freedom and determination, see Charlotte Stough, "Stoic Determination and Moral Responsibility," in John M. Rist, ed., *The Stoics* (Berkeley: University of California Press, 1978).

22. What follows draws on my discussion of Epicureanism in *Freedom, Vol.1*, pp. 187-90. For citations to the ancient texts, see this source.

23. Paul Laurence Dunbar, "Sympathy," from *The Collected Poetry of Paul Laurence Dunbar*, ed. Joanne M. Braxton (Charlottesville: University Press of Virginia, 1993), p. 102.

24. Immanuel Kant, *Groundwork of the Metaphysic of Morals*, trans. H. J. Paton (New York: Harper & Row, 1964).

25. Sidney Hook, "Necessity, Indeterminism, and Sentimentalism," in Sidney Hook, ed., *Determinism and Freedom* (New York: New York University Press, 1958), p. 177.

26. Cited in Charles P. Henry, *Culture and African American Politics* (Bloomington: Indiana University Press, 1992), pp. 79-80.

27. James R. Forman, *Self-Determination and the African-American People* (Seattle: Open Hand Publishers, 1981).

28. V. P. Franklin, *Black Self-Determination* (New York: Lawrence Hill Books, 1984).

29. Porter and Washington, "Black Identity and Self-Esteem," pp. 57-58. For more on this subject, see Gary Marx, *Protest and Prejudice: A Study of Belief in the Black Community* (New York: Harper & Row, 1967); and R. Abeles, "Relative Expectation, Rising Expectations and Black Militancy," *Journal of Social Issues* 32 (1976): 119-37.

30. Judith R. Porter and Robert. E. Washington, "Minority Identity and Self-Esteem," *Annual Review of Sociology* 19 (1993): 139–161. See especially p. 155.

31. Henry Hampton and Steve Fayer with Sarah Flynn, *Voices of Freedom: An Oral History of the Civil Rights Movement from the 1950s through the 1980s* (New York: Bantam Books, 1990), pp. 58-59.

32. Theodore Abel, *Why Hitler Came into Power* (Cambridge: Harvard University Press, 1966), p. 66.

33. Ibid., p. 139.

34. Daniel Jonah Goldhagen, *Hitler's Willing Executioners: Ordinary Germans and the Holocaust* (New York: Knopf, 1996). In this brilliant, chilling account of the Nazi program of eliminationist anti-Semitism, we learn that the "perpetrators, from Hitler to the lowliest officials, were openly proud of the actions, of their achievements" (p. 429).

35. *New York Times*, February 23, 1996.

36. Glenn C. Loury, "One Man's March," *New Republic*, November 6, 1995, p. 20.

37. Albert Camus, *The Rebel* (New York: Knopf, 1961).

38. C. L. R. James, *Beyond a Boundary* (London: Hutchinson, 1963).

39. W. E. B. Du Bois, "The Talented Tenth," in Booker T. Washington, W. E. B. Du Bois, et al., *The Negro Problem: A Series of Articles by Representative American Negroes of Today* (New York: James Pott, 1903), pp. 50-54.

40. The sociologist Gary Marx has shown that the church has worked in both radical and conservative directions for blacks, as has been true of Christian radicals and conservatives throughout the ages. See his *Protest and Prejudice*.

41. Soren Kierkegaard, *Joyful Notes in the Strife of Suffering: Christian Discourses* (New York: Oxford, 1961), p. 114.

42. Camus, *The Rebel.*

43. Frederick Douglass, *The Life and Times of Frederick Douglass* (New York: Bonanza Books, 1972 [1892]), p. 143.

44. Alfred Jospe, "The Threefold Rebellion: Some Reflections on Israel Today," in Alfred Jospe, ed., *Tradition and Contemporary Experience: Essays on Jewish Thought and Life* (New York: Schocken, 1970).

3. The Moral Crisis of Conservative "Racial" Advocacy

1. *Woman's Own*, October 31, 1987.

2. For a good summary of the human investment, risk-sharing and market failure arguments of those economists who do consider these issues, see Rebecca M. Blank, *It Takes a Nation: A New Agenda for Fighting Poverty* (New York: Russell Sage and Princeton University Press, 1997), pp. 192-200.

3. William H. Sewell Jr., "A Theory of Structure: Duality, Agency, and Transformation," *American Journal of Sociology* 98:1 (July 1992):21.

4. In more positive terms, it has been proposed by some that the corporate agency of the state should also seek to coordinate the actions of economic and other corporate agents in an "industrial policy" aimed at optimizing the nation's competitiveness and wealth; this is an interesting proposal, but it is not without even liberal critics and is not required by my argument.

5. William Julius Wilson, *The Declining Significance of Race: Blacks and Changing American Institutions* (Chicago: University of Chicago Press, 1980); idem, *When Work Disappears: The World of the New Urban Poor* (New York: Knopf, 1996).

6. See the brilliant and exhaustive exposé by Connie Bruck, "The Takedown of Tupac," *New Yorker*, July 7, 1997, pp. 46-64. Bruck tells us that on one occasion Knight "forced a black music executive at a rival company to strip in the men's room and then made him walk naked through his company's offices" (p. 46).

7. For one of the best treatments of the ways in which Afro-Americans were systematically excluded from the American industrial revolution of the nineteenth century, and the horrendous social and economic consequences of this exclusion, see Roger Lane, *The Roots of Violence in Black Philadelphia, 1860-1900* (Cambridge: Harvard University Press, 1986); and on the economic and social consequences of the crippling constraints on Afro-Americans in the South after emancipation, see Roger L. Ransom and Richard Sutch, *One Kind of Freedom: The Economic Consequences of Emancipation* (New York: Cambridge University Press, 1977), especially chapters 1, 2, and 9.

8. Robert E. Goodin, "Freedom and the Welfare State: Theoretical Foundations," *Journal of Social Policy* 11:2 (1982):149-75, especially 156.

4. For Whom the Bell Curves

1. Richard J. Herrnstein and Charles Murray, *The Bell Curve: Intelligence and Class Structure in American Life* (New York: The Free Press, 1994).

2. On which, see Michael Schiff and Richard C Lewontin, eds., *Education and Class: The Irrelevance of Genetic Studies* (New York: Oxford University Press, 1986); R. C. Lewontin, S. Rose and L. J. Kamin, *Not in Our Genes* (New York: Pantheon, 1984); Stephen Gould, *The Mismeasure of Man* (New York: Norton,

1980); on the *Bell Curve,* see the reviews by Stephen Gould, Howard Gardner and Richard Nisbett in Steven Fraser, ed., *The Bell Curve Wars: Race, Intelligence, and the Future of America* (New York: Basic Books, 1995); and Sanders Korenman and Christopher Winship, "A Reanalysis of *The Bell Curve:* Intelligence, Family Background, and Schooling" (unpublished manuscript, October 1995, pp. 12-15).

3. The National Longtitudinal Survey of Youth (NLSY) uses the Armed Services Aptitude Battery, a subset of which is the Armed Forces Qualifications Test (AFQT), which many use in national studies of intelligence and skills. The NLSY is a longtitudinal study of a national sample of 12,686 persons ages 14 to 21 as of January 1, 1979. It is generally agreed that these tests are among the most unbiased available.

4. Derek A. Neal and William R. Johnson, "The Role of Pre-Market Factors in Black-White Wage Differences," *Journal of Political Economy* 104:5 (1996): 869–895.

5. Indeed, it is precisely on this issue that Christopher Winship found it necessary to sharply criticize his former advisees after his own careful reanalysis of their data. Not only did he and his collaborator find that "the three components of Herrnstein and Murray's SES index are measured with considerable error," but that education has a powerful effect on the AFQT score amounting to "2.5 IQ points for every year of education." Korenman and Winship, "A Reanalysis of *The Bell Curve,*" p. 25; Lewontin, Rose and Kamin, *Not in Our Genes,* chapter 2.

6. See Jacqueline Jones, "Back to the Future with the Bell Curve," in Fraser, ed., *The Bell Curve Wars.*

7. Herrnstein and Murray, *The Bell Curve,* p. 342.

8. See Daniel Jonah Goldhagen, *Hitler's Willing Executioners: Ordinary Germans and the Holocaust* (New York: Knopf, 1996).

9. Psyche Cattell, "The Fate of National Intelligence: Test of a Thirteen Year Prediction," *Eugenics Review* 42:3 (1951):138-48.

10. James R. Flynn, "Massive IQ Gains in 14 Nations: What IQ Tests Really Measure," *Psychological Bulletin* 101 (1987):171-91.

11. Samuel Preston and Cameron Campbell, "Differential Fertility and the Distribution of Traits: The Case of IQ," *American Journal of Sociology* 98:5 (1993):997-1019.

12. David Lam, "Comment on Preston and Campbell's 'Differential Fertility and the Distribution of Traits,'" *American Journal of Sociology* 98:5 (1993):1033-39.

13. Richard Levins and Richard Lewontin, *The Dialectical Biologist* (Cambridge: Harvard University Press, 1985), p. 93.

14. For a more direct critique of the misuse of IQ in "racial" advocacy, see Lewontin, Rose and Kamin, *Not in Our Genes,* chapter 5.

15. Levins and Lewontin, *The Dialectical Biologist,* p. 111.

16. Ibid., p. 111 and chapter 4 passim. In a brief but enormously important analysis that should be required reading for all psychologists (and for sociologists, too, although for different reasons), Levins and Lewontin sharply criticize the relevance of the usual statistical method used to assign relative causal values to environment and genes—the analysis of variance (ANOVA). This is one of the most commonly used statistical techniques in the social sciences, and it certainly has many legitimate uses, in biology as in the social sciences, but I have always had deep misgivings about many of the causal claims made by means of it. In the case of the genes-or-environment problem, ANOVA does not permit us to know whether an environmental effect is small because the environment itself does not vary very much or because the genotype does not respond to environmental variation; and it is usually limited to specific contexts, telling us nothing about general functional relationships. "What

has happened in attempting to solve the problem of the analysis of causes by using analysis of variation is that a totally different object has been substituted as the object of investigation, almost without our noticing it. The new object of study, the deviation of phenotypic value from the mean, is not the same as the phenotypic value itself, and the tautological analysis of that deviation is not the same as the analysis of causes. In fact, the analysis of variation throws out the baby with the bath water. It is both too specific in that it is spatiotemporally restricted in its outcome and too general in that it confounds different causal schemes in the same outcome" (pp. 113-14).

17. See Peter A. Parsons, "Genetic Determination of Behavior (Mice and Men)," in Lee Ehrman, Gilbert S. Omenn and Ernst Caspari, eds., *Genetics, Environment and Behavior: Implications for Educational Policy* (New York: Academic Press, 1972), p. 93; and, in the same volume, L. Erlenmeyer-Kimling, "Gene-Environment Interactions and the Variability of Behavior," pp. 181-208.

18. Jack R. Vale, *Genes, Environment, and Behavior: An Interactionist Approach* (New York: Harper & Row, 1980). I draw, in what follows, especially on chapters 3, 6 and 9.

19. Ibid., p. 435.

20. More technically, it is the ratio of the *additive* genetic variance to the phenotypic variance of the trait or character being considered: h2= Vg/Vp. The fact that only the additive variance (Va) (i.e., "the variance among individuals due to the differential additive effects of the alleles they carry") enters the equation must be emphasized, since an important additional fact usually goes unmentioned, especially by psychologists, in discussions of heritability. This is the fact that total genetic variance actually contains two other elements, namely, dominance variance (Vd) (i.e., the variance due to interaction of alleles within loci) and epistatic variance (Vi) (i.e., the variance due to interaction among loci). Hence, complete genetic variance is properly given by the additive equation: Vg = Va + Vd + Vi. Further, taking environment (e) into account, total phenotypic variance on a given trait is Vp = Vg + Ve. This measure of heritability has important limitations, especially in the study of social classes and so-called races, as Richard Levins and Richard Lewontin make clear in *The Dialectical Biologist,* chapter 4. It is their view that the analysis of rates of selection and the selection history of a species constitute one of the few areas of population genetics where the analysis of variance may be legitimately used: *The Dialectical Biologist,* p. 122.

21. Vale, *Genes, Environment and Behavior,* p. 435.

22. A friend and colleague, Christopher Jencks, has suggested to me that we may have to distinguish between intelligence in the broad, evolutionary sense, and intelligence more narrowly defined. The former takes place over broad evolutionary time and is of purely academic interest, while the latter may have emerged within recent centuries.

23. See Howard Gardner, *Multiple Intelligences: The Theory in Practice* (New York: Basic Books, 1993), especially chapter 4.

24. Levins and Lewontin, *The Dialectical Biologist,* chapter 2. The authors argue persuasively that it is possible to interpret everything of value in Darwinian evolutionary theory without use of the tautologous concept of adaptation; that indeed, the idea was only later adopted by Darwin when he, unwisely, came under the influence of conservative social thinkers—including the reactionary sociologist Herbert Spencer—who found in it and the related concept of the survival of the fittest (equally irrelevant to the Darwinian theory of selection) a powerful ideological defense of the social horrors of the Victorian capitalist system. Darwin's great contribution to the history of biology is the principle of selection.

25. For a review of regional differences in test performance, see Darrell Bock and Elsie Moore, *Advantage and Disadvantage* (Hillsdale, N.J.: Lawrence Erlbaum, 1986).

26. A classic study claimed that between ages 20 and 60 there is a direct linear decline in intelligence of .3 of a standard deviation, or nine IQ points, per 20 years. For a review of the evidence, see Philip V. E. Vernon, *Intelligence: Heredity and Environment* (San Francisco: W. H. Freeman, 1979), pp. 79-81.

27. George C. Myers, "The Demography of Aging," in R. H. Binslock and L. George, eds., *Handbook of Aging in the Social Sciences* (New York: Academic Press, 1990), p. 29.

28. According to one estimate, if present trends continue, by 2025 fully 63 percent of the federal budget will be devoted to retirement spending. See G. Hendricks and R. Storey, "Economics of Retirement," in M. Morrison, ed., *The Economics of Aging* (New York: Van Nostrand, 1982).

29. On which, see E. Howard et al., "Age Discrimination and Mandatory Retirement," in Malcolm H. Morrison, ed., *Economics of Aging*, pp. 217-46.

30. It should be noted that more recent research has drawn a less pessimistic picture of the decline of cognitive competence among the elderly. I find it extremely revealing, and somewhat amusing, that after nearly a century of consensus among psychologists that aging and intellectual impairment are positively and strongly related, psychologists began to change their views on the subject, amounting almost to a volte-face, at exactly the same time that the over-65 segment of the population became large and powerful. Is this merely coincidental? See P. Coleman, "Psychological Aging," in P. Coleman and J. Baird, eds., *Ageing in the Twentieth Century* (London: Sage, 1990).

Equally revealing is the way in which psychologists who work in this area dramatically altered their concept of intelligence so as to facilitate a more favorable and sensitive interpretation of aging, one which protects the honor and intellectual integrity of the aged. We are now, for example, urged to take seriously the distinction between "fluid" and "crystallized" abilities, the latter, based on experience and wisdom, actually growing with age.

Oh that colored folks could command such power and respect! Never mind. See Raymond B. Cattell, *Abilities: Their Structure, Growth and Action* (Boston: Houghton Mifflin, 1971), who discusses the two kinds of intelligence at some length.

31. The situation is different in Britain, where the elderly have less respect and there is much talk of "disaster" and "impending crisis," on which see P. Coleman's introduction to *Ageing in the Twentieth Century*.

32. Mike Featherstone and Mike Hepworth have argued that there are persisting negative conceptions of age in society. Perhaps so, but these in no way vitiate my argument. In a beauty-conscious society such as our own, one would be surprised not to find such negative images. In any case, the way things are going, in terms of the shifting of the nation's resources toward the elderly, such carping may soon be the only thing younger people will have left to assuage their penury. See Featherstone and Hepworth, "Images of Ageing," in Coleman and Baird, eds., *Ageing in the Twentieth Century*, pp. 250-75.

33. See Gordon L. Patzer, *The Physical Attractiveness Phenomenon* (New York: Plenum Press, 1985); Elaine Hatfield and Susan Sprecher, *Mirror, Mirror...The Importance of Looks in Everyday Life* (Albany: State University of New York Press, 1986); Naomi Wolff, *The Beauty Myth* (New York: Morrow, 1991); and Linda Jackson, *Physical Appearance and Gender: Sociobiological and Sociocultural Perspectives* (Albany: State University of New York Press, 1992).

34. K. K. Dion and S. Stein, "Physical Attractiveness and Interpersonal Influence," *Journal of Experimental Social Psychology*, 14 (1978), 97-108; and

Karen Dion, Ellen Berscheid, and Elaine Webster, et al., "What Is Beautiful Is Good," *Journal of Personality and Social Psychology* 24 (1972): 285-90.

35. Patzer, *Physical Attractiveness Phenomenon*, pp. 44-46.

36. Patzer, *Physical Attractiveness Phenomenon*, pp. 101-16.

37. R. Keyes, *The Height of Your Life* (Boston: Little, Brown, 1980); Patzer, *Physical Attractiveness Phenomenon*, pp. 167-68.

38. Of course, all three can, and often do, overlap, and when they do the effects can be devastating: our by now familiar interaction problem.

39. Darwin, *The Origins of Species by Means of Natural Selection* (1871).

40. Kin Hubbard, *The Best of Kin Hubbard*, ed. David S. Hawes (Bloomington: Indiana University Press, 1984).

41. Alan Wolfe, "Has There Been a Cognitive Revolution in America?" in Fraser, *The Bell Curve Wars*, pp. 109-23.

42. Patzer, *Physical Attractiveness Phenomenon*, p. 6. Others have made the same point, on which see Alice S. Rossi, "Eros and Caritas: A Biopsychological Approach to Human Sexuality and Reproduction," in Alice S. Rossi, ed., *Sexuality Across the Life Course* (Chicago: University of Chicago Press, 1994), p. 14.

43. In this regard, we face the paradox that what circumstances dictate as the most efficient and socially intelligent means of group survival may be in sharp conflict with what is required for optimal survival within that same environment, a contradiction not uncommon in human and nonhuman populations. Thus the sickle-cell trait may have promoted greater group survival of West Africans in the malaria-infested environment, but it may well have reduced their energy level to a degree that prevented optimal exploitation of the otherwise abundant African physical environment. The pathological social behavior of the urban underclass in the face of a social environment infested with racism and a once predatory, and still punitive, dominant group may be a tragic social parallel to the sickle-cell trade-off.

44. Gardner, "Cracking Open the IQ Box," in Fraser, ed., *The Bell Curve Wars*, pp. 30-31.

45. Nisbett, "Race, IQ and Scientism," in Fraser, ed., *The Bell Curve Wars*, p. 41.

46. Of course, it is acceptable, indeed, politically most correct, to speak at length of Afro-American culture if all we intend to do is praise it.

5. Why We Still Need Affirmative Action

1. Data from: National Opinion Research Center, *General Social Survey Database 1990*, The University of Chicago.

2. At the .06 probability level. In plain English, there is a 94 percent probability that this is a meaningful difference, and not due to chance or sampling error. On the other hand, there is no difference whatsoever between Euro-American men and women on this issue.

3. Humphrey Taylor, "White Backlash, If It Exists, Is Not Based on Personal Experience in the Workplace," Louis Harris & Associates, Harris Poll 1995, No. 44.

4. Ibid. I would like to thank Mr. Taylor for sending me this material, which he kindly did after reading my *New York Times* op-ed piece (*"Affirmative Action, on the Merit System,"* August 7, 1995) reporting the NORC data. It is very revealing that the press paid scant attention to this very important survey finding, in spite of the prominence and authoritative nature of its source.

5. For an account of the extraordinarily devious route by which affirmative action became established government policy during the Nixon administration, see John David Skrentny, *The Ironies of Affirmative Action: Politics, Culture, and*

Justice in America (Chicago: The University of Chicago Press, 1996), especially chapter 7.

6. Report by the Council of Economic Advisors, *Job Creation and Employment Opportunities: The United States Labor Market, 1993-1996* (Washington, D.C.: Council of Economic Advisors, April 1996).

7. See letter of J. W. Peltason, president of the University of California, to the Regents of the University of California, May 12, 1995: "On the Use of Ethnicity in University of California Undergraduate Admissions." See also Chancellor's Office, "UC Fact Sheet: Myths and Facts About Undergraduate Admissions," July 27, 1995. My thanks to President Peltason for sending me this information.

8. Richard Hofstadter, *Anti-Intellectualism in American Life* (New York: Knopf, 1963).

9. See Orlando Patterson, "Ecumenical America: Global Culture and the American Cosmos," *World Policy Journal,* Summer 1994, 103-17.

10. Claude M. Steele discussed this experiment at a conference on race and inequality held at the University of Chicago, 1994. See his article, "Race and the Schooling of Black Americans," *Atlantic Monthly,* April 1992, pp. 68-78.

11. See Skrentny, *Ironies of Affirmative Action,* chapter 2. This is perhaps the best work on the development of affirmative action and the complex political, cultural, and moral issues which it poses. See also S. M. Lipset and W. Schneider, "The Bakke Case: How Would It Be Decided at the Bar of Public Opinion?" *Public Opinion* (1978), 1: 38-44; and Nathan Glazer, *Affirmative Discrimination: Ethnic Inequality and Public Policy* (Cambridge: Harvard University Press, 1987), especially chapters 1 and 6.

12. *New York Times,* "The Downsizing of America," The New York Times Co., March 3-8, 1995.

13. See, in particular, Glenn C. Loury, *One by One from the Inside Out: Essays and Reviews on Race and Responsibility in America* (New York: Free Press, 1995), chap. 6.

14. George Caspar Homans, *The Human Group* (New York: Harcourt, 1950).

15. Harry H. L. Kitano and Roger Daniels, *Asian Americans: Emerging Minorities* (Englewood Cliffs, N.J.: Prentice Hall, 1988), pp. 166-71.

16. Charles Moskos and John Sibley Butler, *All That We Can Be: Black Leadership and Racial Integration the Army Way* (New York: Basic Books, 1996).

17. See Daniel Bell, "Ethnicity and Social Change," in Nathan Glazer and Daniel Patrick Moynihan, eds., *Ethnicity: Theory and Experience* (Cambridge: Harvard University Press, 1975), 141-174, and more generally Bell's *The Coming of Post-Industrial Society: A Venture in Social Forecasting* (New York: Basic Books, 1993).

18. Noel Ignatiev, *How the Irish Became White* (New York: Routledge, 1995), p. 41.

19. William V. Shannon, *The American Irish* (New York: Macmillan, 1963), p. 38.

20. Ibid., p. 37.

21. Ibid., p. 40.

22. George Potter, *The Golden Door: The Story of the Irish in Ireland and America* (Boston: Little, Brown, 1960), p. 407.

23. Christopher Jencks, *Rethinking Social Policy: Race, Poverty, and the Underclass* (New York: Harper Perennial, 1992), p. 28.

24. Joseph O'Grady, *How the Irish Became Americans* (New York: Twayne Publishers, 1973), prologue.

25. Jean Jacques Rousseau, *The Social Contract,* trans. Willmoore Kendall (Chicago: Henry Regnery Co., 1954), book 2, chapter 11.

Conclusion: What Is to Be Done

1. The Washington Post/Kaiser Family Foundation/Harvard University Survey Project, *The Four Americas: Government and Social Policy Through the Eyes of America's Multi-Racial and Multi-Ethnic Society* (Menlo Park, CA: Kaiser Family Foundation, 1995), Figures 3.1 and 3.2.

2. Anita Haya Patterson, *From Emerson to King: Democracy, Race and the Politics of Protest* (New York: Oxford University Press, 1997), chapter 8.

3. Data from the National Opinion Research Center, General Social Survey database, 1994.

4. The Gallup Poll Social Audit, *Black/White Relations in the United States,* (Princeton, N.J.: The Gallup Organization, June 1997), pp. 22-25.

5. Paul M. Sniderman and Thomas Piazza, *The Scar of Race* (Cambridge: Harvard University Press, 1993), pp. 67-68. While the fascinating survey experiments of these authors partly address this side of the distinction I am making, they really do not apply to the second category of ethnic prejudice discussed below, namely individual ethnic prejudice in the absence of collective or group prejudice otherwise known as "statistical discrimination." This second kind of prejudice cannot be properly studied with the questionnaire instrument, since it requires observation of the actual behavior of the person being discriminated against. It is also not the same thing as ideological prejudice. Sniderman and Piazza find that conservatives have been unfairly labeled racists by advocates of the "new racism" who identify conservative values with covertly racist attitudes. They show convincingly that educated conservatives are opposed to government spending on behalf of Afro-Americans not because of ethnicity but because of their principled opposition to government spending. This, however, is a quite separate issue from the problem of statistical discrimination, which, as I argue, is frequently practiced by Afro-American employers who, however, depart from conservative ideology in their support for strong government intervention such as affirmative action.

Note too that the Sniderman and Piazza experiments do not necessarily tell us anything about the contradictory attitudes of the same respondents, but rather of randomly selected categories of persons.

6. William Julius Wilson, *When Work Disappears: The World of the New Urban Poor* (New York: Knopf, 1996), chapter 5, especially pp. 129-32. See also Joleen Kirschenman and Kathryn M. Neckerman, "'We'd Love to Hire Them, But...':The Meaning of Race for Employers," in Christopher Jencks and Paul E. Peterson, eds., *The Urban Underclass* (Washington, D.C.: The Brookings Institution, 1991), pp. 203-32.

7. See Orlando Patterson, *Ecumenical America* (Washington, D.C.: Civitas/Counterpoint, forthcoming).

8. Sniderman and Piazza, *The Scar of Race,* p. 66.

9. Ibid., p. 87.

10. Clyde W Franklin II, "'Hey, Home—Yo, Bro': Friendship Among Black Men.'" This is true, however, of working class Afro-American men. Middle-class Afro-American men tend to be no more involved with intimate friendships than Euro-Americans.

11. See Orlando Patterson, *Ethnic Chauvinism: The Reactionary Impulse* (Briarcliff Manor, N.Y.: Stein and Day, 1977), pp. 170-72.

12. Carl H. Nightingale, *On the Edge: A History of Poor Black Children and Their American Dreams* (New York: Basic Books, 1993).

13. Mary Jo Bane and David T. Ellwood, *Welfare Realities: From Rhetoric to Reform* (Cambridge: Harvard University Press, 1994), pp. 161-62.

14. Raymond J. Struyk and Marc Bendick Jr., *Housing Vouchers for the Poor: Lessons from a National Experiment* (Washington, D.C.: The Urban Institute, 1981), p. 108.

15. Ibid, p. 124.

16. Susan Mayer, *What Money Can't Buy: Family Income and Children's Life Chances* (Cambridge: Harvard University Press, 1997), p.145.

17. Ibid., pp. 152-56.

18. Gary Orfield, Mark D. Bachmeier, David R. James, and Tamela Eitle, *Deepening Segregation in American Public Schools* (Cambridge: Harvard Project on School Desegregation, April, 1997).

19. Ibid., pp. 5-8.

20. Ibid., p. 41.

21. Ibid., pp. 12-13.

22. The Gallup Poll Social Audit, *Black/White Relations in the United States*, p. 15.

23. Orfield, et al., *Deepening Segregation in American Public Schools*, pp. 16-23.

24. The Gallup Poll Social Audit, *Black/White Relations in the United States*, p. 19.

25. Steven A. Holmes, "At N.A.A.C.P., Talk of a Shift on Integration," *New York Times*, June 23, 1997.

26. See, for example, Stanley Lieberson and Mary Waters, *From Many Strands: Ethnic and Racial Groups in Contemporary America* (New York: Russell Sage Foundation, 1988).

27. The Gallup Poll, *Black/White Relations in the United States*, p. 20.

28. These unpublished figures were kindly provided to the author by the Gallup Organization in a personal communication. They are from the June 1997 poll that led to *Black/White Relations in the United States*.

29. Douglas J. Besharov and Timothy Sullivan, "One Flesh: America Is Experiencing an Unprecedented Increase in Black-White Intermarriage," *New Democrat*, July-August, 1996.

30. Ibid.

31. Mary Waters, *Ethnic Options: Choosing Identities in America* (Berkeley: University of California Press, 1990).

32. Edward Laumann et al., *The Social Organization of Sexuality: Sexual Practices in the United States* (Chicago: The University of Chicago Press, 1994), p. 246.

33. Herbert Gans, "Symbolic Ethnicity: The Future of Ethnic Groups and Cultures in America," *Ethnic and Racial Studies* 2:1 (1979):9-17.

34. Peter J. Boyer, "Ron Brown's Secrets," *New Yorker*, June 9, 1997, pp. 63-75.

35. The Gallup Poll, *Black/White Relations in the United States*, p. 15.

36. Sniderman and Piazza, *The Scar of Race* (Cambridge: Harvard University Press, 1993), p. 136.

37. Ibid., p. 14 and chapter 6, passim.